MAN'S DISORDER AND GOD'S DESIGN

Volume IV

THE CHURCH
AND THE
INTERNATIONAL
DISORDER

MAN'S DISORDER AND GOD'S DESIGN

The Amsterdam Assembly Series

I. THE UNIVERSAL CHURCH IN GOD'S DESIGN
    (i) The Doctrine of the Church. (ii) Shame and Glory.
    (iii) Signs of His Appearing. (iv) The Ecumenical Movement.

   By G. AULÉN, KARL BARTH, C. T. CRAIG, P. DEVANANDAN,
   A. FJELLBU, G. FLOROVSKY, J. GREGG, RICHARD NIEBUHR,
   E. SCHLINK, K. E. SKYDSGAARD, W. A. VISSER 'T HOOFT, OLIVER
   TOMKINS, M. VILLAIN, OLIVE WYON.

II. THE CHURCH'S WITNESS TO GOD'S DESIGN
     (i) The Church's Commission. (ii) Our un-Christian World.
     (iii) Some Axioms of the Modern Man. (iv) The Relevance
     of the Gospel. (v) The Gospel at Work. (vi) The Approach
     to Other Faiths.

   By FRANK BENNETT, EMIL BRUNNER, W. M. HORTON,
   H. KRAEMER, PIERRE MAURY, S. C. NEILL, L. NEWBIGIN,
   W. PAUCK, S. SAVARIMUTHU, P. TILLICH, G. VICEDOM.

III. THE CHURCH AND THE DISORDER OF SOCIETY
      (i) God's Design and the Present Disorder. (ii) Technics and
      Civilisation. (iii) The Situation in Europe, Asia and U.S.A.
      (iv) Personal Relations in a Technical Society. (v) The
      Involvement of the Church. (vi) New Beginnings in the
      relations of the Church with Society. (vii) A Responsible Society.
      (viii) The Strategy of the Church.

   By S. BATES, J. C. BENNETT, KATHLEEN BLISS, EMIL BRUNNER,
   J. ELLUL, REINHOLD NIEBUHR, J. H. OLDHAM, C. L. PATIJN,
   M. M. THOMAS, E. C. URWIN.

IV. THE CHURCH AND THE INTERNATIONAL DISORDER
     (i) The Churches' Approach to International Affairs. (ii) The
     Church and the Disorder of International Society. (iii) Chris-
     tian Responsibility in our Divided World. (iv) Freedom of
     Religion and Related Human Rights. (v) Christian Responsi-
     bility in a World of Power.

   By R. P. BARNES, E. BRUNNER, JOHN FOSTER DULLES, K. G.
   GRUBB, J. L. HROMADKA, O. F. NOLDE, F. M. VAN ASBECK.

V. THE OFFICIAL ASSEMBLY REPORT

THE
CHURCH AND
THE INTERNATIONAL
DISORDER

AN

ECUMENICAL STUDY

PREPARED UNDER THE AUSPICES OF THE

WORLD COUNCIL OF CHURCHES

S C M PRESS LTD

56 BLOOMSBURY STREET, LONDON W C 1

First published October 1948

Distributed in Canada by our exclusive agents
The Macmillan Company of Canada Limited
70 Bond Street, Toronto

Printed in Great Britain by
The Garden City Press Limited
Letchworth, Hertfordshire

GENERAL PREFACE

THIS book, with its companion volumes, was written in preparation for the First Assembly of the World Council of Churches in Amsterdam, Holland, August 22-September 4, 1948.

Two years and a half in advance of the Assembly, the Provisional Committee of the Council determined that the main theme for the Assembly should be:

MAN'S DISORDER AND GOD'S DESIGN

and that this theme should be considered under four aspects:

1. The Universal Church in God's Design.
2. The Church's Witness to God's Design.
3. The Church and the Disorder of Society.
4. The Church and the International Disorder.

These topics were not chosen at random. They represent burning concerns of all the churches in this crisis of civilisation. The first reveals the growing determination of the various churches to rediscover the divine intention for the Church, and the right relationship of the various churches to one another. Of that determination, the World Council itself is both an evidence and a concrete result. The second testifies to the obligation recognised by all churches alike to claim for Christ the whole world and all aspects of life. From the outset it has been recognised that the World Council would be still-born unless evangelism were its life-blood. The third and fourth subjects bring Christian faith directly to bear upon two critical areas of disorder in contemporary civilisation, the social and the international. They deal with the familiar query: What has the Church to contribute to society in its present extremity?

Preparation of the delegates for the consideration of these issues at Amsterdam was entrusted to the Study Department Commission of the World Council of Churches. Commissions consisting of leading Christians, both clerical and lay, from various parts of the world, were formed to deal with the four topics. Each Commission held two meetings and came together again on the eve of the Assembly for the final stages of preparation. A volume was outlined on each topic, and writers of chapters were carefully selected. In almost every instance, their contributions have been subjected to searching criticism by the Commission concerned, both individually and corporately, and by a considerably wider circle of experts. In most cases, chapters have been rewritten in the light of this truly ecumenical scrutiny at least once, in some instances two or more times. Thus, the volumes which are here presented represent the outcome of a comprehensive interchange of thought and conviction among leaders of virtually all Christian Communions (except the Roman Catholic). It will be understood that in these circumstances the World Council of Churches itself is not committed to the opinions expressed in the volumes.

But quite apart from its literary results, the process of ecumenical thinking possesses in itself an educational and inspirational value which should not be underestimated. Especially for people in isolated areas of the world, this interchange of documents and comments means an opportunity, eagerly grasped, to share in a vital conversation with brethren from other churches and countries. The wide interest taken in the theme of the Assembly is also evidenced by the fact that several collaborating groups are now preparing similar volumes, dealing with the same set of subjects from a national or confessional perspective.

All these studies are founded on earlier work—the sequence of ecumenical conferences of the past two decades, especially the Oxford Conference on " Church, Community and State " in 1937, the patient enquiries of the Faith and Order movement, the labour of ecumenical study groups in many lands, and the programme of the Study Department of the World Council which continued, hampered but unabated, through all the years of the war.

Serious effort has been made to assure that this discussion be truly ecumenical, representative equally of Christian churches in every part of the world. But difficulties of effective communication have to a considerable degree frustrated that aim. It has not been possible to secure as many contributions as was hoped from the Eastern Orthodox world and from the Churches of Asia, Africa and Latin America. This limitation, while real and regrettable, is less grave than might at first be supposed. For no fact stands out more clearly than that, in the basic problems confronted both by the Churches and by the societies in which they are set, ours is in truth one world.

Although the volumes of the present series were prepared to serve the particular occasion of the Amsterdam Assembly, they deal with issues of continuing and urgent importance for the whole of Christendom. It is hoped, therefore, that they may have a wide usefulness beyond and after the Assembly, and they are here presented to all thoughtful people, within and outside the churches, for that purpose.

GENERAL INTRODUCTION

T HE World Council of Churches has come into being at a moment of peril for all mankind which is without precedent in the whole of human history. Frustration and fear grip the minds of men and women. This is true not only of the masses who feel themselves caught in a fate over which they have no power, but hardly less of their leaders who hold in their hands the guidance of events which they are unable to control.

At this fateful moment, the theme of the first Assembly of the Council—MAN's DISORDER AND GOD's DESIGN—is singularly relevant and needs little interpretation.

MAN's DISORDER is inescapably manifest in every aspect of the world's life to-day. It is not merely a result of the recent war. Before the war, the sickness of civilisation was far advanced. The disappearance of common standards, the denial of a law of God above the wills of men and states, the disintegration of family life, the dissolution of community, loss of faith save the false faith in human wisdom and goodness, emptiness and meaninglessness in the souls of men—these symptoms of sickness were clear enough. At almost every point, war and its aftermath have aggravated MAN's DISORDER. And now has been added the greatest dread of all, that man's mastery of atomic energy foreshadows the annihilation of man and all his works.

The Church carries a large share of responsibility for MAN's DISORDER; and it is for that responsibility that the churches must give account. This is true : if the churches had been faithful to their commission from Christ, if they had spoken the word of truth committed to them, if they had rightly interpreted to the world the causes of its sickness, if they had ministered to the world grace and power, above all if they had manifested in their own life the only true medicine for the healing of the nations— if they had done all this, humanity might not have come to its present extremity. On the contrary, MAN's DISORDER finds its most pointed expression in the disorder of the Church itself.

We live in an age when the Christian Church in many parts is rediscovering its divine mission. But precisely at that moment it discovers also its own weaknesses. To men whose deepest need is spiritual rebirth, it has not exhibited the power of the Spirit. To a world whose deepest need is community, the Church which claims to be the Body of Christ, professing one Lord, one faith, one baptism, one God and Father of all, has presented division and disunity. These are sins for which the Church is responsible to God and to man. Its first act must therefore be, not condemnation of the world, but confession and contrition.

In this plight, our only hope lies in GOD's DESIGN, His design for the world and for the Church.

GOD's DESIGN is the divine purpose for men and nations, manifest in the acts of God in Christ. In His life, death and resurrection, in the coming of the Church and the outpouring of the Holy Spirit, a new beginning has been made in human history. In Him, God has begun a work of new creation and redemption. In Him, a reign of love and forgiveness has been inaugurated, moulding the hearts and lives of men, calling them to find their common centre and desire in Him, and so to discover that real community for which mankind is longing. In Him, the Church is continuously reborn from death to life. In Him, there is also revealed GOD's DESIGN for the ordering of human society, a design that is an act both of judgment and of redemption.

Adopting MAN's DISORDER AND GOD's DESIGN as the theme for its first Assembly and as the title of the present series of volumes, the World Council of Churches has committed itself to a double task. It must seek to comprehend MAN's DISORDER in the light of GOD's DESIGN, in order that the churches may mediate to the world both a true understanding of its distress and the grace and power to find the way out. And it must bring the churches to face, with relentless realism, their involvement in the world's folly as well as their own distinctive disorders, in order that they may be ready to receive from God the rebirth and true unity which He purposes for them.

HENRY P. VAN DUSEN,
President of Union Theological Seminary
Chairman of the Study Department Commission

CONTENTS

CONTRIBUTORS

BARNES, Roswell P., Associate General Secretary, Federal Council of Churches, U.S.A. Author of *A Christian Imperative*.

BRUNNER, Emil, D.Theol., Professor of Systematic Theology, Zurich. Author of *The Mediator, Justice and the Social Order*, etc.

DULLES, John Foster, LL.D., Chairman of Committee on Policy, Department of International Justice and Goodwill of American Federal Council of Churches; Member of United States Delegation to many international conferences, including United Nations Assembly. Author of *War, Peace and Change*.

GRUBB, Kenneth G., C.M.G., Chairman, Commission of the Churches on International Affairs, and of International Department, British Council of Churches; Secretary General, Hispanic Council.

HROMADKA, Joseph L., D.D., Professor of Systematic Theology, John Hus Faculty, Prague. Author of *The Legacy of Calvin, Doom and Resurrection*, etc.

NOLDE, O. Frederick, D.D., Professor, Lutheran Seminary, Philadelphia, and Director of the Commission of the Churches on International Affairs. Author of *Power for Peace*, etc.

VAN ASBECK, Baron F. M., LL.D., Professor of International Law, Leiden, formerly Government Secretary, Netherlands Indies. Author of *Le Régime des étrangers dans les colonies*, etc.

I

CHAIRMAN'S INTRODUCTION

Kenneth G. Grubb

THE papers in this volume treat some of the problems in the field of international affairs which claim the attention of Christians, and frequently require the adoption of definite attitudes. The Disorder of Man is to most men nowhere more painfully apparent than in international relations ; the Design of God for the nations is difficult to perceive. It is often said that national socialism, communism and democracy are the great designs of the present time to overcome Man's disorder and to evoke order. The differences between these systems or the nations that adopt them account for no small part of international disorder.

It is tacitly assumed that the relations between nations are reasonably satisfactory, if their differences are not expressed with such violence as to threaten harmony and provoke rupture, and perhaps war. The nations, indeed, desire peace, not usually at any price, nor even at the price of national sovereignty, and most nations are willing to adopt an attitude of " live and let live " in regard to their neighbours. It is possible that societies with very diverse outlooks may live side by side for long periods on such terms, but the possibility is less than it has been at any previous stage in history. For, whereas there is a widespread appreciation of tolerance and a desire to secure basic rights and liberties for all men, there is also a more general consciousness of nationality and dignity, a closer contact through modern communications, and an unprecedented recourse to sources of power.

How far, therefore, nations which have built up their domestic policy on contrary principles can live side by side to their mutual peace and profit, it is not unreasonable to question. It is easy to disclaim any desire to export the domestic political product, and this intention is often genuine. But the appetite grows by what it feeds upon : and all aspects of national policy are infected, as they should be, by a nation's fundamental assumptions about the state and the citizen and the purposes of national existence.

It is a mistake to suppose, therefore, that conduct in the kitchen has no bearing on conduct in the park. International relations will not be harmoniously solved if there is unresolved disharmony between men as men, and between man and God. The truth of essential human interdependence has yet to be learned : attitudes that are wrong at home cannot be right abroad. If this is so, it must have a bearing on the Christian approach to international affairs. If the ordinary members of the Christian churches of the world succumb to the feeling that they can do nothing to influence the clash of the nations, then they are right, because they have succumbed. But if they do not succumb, then they can do something simply by their attitude. How much they can do varies greatly from country to country, for in some countries it is difficult for the ordinary citizen or churchman to defend publicly what he has chosen privately.

Some will be surprised that little is said in this volume about the problem of peace, as such. This is due to both a reaction from the past, and a realism in the present. Much more is said about human rights and liberties. Christians must repudiate the search for peace merely as an insurance for selfishness or as scope for overweening ambition. Subordination of the life of the nations and of individuals to God's will is indispensable to peace. Peace, as a supreme end in itself, has ceased to be the final objective of men's efforts.

A lot is said in the volume about Great Powers. In most historical eras there have been great Powers. Their position is one of more than ordinary responsibility to-day. They have a preponderant influence at the United Nations ; their military, naval and air resources are vast, and their differences not easy to harmonise. The situation for small Powers has deteriorated. The Second World War showed once more that they have no security in being small and professing neutrality. Great Powers can exercise a beneficent influence if they are tolerant and responsible ; if not, they may be fatally dangerous.

The fear and fact of power overshadows men's minds. But it remains true that states as well as individuals subsist under the governance of God. All power, small and great, and all persons in authority, need to be reminded of this truth, especially in an age of atomic power. But although men may fear power, they cannot forgo its use and its fascination. Christian men, for their part, stand for the reality of moral power. It is slow in its effects and incapable of determining situations which have got out of hand when passions are enraged, or issues decided without reference to the people. But it counts, as the course of history shows, if there exist those who express it.

Moreover, although there is much human cause for misgivings and apprehension in the world of nations, God still reigns. His intervention in history, centred above all in the Incarnation, is history's most decisive feature and the basis of eventual and Christian hope. He is not deaf to prayer, nor indifferent to pain. The sufferings of the just are still the saving principle in human experience. Evil brings its own retribution, and righteousness its reward, not to-day, nor to-morrow, but equally not in a future so distant as to be irrelevant to life.

National diversity is a creative element in international life, but its beneficent ends have repeatedly been prevented by an excessive nationalism. The ideal of world government is to many a legitimate objective, but practical schemes are in advance of world opinion, and the present development of man's moral capacities. The risk of a centralised tyranny is, in any case, great. The immediate possibility is to work for an international order based on a rule of law, limiting national sovereignties and providing procedures for peaceful changes. This means the development of international law from a contractual law between nations to a law above them.

A step towards this end lies in the more constructive use of the United Nations. So far, the United Nations has not shown any capability of succeeding at one of the important points where the League of Nations failed, namely, the formation of a body of authority, experience and policy which will truly be above the nations. The decisions of the United Nations are the decisions of nations agreeing or differing from one another. The emergence of a truly supra-national body with influence and standpoints of its own, and policies which are not merely the highest degree of possible compromise between the nations, is a matter for the future. If it is unobtainable, it is even more impracticable to think in terms of such a limitation, or even abolition of national sovereignties, as would make world government a possibility. Meanwhile, it is urgently necessary that the rule of law and the recognition of moral responsibility in international relations be extended.

The demand for guarantees of human rights and freedoms has occupied men's minds in many countries. The state assumes the prerogatives of God when it supposes that it is free to grant or to deny fundamental rights and freedoms to men. The authority of the state must support that law which expresses these rights and safeguards such freedoms. Internationally, a constructive step lies in the acceptance of an international covenant of rights with adequate measures to protect it. Since the churches are concerned with ultimate loyalties, the state's recognition of their essential freedom is the crucial test of its own moral responsibility.

The effectiveness of securing human rights, however detailed the measures of enforcement may be, depends largely on good faith. The whole structure of international relations, in so far as it is expressed in agreements, depends on respect for the plighted word. If a world of restraints can be removed by the mere decision to regard none except those of brute force, then trust gives way to suspicion and suspicion to war or anarchy. Up till recently the history of human development was one of gradually increasing respect for justice and honourable dealing. The main problem of statesmanship must be to restore that respect, and at the same time to allow room for adjustment of the reasonable demands that arise from the social vitalities of the peoples.

It is the essence of the dilemma that such respect cannot be restored by statesmanship alone. The sanctity of solemn obligations depends on the recognition of absolute justice. Else, all conceptions of justice are relative both as to their bases and the respect due to them. Justice becomes the will of the state symbolised in its leader or the voice of the people heard in its assemblies. There is no higher corrective to either. The decay of justice has been hastened by oppression exercised in the name of order, especially in war ; its restoration can only be effected by a legal order which expresses rights and freedoms derived from man's ultimate loyalties.

The defeated nations of the Second World War, Germany and Japan, deserve special consideration from this standpoint. In the administration of conquered peoples it is inevitable that the victors should be to some extent judges on their own behalf. No man, or group of men, who live in the fear and obedience of God, can sustain such a responsibility with equanimity. The demands of government and of proper discipline are only respected when justice is not only done, but is seen to be done. If justice cannot in some measure be achieved in the legal order, it is unlikely that it can be secured in the economic order where its demands are difficult both to define and to satisfy.

The modern world is the stage of a new movement of national emergence and popular consciousness. The short period since the war has witnessed the acquisition of autonomous nationhood by some 500,000,000 persons. The nations of the East have suddenly taken an active part in world affairs, and precisely at the time when many in the West are disillusioned about progress, in Africa and the East men are embracing it with new fervour. From now on, the statesmen and people of the newly born nations will be concerned not so much with self-government as with good government. For the one, passion and combative conviction are mainly required ; for the other, righteousness and wisdom.

Finally, the whole international scene is the scene where communism and Christianity meet. They meet not only as rival ideologies or faiths, but as ingredients in the total attitude of peoples to concrete situations. Their confrontation as systems of thought and faith extending dominion over the allegiance of men is not the subject for this volume.

So much has been written on this that it is hard to choose words. The deterioration in relations between the U.S.S.R. and the U.S.A., and to a lesser extent, Great Britain, has been a sad feature of the post-war years. The obstructive use of the veto in the Security Council, the failure of the Foreign Ministers' conferences with consequences for the future of Germany, the apparently uncompromising character of Soviet policy in special incidents, and the tone of Soviet propaganda (sometimes, however, rivalled by irresponsible journals elsewhere) are all well known. Men differ over the interpretation of these things. There seems no real reason to believe that the U.S.S.R. wants war on a global scale ; primarily nations want security. No nation wants war if it can obtain its fruits otherwise. But a limited demand easily becomes unlimited, and passions and anger of expression lead to positions from which shame or pride prevent retreat.

What contribution can the fellowship of churches represented in the World Council of Churches make ? To their regret, the

B

churches of the West know little of the real influence of Christianity in Russia, and have little opportunity for seeking a clearer understanding with Russian Christians. It is easy to advocate an experiment in friendship between the peoples of the U.S.S.R. and the other nations, East and West. It is also easy to affirm that, above all political differences, Christians believe in certain fundamental assertions about the nature of God and His redemptive action in human history. But if there is no form of access and contact, what progress can be made ? It is difficult to answer this. At least, Christians can strive so to form their views and influence those of others as to exercise a moderating influence where matters of fundamental conviction are not involved ; to forgive while conscious of their own need of forgiveness ; and to recognise all that communism has done for peoples for whom Christianity had apparently accomplished little. In the larger view, it may yet prove that the fellowship of Christians may be the most effective starting point for a development of open relations between the U.S.S.R. and other countries.

In the field of international affairs the ecumenical nature of the Church is of particular significance. This is a truth so obvious that it hardly needs repeating. But there is need for a more thorough exposition of the meaning of this luminous idea. At what points does the ecumenical Church effectively touch the world of international relations ? What Biblical truths, common to the faith of all the churches, provide the foundation for a Christian approach ? What is involved in bringing the influence of ecumenical bodies to bear on international ones ? The World Council of Churches has undoubtedly been well advised in including the intractable field of international relations in its official purview, but in so doing it has raised more questions than can readily be answered, and some that cannot be answered in print, and only by a divine miracle in life.

II

THE CHURCHES' APPROACH TO INTERNATIONAL AFFAIRS

Roswell P. Barnes and Kenneth G. Grubb

T*HE particular purpose of this section is to enquire how the influence of the churches can best be employed in the field of international affairs. It is widely felt in the churches that some of the most crucial questions that confront the Christian conscience are being posed by the relations between the nations ; and yet spiritual and moral influence seems to be impotent. The renewed possibility of war, a continuing testimony to sin and to inability to define the purpose of the power of the state and to confine it, still gloomily dog men's minds. The discovery of the means of using atomic energy has multiplied a thousand-fold the danger, but has also offered new possibilities for peaceful control of power, which it is a duty of the Churches to use. What Christians can do must be done now and maintained constantly ; for when conflict between nations has once broken out, the opportunity for remedy by Christian action, or the chances of limiting the conflagration, are small.*

The relations between nations are therefore of importance to the churches long before they reach the stage of threatened conflict. Wars may be planned, or they may be the almost unavoidable consequence of attitudes which have been nursed and fed until they have grown into uncompromising demands. It is often difficult to foresee what will be the ultimate outcome of economic or political tendencies. They may appear capable of harmonisation with the ambitions of others but, even if the spectator holds that they are, the actors on either side may not believe it. It is similarly difficult to know what will be the ultimate result of any policy. Benevolence of intention provides no assurance of effectiveness. There are many situations in which inaction or a gesture intended as conciliation leads, to all seeming, to greater disaster than the timely, if vigorous, use of power. To the Christian, the difficulty is not to find situations which are interesting because they appear to involve the application of Christian principles, but to refuse to squander energy over the relatively secondary.

THE CHURCHES' APPROACH TO INTERNATIONAL AFFAIRS

I. TYPES OF PROBLEMS

A. *Aspects of International Relations*

What does the task of exercising influence in international relations mean for the churches? In a narrow sense, international relations are direct relations between states as such, negotiating directly with one another through their governments. A dispute over a frontier, a treaty, the exchange of plenipotentiaries are examples. The interests of the churches may be involved in international exchanges of this type, although it more frequently happens that their concern is not sufficiently evident to justify special action. But it is impossible to say so in advance and constant vigilance is needed. The exchange of a few square kilometres of forest may conceivably affect freedom of education or preaching. A treaty may contain conditions safeguarding the rights of minorities or omitting to do so. Such actions as the removal of large masses of people must, on any count, affect the situation of religion as well as the organisation of human welfare.

In a broader sense, international relations are relations between peoples. Governments generally represent in some measure the will of their people, though this representation may vary from a considerable measure to an almost negligible degree in totalitarian régimes. Even in a " police state " it is likely that the government will seek to influence and control the will of its people so as to induce acceptance, if not support, of the government's policy. Consequently, any contact or communication between people across national frontiers may have some bearing on the relations between their nations. " Since all relations within a State, and all supra-national relations, are ultimately relations between one human being and another, the Christian understanding of man is the starting-point for all questions of international relations."[1]

[1] Max Huber, *The Universal Church and the World of Nations*, p. 99.

Thus it is important, in considering the approach of the churches to international affairs, to keep in mind the distinctions between the narrower and the broader aspects of international affairs : between the state and the nation, the government and the people, the technical and the psychological, the scientific and the moral, the impersonal and the personal. While these distinctions are useful for purposes of analysis, the close relationship between the two sets of factors is also important ; for example, the codification of international law and the development of a common moral atmosphere must go hand in hand ; the negotiation of tariff agreements, a highly technical task, is futile unless the government will ratify and the people will support the resulting measures ; an international convention on human rights would be of little value without the will in the several nations to support it.

A different type of relationship was introduced by the League of Nations, and resumed by the United Nations and its Specialised Agencies, including such bodies as UNESCO, and the International Labour Office. The Charters of such bodies frequently contain principles or provisions which are of special importance to Christians. Article 71 of the Charter of the United Nations is an example. The Constitution of UNESCO, by the very nature of its subject, is in this class, and it deserves careful study. It is a feature of the basic documents that govern the policy of some of these recent bodies that they specifically express a willingness or desire to co-operate with recognised non-governmental international bodies. This, perhaps, is not so significant as the more general considerations of the obligations involved and stated in a Charter. The nations which are members of the United Nations do, in effect and in respect of certain policies, agree to accept certain standards of conduct. Constant exposure to comments, strictures and possibly measures of an international body, and the public opinion which is liable to form, can be very effective, but just in what degree depends ultimately on the respect of members for the authority in question, and on the provision for the use of sanctions, or force, against offenders. The effectiveness of this type of internationalism is precisely one of the great issues at stake to-day. In the past it has been effective in minor but useful decisions, but has broken down in great and crucial ones. It is hoped that the curative and creative work of the United Nations will become proportionately more important.   At least, it is worth while for the churches to be so organised as to make their voice heard and views felt in all such organisations, and this is best done if they make their own international instrument for the purpose.

There are occasions when an internal situation may arise within any nation which is repugnant to the Christian conscience outside national bounds, but which is defended on grounds of the sanctity of national sovereignty.   There are also general standards of conscience which do not needlessly interfere with the customary functioning of national governments.   Thus the right of every man to obey his conscience is to be safeguarded by the churches.   But special communities or sections of the populace may be treated wrongly, done out of their reasonable rights, or even persecuted, and the offences condoned if not defended on the ground of the inviolability of domestic sovereignty.   Justification of these lapses from standards of behaviour expected from members of the United Nations may be sought on grounds of public order or the necessity of homogeneous national development.   Remedies may be available but may not be effective. There is an alleged lack of information, differences about the facts, and delay in establishing them.   These cases are apt to be intractable ;   in the end the world loses interest and passes on to the next sensation.

There is also widespread doubt whether the world can go any further on the lines of separate national sovereignty without courting disaster ;   but, in practice, nationalism remains a powerful and almost irreducible force.   It is the responsibility of the churches to remind governments and peoples that nations subsist under the governance of God.   Aside from this consideration, the nation tends to regard itself as morally autonomous and therefore to accept what is, in effect, moral anarchy in the world community.   The Oxford conference stated :   " A true conception of international order requires a recognition of the fact that the state, whether it admits it or not, is not autonomous but is under the ultimate governance of God."

B.   *The Position of the Churches*

In regard to all these different situations the question has not merely to be asked whether the churches have the right to recommend certain action, but what is their competence to do so.   It can be argued that if Christian principles are ignored in the handling of public affairs, Christians must at all costs at least protest. Protest they may, and in so doing relieve their consciences, but it does not follow that the situation will be relieved. The effectiveness of action depends on its being closely matched to the real demands of the situation which are not always candidly declared, or, indeed, easy to identify. Moreover, to endeavour to correct injustice by the application of absolute justice, is not usually possible, and if not possible, to seek to do so may merely mean the creation of tensions in which further injustices will be committed.

On the other hand, immediate effectiveness is not the only consideration in determining Christian action. It is not necessarily demanded of the Christian that he be successful ; it is demanded of him that he be faithful. The churches must raise their voices even if they do not seem to be heard. The Christian always labours in tension between the seeming irrelevance of the absolute on the one hand and the questionable validity of the immediately practical on the other hand.

It is true that Christianity is concerned with the whole life of man. Nevertheless, a useful practical distinction can perhaps be drawn between those questions on which the churches can claim special competent knowledge and others on which they can advance no such claim seriously. An individual Christian may be a first-rate economist, and as such he may have something of weight to say on the technical aspects of an economic question. It is not for the churches, as churches, to claim competence to make similar pronouncements. But the churches can take a firm stand on their own ground : they can expose the fallacies that underlie some of the aims and many of the methods which the modern manipulations of economic society embrace, in the light of the Christian view of the purposes of man's life. They can also speak out of much experience, and from a broader than national or class perspective, on the nature of those inner forces and compulsions which compel men, in spite of natural misgivings, to be ready to suffer for convictions. Thus they may condition the decisions of the Christian economist. They can add to this a wealth of practical wisdom in the promotion of welfare, literacy and the healing of disease of mind and body, and these are questions which are receiving much attention in the discussions of international bodies.

But it is one thing to admit the competence of the churches

to exercise an influence on certain aspects of international affairs, and another to secure agreement as to the objectives they should seek and the methods they should use.   The relations between the nations are fraught with such critical potentialities that it can be argued that every major international issue should engage the close attention of the churches.   At the other extreme stand those who contend that it is impractical to hope to influence the general relationships of the nations or the standards of human rights which they will, in practice, observe, and the churches should concentrate on securing those minimal rights and freedoms which are essential to their own existence.   Another wide body of Christian opinion finds a middle ground and claims an intimate concern in all international measures and national policies designed to promote the social rights and welfare of men, the stability of family life, the advance of literacy, and the improvement of public health, the maintenance of peace and the access to opportunity.   They would not consider that complicated international financial settlements or transport agreements should make detailed claims upon their attention ; but they will recognise a responsibility to create a favourable atmosphere for the negotiations of even such agreements and to comment on broad relevant principles.

The main difference is between those who hold that it is the duty of the churches to influence and form a view upon international relations as such, and those who hold that it is their duty to state and guide the attitude of Christians to them.   It is difficult to draw this line with exactitude, and may not be desirable to do so.   The advocates of the first of these views are faced with an immense task.   The advocates of the second assume that certain political outlooks are unlikely to be changed and that the appetite for power takes little real account of formal and legal obligations.   Therefore, they seek to define the attitude of the churches in the face of these conditions, and to identify a few points where Christian action seems unavoidable.

These differences in approach and temper are partly traceable to the theological and historical background of the churches. Examined more factually, they are also due to the different positions occupied by nations in world affairs, and the very different degrees of influence exercised by the Church within the nation.   A vigorous church movement, exercising influence in its own nation while that nation commands weight among the world

of nations, finds no field of international action alien to it. Great
Britain was in this position in the nineteenth century when
religion was conventionally popular and the nation energetic
and assertive. The United States, for different reasons, occupies
a place of great influence in the world to-day and the churches
are, in turn, influential in the country. But when a church is
very small, or is shrinking rather than growing, or has been the
victim of persecution, or is faced with an unsympathetic and
restrictive political régime, it tends inevitably to concentrate
on the maintenance of its own essential life, and to limit its
interest in international affairs to a minimum. It is, therefore,
impossible to say that either of the two tendencies in question is
right to the exclusion of the other. Which is followed will, in
practice, depend on the standing of the churches in a nation,
their tradition and their relation to the state. A lively sense
of interdependence and mutual obligation between churches all
over the world is one way by which to fortify their influence
and incidentally to strengthen their own position. But no one
who is conscious of the strength and jealousies of nationalism and the conscious repudiation in many quarters of a
Christian approach to politics will underrate the difficulties in
practice.

Despite these differences, there has been a tendency during
recent years to converge upon a common ground where there
is a large measure of agreement. This agreement, already hinted
at above, is furthered by emphasising the distinction between
the more limited and technical aspects of international relations,
on the one hand, and the broader moral and psychological aspects
on the other hand. It is recognised that the churches seldom
have a responsibility to advocate one specific technical measure
among several when their respective merits can be judged only
on the basis of highly specialised knowledge and information.
But behind the technical questions there are usually questions
of purpose and motive, upon which, it is generally agreed, the
churches must speak. By speaking in this field, decisions are
conditioned rather than determined. The distinction between
conditioning and determining decisions cannot be clear-cut,
but it implies that influence intended to condition decisions is
less direct and specific than influence intended to determine
decisions. Even in the technical field, the proficiency and
effectiveness of the experts and professional diplomats has not

been so conspicuous during recent decades as to justify the relegation of all responsibility to them.

The churches possess certain assets and suffer from certain limitations or disadvantages in organising to influence international affairs. Their most obvious and valuable advantage is the widespread distribution of Christians. Thanks largely to the past 150 years of missionary expansion and to the character of emigration to the British Dominions, Christian churches of Protestant, Orthodox or Anglican allegiance are scattered over the world. Much has been said of the significance of this : Archbishop Temple called it this " great new fact " of our time. Potentially it is unquestionably a development of great significance, for it means that between and among the nations there are numbers of persons, themselves citizens of " sovereign states ", who owe obedience to our Lord and Master, and are constantly striving to maintain that obedience amid the cogent and necessary loyalties of national life.

The Christian testimony to the permanence of absolute principles, to the existence of values which have not been, and cannot be, created by the unaided effort of statesmen, philosophers or scientists, is a contribution to an approach to international affairs that is badly needed. Belief about man's place in society and the unconditional obligations which the existence of God and his neighbour lay upon him, is an essential constituent in enduring human relationships. The churches may be divided on many questions of order, theology and tradition, but in those beliefs which are the decisive ones for the establishment of human rights they are very largely at one. It is certainly the case that there have been and will continue to be differences about the precise relationship between church and nation which may best express the truth of such assumptions, but there is a Christian conception of the relation of man to his neighbour, of the reverence due to personality and of the obedience to be held towards reasonably and properly constituted authority and the inviolability of the pledged word, which are not to be found, and may be explicitly repudiated, where the Christian conscience is unheard.

But to leave the matter at that is to overstate the case. The value of this world-wide witness of the Church is seriously reduced by its actual condition. In most nations the churches are small, and it is correspondingly more difficult for them to maintain their own due freedom and rights under circumstances of discrimination, and to influence the international conduct of the nation. The Christians of India, of every ecclesiastical allegiance, are two per cent. of the population ; of China, less than one per cent. In the Near and Middle East the question has to be asked whether the ancient Orthodox and Eastern minorities can prosper. There are, however, hopeful signs in many places that Christian influence is not solely dependent upon numerical strength. While in most countries there are not many citizens who vote for a policy because it appeals to an enlightened Christian conscience, yet it is true that where Christians are few in number they are sometimes prominent in leadership. In a democracy, however, the quality of counsel is commanded by its popularity, and any estimate of the international influence of the churches must be tempered by a sense of these limitations, and of the final aims of human society.

It follows that the concerns of the churches, even if acutely involved in any situation, will be only one of many factors which will weigh in the formulation of official policy. A general negotiation which in its consequences may affect the interest of the churches, may be pursued and completed on grounds only remotely connected with it. It may often be right for the churches to endeavour to secure that due attention should be given to their case, but it cannot be right that they should over-state it, or press it beyond a due point. The consequences of human actions are frequently very different from the intentions of human agents, and a certain prudence must be exercised in pressing for policies whose ultimate repercussions may be unexpected and not generally profitable.

In practice, religious motives are usually found in dilution, not in a pure state. The protection of weak Christian minorities may be assumed by powerful Christian neighbours desiring to advance national influence under the guise of religious zeal. In such cases a genuine Christian approach is rendered nugatory almost from the start. It is partly the sense that these situations involve so many tangles that caused enlightened opinion to advocate a general approach to human rights as the best way to attempt to solve the specific problem of the rights of minorities.

Finally, it must be remembered that the international action of the churches is frequently powerless in the face of the extra-ordinary resistant amalgam produced by the integration of

religion and national life, and constantly hardened by the
nationalist appeal to cultural homogeneity.   In some countries
the attitude of the State to its own political and social problems
has been powerfully, if insensibly, affected by the outlook of
popular religion, and the attitude of religion similarly influenced
by the State.   The massive and impressive religious and national
cultures of the East are not easily penetrable.   In the Christian
world the same resistance is found in the hardening of the Roman
Catholic centres of influence and power in Latin America against
the liberties and rights of other Christians.   These tendencies and
attitudes of nations may effectively nullify the paper decisions
of the most solemn international guarantees.

Moreover, it frequently happens that influence can be
exercised only or mainly through ways that are uncongenial
to Christians.   Christianity makes unconditional claims.   The
execution of policy in international relations is, as is the case in
politics generally, the art of the possible.   Only in certain
countries can the churches arouse popular interest, and then only
over certain questions.   Matters of some importance to the
Christian conscience may be settled in negotiations between
governments and only a few people will be aware, and then too
late for action.   In the long run, the advocacy of general principles does have its effect, or rather in the past it has had, but
in the process many just causes may be lost and apparent
injustices done.

The Christian is, therefore, faced with the task of tirelessly
pursuing valid objectives by the methods of compromise and
adjustment to the possible.   In this process the objectives lose
their clarity and not infrequently their original value.   Ends are
inevitably coloured by the kind of means used to achieve them,
and it is always questionable how far it is right to lower the level
of even proximate aims in order to enjoy a partial success.   On
the other hand, in such an atmosphere it is frequently possible to
combine forces with those who are moving in the same direction,
although they start from different assumptions.   All who believe
generally in the respect due to human personality, although they
may not agree with Christians on the ultimate grounds on which
that respect must be based, are concerned in the struggle to
secure effectively certain human rights.   Most minorities appeal
to a broad cultural liberalism and some hold to the same principle when they become majorities.   The advisability of the

churches correlating efforts with those of other faiths or of no
fundamental faith in the struggle for standards and conditions
rests upon considerations of prudence and convenience rather
than of principle or conviction.   But even while they accept
compromise in a given situation, the churches must remember
that it is their responsibility always to maintain a tension between
the absolute and the immediately possible.

2. ACTION OF THE CHURCHES

Whereas the political forces of the modern world are to-day
so aligned as to offer some new possibilities for Christian action,
they also present very serious obstacles.   In the nineteenth
century the British influence was at its height and was widespread
throughout a large part of the world, and this corresponded with
a period when nascent nationalisms of the modern regimented
type were only beginning to rise to self-consciousness.   It was,
therefore, possible for Britain to champion humanitarian causes
whether on disinterested or self-interested grounds, to intervene
actively for the protection of missionaries, and to press for and
often obtain substantial concessions to the demand for religious
and cultural freedom.   Britain was not alone in these aims and
such accords as the Berlin Act, establishing minimum standards
for the powers in Africa, were the joint result of the efforts of
several nations.   But Britons played a prominent part, which in
the view of some should be assumed by the United States.   But
to many the idea that any one nation should enjoy excessive
power, even if it uses it beneficently, is distasteful, and inevitably
savours of an imperialism meaning little more than the domination of one people by another to the latter's advantage, or at the
best complacent and unprogressive patronage.

By the end of the War of 1914-1918, the growth of modern
nationalistic feeling was in full swing.   The break-up of the
Turkish Empire marked the end of the old order in the Near
and Middle East ;   the constitutional struggle was soon to
develop intensely in India ; China and Japan were in various
stages of national growth, internal coherence or assertiveness.
But a totally new factor was introduced by the creation of the
League of Nations.   This raised the question of the ultimate
meaning and possible limitations of national sovereignty, but this
proved incapable of solution. After the war of 1939-1945, the same
question remained and, in the view of many, is still the most crucial

single one in this field. All nations claim the right of national self-government but, through the United Nations, an attempt has been made to secure adhesion to certain standards of conduct, and to provide, in some cases, for measures by which they will be observed. But the difficulty of reconciling national sovereignty with international obligations is still unsolved in practice.

It seems inadvisable that reliance should be placed on the direct intervention of any one nation in order to sustain the principles of Christian action in the affairs of other states. Politically it is impracticable and, religiously, it is a principle of inadequate strength and justice. If, in special cases, pressure is to be brought from outside on any nation to ensure the fulfilment of agreed standards of human rights, it should only be through the process of representation at the United Nations and its specialised agencies, and through other appropriate international institutions. The times are past when any one or more nations can, or should, assume the position of advocates of special privilege or status for Christians or for churches. The fact must be faced that the modern atmosphere of cultural relativism and the sanctity accorded to national autonomy make this difficult. But the dangers of the present international situation must be taken into full account. The Charter of the United Nations is not regarded by most Christians as an ideal international instrument : it represents, as was plainly stated at the time, what was possible under all the circumstances. Moreover, it is as well to remember that a great war necessarily undermines the effective moral assumptions current in international relations. The success of force, however justified, breeds respect for force. The repudiation of accepted codes under the supposed necessity of circumstance, and the pressure to sacrifice standards of moral conduct for the sake of victory, lower the temperature of international sensitivity. The public conscience becomes hardened, and the motive of self-interest, always dominant, becomes over-powering. When even the strong are preoccupied with the problem of survival, the rights and liberties of the weak receive scant respect. While, on the one hand, it should be recognised that in such an atmosphere it is sheer optimism to expect that the representations of churchmen will easily result in positive and favourable action, on the other hand it should be remembered that the calculation of immediate success or failure is not for Christians decisive.

It is pertinent to ask whether the churches are equipped to maintain in this field the activity necessary to make their influence felt. Theoretically, there is no reason why they should not be. The expansion of Christianity, the leadership which the churches possess, and the basic assumptions of the Christian Faith are all assets. The formation of the World Council of Churches has come at a time when not only the internal consciousness of the churches has demanded it, but when also the external situation may only be susceptible to a central and united approach. The younger churches may express their concerns through the International Missionary Council as well as the World Council. Moreover, ever since the Edinburgh Conference of 1910 the churches have been at work improving their own techniques of co-operation across the boundaries of the nations and the divisions imposed by their own traditions. More recently (1946) these two representative bodies have combined to establish a Commission of the Churches on International Affairs.[1]

But certain conditions must be observed if Christian action in international affairs is to be appropriate. It is important to decide whether, in general, the churches should pursue those requisites which belong especially to their own life or should immerse themselves in the struggle to secure the general conditions which they believe to be essential to the well-being of the peoples. Should they concentrate on the fight to obtain effective guarantees, and the effective practice of religious liberties, or should they join with all those who are promoting a general and effective Bill of Human Rights ? Should they seek privileges for any religious minority, Christian, Moslem, Jewish or other, or should they advocate the acceptance of a general standard and formulate a broad policy accordingly ? It will probably be agreed that they should not be concerned to seek any privileges at all, but such rights as all men should enjoy ; but when energies and resources are limited there will be differences of opinion over the priorities. It may be argued that unless the churches protect their own interests, no one else will do so. But the churches do not have interests which they do not earnestly desire to share with all men. In the long run, therefore, they may be well advised to pursue a standard of general human rights to which at least all members of the United Nations will be expected

[1] For a review of its programme and work, see Section 3, p. 37

to conform. But, within such a programme, the rights and liberties of special value to organised religion are committed to their special care.

Agreed provisions could only express the churches' policy in the limited field discussed. If the concern of the churches is with such matters as disarmament, the conditions of dependent peoples, the assumption of a true international culture and a host of other questions, it is clear that agreement could only be reached among the churches on very general statements. This is not to say that the churches cannot take any action, but it is often the case that the most effective action in such negotiations is not inspired by any very clear or detailed understanding of policy. It is impossible to lay down hard-and-fast rules in advance for the elaboration of the best procedure. Every situation requires to be studied on its own merits and with reference to its own importance and the vigour and weight of the forces which seek to control it. All that can be done here is to point to some of the various approaches which may have to be followed.

It is a commonplace that the soundness of a policy depends largely on accurate, continuous and up-to-date intelligence. Large sums are spent by the departments of external affairs of the governments of the world, and millions of cabled words translated into cypher or code in order that the policies of states may be perceived, the state of public opinion foreshadowed and the probable moves in the game correctly estimated. Much of this work of accumulating information and compiling intelligence must be done with great secrecy : no reasonable person would expect it to be a transaction of the market-place. It is not suggested that the churches should imitate such a system. It would be contrary to their habitual outlook and would require expenditure which they ought not to contemplate when the more urgent primary needs of mankind are so largely unsatisfied. Nor would the situations which the churches may be called upon to consider usually be such as to require so elaborate an apparatus.

It is nevertheless true that to determine policy in any situation without good intelligence is to court disaster from the start : it implies what is too often true, that the churches under-rate the resources both of governments and of other organisations in the field. The churches are not badly equipped for the development of a centralised system of necessary intelligence. Their own members are scattered throughout the world. In their ranks are found persons of judgment and experience in contact with many aspects of the national life and capable of forming reliable estimates on the trend of official policy and the real outlook of different sections of the people. The churches naturally speak with authority and understanding on the movements of religious thought and the temper of the religious life. But if they are to render good service to internal relations, it is essential that their analysis should not be vitiated by undue optimism or over-simplification.

An international Christian body equipped with a good service of intelligence from informed church sources on matters which by general consent touched immediately the Christian conscience might render useful service. This would be enhanced if such intelligence proved to be a reliable shadow of events actually to come—but prophecy is dangerous because it is usually misleading. Anyhow, a really adequate scheme could hardly be envisaged as it would require a central staff, for the digestion of material, which could not be provided without considerable resources. At present the opposite error is frequently inevitable. Action is frequently suggested at the last moment and backed up by a presentation of the case that may be informative and accurate to men on the spot, but unconvincing to men off it. Time is not allowed for facing coolly the objections that those less interested in the cause of religion may very properly raise, and, in fine, the case proves difficult to sustain.

But information is not enough, either for governments or for churches. Wisdom is as essential as knowledge, and no amount of knowledge evaluated and analysed within a pattern of reference of secular pragmatism can provide sound policy. A Christian understanding of history is fully as important as political science for understanding the behaviour of people. Consequently, the churches should give attention to supplementing the competence of governments rather than to attempting to duplicate it.

But to possess the facts and understand them and leave it at that is inexcusable in a world where anxiety is more common than hope, and war easier to organise than peace. Action can take one or all of six forms—prayer, negotiation, consultation, reconciliation, education and publicity.

C

A. *Prayer*

It is a duty of Christians to pray for constituted authorities and for international bodies, and if it sometimes seems all that can be done it is never the least important thing to do. The efficacy of prayer should not be questioned, for not only does Biblical history testify to the influence of prayer upon political events, but also the experience of present-day Christians corroborates the faith of prophets, apostles and martyrs who called upon God in prayer. Spiritual forces are liberated by prayer which create peace and destroy evil.

B. *Negotiation*

Action through negotiation can take various forms. An international, non-governmental body, as is the World Council of Churches, can properly negotiate directly with international organisations, the United Nations and its specialised agencies including such bodies as UNESCO, the International Labour Office, the International Refugee Organisation and others. These bodies sometimes have, as in the case of the Economic and Social Council of the United Nations, elaborate provisions for co-operation in certain questions with the non-governmental organisations. In other cases they allow for the appearance of recognised observers at conferences and for consultative committees of a " mixed " type when non-governmental representation may be admitted. It can be determined only by a careful examination in each separate case whether the churches, through the World Council of Churches or any body acting on its behalf, should avail themselves of these opportunities. On the one hand, the expenditure of mind and time may be considerable if policy is to be thoroughly and continuously discussed and the churches' viewpoint effectively pressed. On the other hand, it is useless to complain afterwards that the process of international debate and possible agreement has ignored the legitimate interests of the churches, if use has not been made of the openings afforded for representation.

There are, however, many questions which are not international in the broad sense: they only concern the interests of one or two countries or are matters which are most likely to be settled by negotiation between two or three states or powers, without being raised at the United Nations or its councils and specialised agencies. In such cases, if action is to be taken by the churches at all, it is often better taken by the competent representative national organisation, by national councils of churches, or one influential church. If such matters are raised with the World Council of Churches or any of its agencies, it may or may not be desirable for the World Council or the appropriate committee to express an opinion, but it is usually proper to refer action to the national church bodies concerned. This is not a universal procedure, but unless it were clearly evident that agreed Christian principle had been flagrantly transgressed, it is difficult for a body such as the World Council to press for any particular solution. The same principle usually applies to the not infrequent case of an appeal by a Christian minority against a constitutional injustice. It may be possible for the World Council to have the matter raised at the United Nations, but frequently the only remedy lies in access to the seat of power of the one or two countries concerned.

C. *Consultation*

Consultation with those directly responsible for governmental policy and action is generally more appropriate and effective than formal negotiation. Or it may be a correlative to negotiation. A conference, formal or informal, of a church leader or group of leaders with government officials provides an opportunity to ask questions and offer suggestions and warnings which may correct perspective, deepen insight, or call attention to a neglected interest. It may serve also to inform the churchmen and to increase their understanding of the government.

Consultation may also serve to encourage the responsible government leaders to give due weight to Christian considerations, including the wider interests of humanity. Such leaders are under constant pressure from groups seeking to further their own interests. They are also under pressure to serve the immediate and obvious interests of the state to the neglect of the welfare of other peoples. One of the functions of the Church is to keep the leaders of the state under tension in the face of the demands of the moral law, lest the necessary compromise in political action go farther than is necessary in the direction of mere expediency and so bring disaster. Moreover, public leaders need to be assured that, in their highest purposes, they have the fellowship and support of the Christian forces. A consultative visit may be more helpful than a carefully formulated petition.

D.   *Reconciliation*

The churches in their own life, relationships and behaviour can set an example of reconciliation for the world of nations. This example may have a more persuasive influence on international affairs than hortatory resolutions.   On at least these three propositions there is widespread agreement : (1) The several churches, in their relationships and in their life as members of a world-wide fellowship, should give a demonstration of the achievement of an orderly and mutually helpful community. The basic problem of world order is that of achieving world community in a moral or spiritual sense.   This requires that peoples of different nations, races and cultures should learn to live together as members of a community.   If the churches in their fellowship can achieve mutual understanding and community of essential purpose, they can bind the world together and thus build the necessary foundations for political order. (2) The churches in the ecumenical fellowship should achieve common agreement on the basic moral principles of national and international policy inherent in their common faith.   Such agreement among the peoples of various nations, races and cultures is the basic need of the world to-day.   Moreover, the aggressive promulgation of such principles is generally the most appropriate and most effective way of influencing and guiding political policies.   (3) The churches of various communions and in all nations should continue and enlarge their programme of mutual aid, bearing one another's burdens.   By extending assistance in relief and reconstruction across national, racial and ecclesiastical boundaries, Christians show the better way, strengthen faith, and further reconciliation.

E.   *Education*

Education is another form of action.   The churches have a responsibility for educating and influencing public opinion concerning the basic ethical and moral principles which should underlie national policy with regard to international relations. The basic Christian principle that all men are brothers presupposes the need of educating mankind in the recognition of the great human family.   The churches should urge upon their members especially the acceptance of the responsibilities of Christain vocation in citizenship which requires (1) that the individual, on the basis of his enlightened Christian judgment, support as a citizen those national policies which most closely approximate to an application of Christian principles and oppose measures that are objectionable ; and (2) that he vote for, and support, public leaders who are committed to such policies. The educational programme may include the publication of analyses of current government policies in the light of Christian principles.

F. *Publicity*

The value of publicity in relation to international questions varies enormously from one country to another. In the United States, for example, it is relatively easy to secure and the American people are influenced by publicity when it is done with skill. The public nature of modern official conferences creates an atmosphere which is favourable to the use of publicity. But it is precisely in countries where publicity might be most helpful that it is impossible to secure. There are usually one or more of four reasons for this. Either the Press and radio are strictly controlled by the authorities and access cannot be had by unofficial bodies ; or the question which may be of great importance to the Christian community has little or no general appeal ; or editors and radio directors wish to avoid controversy ; or the churches, representing only a small minority ; are unable to carry the necessary influence.

3. THE COMMISSION OF THE CHURCHES ON INTERNATIONAL AFFAIRS

Effective Christian action in international affairs calls for an organisation which will give due regard to the responsibilities of churches in different countries and which will at the same time capitalise on the world-wide resources of non-Roman Christianity. A brief description of work now being carried on under international Christian auspices may serve as a basis for fashioning a plan for further procedure.

The Commission of the Churches on International Affairs (C.C.I.A.) has been set up jointly by the World Council of Churches and the International Missionary Council to work on their behalf in the field of international affairs. The Commission was established at a conference at Cambridge, England, in 1946. It consists of twenty-eight members in different countries of the world, many of whom are laymen. While the duties of the Commission member have not been formally specified, initial experience has suggested the following functions : (*a*) to correspond with the officers of the Commission, drawing their attention to matters which call for study or possible action and advising them on relevant data ; (*b*) to co-operate with recognised church agencies and committees in his own country in educating public opinion or in making representation to public authorities on matters in the international sphere that are of concern to the Christian conscience ; and (*c*) to participate in duly convened meetings of the Commission.

The primary responsibility of the Commission is to serve the churches, councils ; and conferences which are members of the World Council of Churches and the International Missionary Council as a source of stimulus and knowledge in their approach to international problems, as a medium of common counsel and action, and as their organ in formulating the Christian mind on world issues, and in bringing that mind effectively to bear upon such issues.   The specific purposes of the Commission are defined in the statement which was adopted at Cambridge and subsequently approved by the parent bodies.   (See Appendix A.)   In accordance with these provisions, the Commission, which has offices in London and New York, has begun the work committed to it.

Contacts with International Authorities

Contact with the United Nations and its organs is maintained in two ways.   The Commission is officially registered with the United Nations Department of Public Information at its New York headquarters ; by this provision it regularly receives all unrestricted documents and is entitled to be represented by an observer at all open meetings.   The documents are catalogued and filed daily with a view to communicating any items of importance to appropriate church leaders or agencies.   A staff member of the C.C.I.A. attends most of the United Nations meetings where matters of concern to the churches are under discussion.   Moreover, the Commission holds consultative status with the Economic and Social Council (Category B), as provided under Article 71 of the United Nations Charter and is represented by an officially accredited consultant.   This offers a channel for bringing to the Council and its commissions any views which the Churches' Commission itself may desire to submit or which churches request it to transmit.

Contact is further maintained with related and specialised agencies. Through arrangements at the London office, the Commission has been represented by an observer at the Paris and Mexico City Conferences of the United Nations Educational, Scientific and Cultural Organisation and has maintained continuing contact with the work of this agency. While such informal, friendly relations have proved helpful, there are strong arguments favouring a more formal relationship in accordance with arrangements which UNESCO has set up. Through unofficial relationships at London and Montreal, the Churches' Commission has also followed the activities of the International Labour Office.

National or Local Commissions

It was recognised at Cambridge that the strength of international Christian action in international affairs would be in proportion to the interest and activity of the churches in their national settings. In accordance with the first aim of its Charter, the Commission has sought to encourage the formation of national commissions through which the conscience of Christians may be stirred and educated as to their responsibilities in the world of nations. The World Council of Churches and the International Missionary Council supplied lists of addresses, including existing ecumenical committees, Christian councils, correspondents, and the like. Circular letters and inquiry forms were sent to these inviting their advice on the best means of establishing contacts within their particular countries.

Nine national commissions concerned with international affairs are now known to be in existence, and one has been authorised but not yet established. In sixteen countries, correspondents have been appointed, either provisionally or by official church bodies, to serve as a point of contact with the international Commission. In a few countries two correspondents have been named to care for the local church and the missionary interests. Where commissions have not yet been set up and correspondents not yet named, church leaders, including members of the C.C.I.A., have been temporarily designated to receive communications and to refer them for study and action to the proper agencies of the churches. While the results thus far achieved by letters are encouraging, there is general agreement on the need to strengthen and extend these contacts through personal visits.

Information to the Churches

Utilising the points of contact thus provided, the officers of the Commission have sought to keep its constituency informed about its activities. They have brought to the attention of the churches certain issues with which Christians were apparently concerned or on which judgment could helpfully be expressed. Memoranda on United Nations activities in the field of human rights and on the general work of UNESCO have been distributed. Information has been sent out covering the decisions of the United Nations General Assembly and of other organs. A few statements by national church commissions have been circulated.

Particular attention has been given to the process of writing an International Bill of Human Rights. Drafts of the first Working Papers for a Declaration and Convention, prepared by a United Nations drafting committee, were widely distributed and critical reactions solicited. Similarly, the draft Declaration and Covenant prepared by the United Nations Commission on Human Rights at Geneva in December, 1947, were forwarded to church leaders in over forty countries with a request for appraisal.

It should be recognised that only a meagre beginning has been made in the effort to keep the churches informed about international developments. While the contacts with the United Nations and related agencies make available relatively full information, the resources of the Commission have been inadequate for necessary analysis and distribution.

Representation to International Authorities

By its Charter, the Commission of the Churches is authorised to represent its constituency before international bodies such as the United Nations and related agencies. The contacts which the Commission maintains with the United Nations, particularly by virtue of its consultative status with the Economic and Social Council, open the way for a ready transmission of Christian views. In a few instances, the officers have presented to the Secretariat of the United Nations statements which were formally adopted by national church bodies or by their officially constituted departments. Since the Commission is known to represent many churches throughout the world, such transmission has been possible on behalf of a single church group without implicating others or the parent bodies.

In only one field—human rights and, more particularly, religious freedom—has there been sufficient evidence of a common mind to enable the Commission to speak directly on behalf of the churches. Here it drew upon statements of the Oxford and Madras Conferences, current actions by officially constituted groups of the World Council and the International Missionary Council, and the replies received from critical study of the draft Declaration and Convention on Human Rights. As a result of this representation, numerous changes were brought about at the next stage of drafting : the United Nations proposals for provisions to safeguard religious freedom and related human rights, as provisionally accepted in the Geneva drafts of the Declaration and Covenant, conform closely to the position taken by representatives of the churches. On behalf of the Commission, the Executive Chairman and the Director addressed a letter to the Secretary-General of the United Nations urging prompt action on a convention to outlaw genocide.

On many other subjects where an expression of Christian opinion could reasonably be expected, the Commission has been unable to take a stand, primarily because (1) the churches have not formulated the general principles to express a Christian mind on these subjects ; and (2) the speed with which action was required could not be matched by the present facilities for communication with churches all over the world. However, by processes of informal consultation and clearly without commitment of the Commission or its constituency, officers of the Commission have conferred with officials of the United Nations and related bodies on numerous matters in which the churches are vitally interested.

Action by Separate Church Groups

As occasion demanded, churches in various countries have taken independent action on problems of international relations or have communicated directly with their own governments. In a number of cases, the Churches' Commission on International Affairs has brought problems with relevant information to the attention of various agencies of the churches of their national councils, and constructive steps have followed. A limited number of issues are here cited to illustrate this type of procedure : (1) revision of original Trusteeship Agreements to include more adequate safeguards for religious liberty and missionary freedom ; (2) provisions for human rights with special reference to religious freedom in treaties with the Axis satellite powers ; (3) consideration of the Palestine problem, to make available important information and to stress especially the historical and contemporary interests of the Christian community ; (4) investigation of the refugee problem with a view to possible representation by the C.C.I.A. when the basic information had been compiled by the Ecumenical Refugee Commission ; (5) provisions for religious freedom in the Italian constitution and the import of these in face of discriminatory articles in the Lateran Pacts ; (6) the alleged treatment of natives in S.W. Africa ; (7) violations of religious freedom in Spain ; (8) protection of German missionary property and the status of German missionaries ; (9) general problems of the peace settlement with Germany, with special reference to human rights.

International issues will continue to arise in which Christians in one or another country have particular interest or peculiar competence. Moreover, many problems will appear on which a common world Christian mind is difficult to reach, or to reach rapidly enough. While international Christian action must be sought wherever imperative and feasible, the procedure through separate church agencies or national churches will obviously play an important part.

Study Programme

The Commission of the Churches on International Affairs has been made responsible for special studies on international issues in preparation for the Amsterdam meeting and, in that connection, has served as Commission IV of the study programme. This assignment has involved considerable time and effort, as well as correspondence and travel. Little opportunity has been at hand for additional investigations. However, the Commission has under consideration various studies, among which those projected in co-operation with the Younger Churches of the Far East hold a prominent place.

This report is in no sense an exhaustive description of the work thus far attempted under the auspices of the Commission of the Churches on International Affairs. While it recounts in part what has been undertaken, it is intended primarily to illustrate a programme which, with necessary modifications, will permit Christian testimony in current world affairs. The examples cited are largely within the types of action described above as negotiation, consultation and education, but prayer, reconciliation and publicity have played an important part. The churches will have to decide whether the kind of organisation here projected and the kind of work here done represent the manner in which their responsibility can be most adequately met. They will further have to decide whether their activities in the field of international relations shall be carried on at a minimum level, or whether the resources which they make available shall be more nearly in proportion to the gigantic nature of the task.

All private bodies dealing with international affairs are at a disadvantage in matters of technical skill and information compared with official ones. The expansive strength of bureaucracy, the discipline of organised departments of state in the best civil services, and the quality of personnel employed, give governments a long lead. This is increased by lavish expenditure on cables, transport and accommodation. Even so, their achievements leave something to be desired. On the other hand, the churches enjoy the advantages of clearly defined and limited aims, of spiritual cohesion and world-wide extension, and of the service of mind and heart which derives from deeply-felt loyalties. It should not be impossible to devise means to use these assets to the best advantage in a world which sorely needs justice between the nations and mercy between men.

APPENDIX A

CHARTER OF THE COMMISSION OF THE CHURCHES ON INTERNATIONAL AFFAIRS

The primary responsibility of the Commission on International Affairs shall be to serve the Churches, Councils and Conferences which are members of the World Council of Churches and the International Missionary Council, as a source of stimulus and knowledge in their approach to international problems, as a medium of common counsel and action, and as their organ in formulating the Christian mind on world issues and in bringing that mind effectively to bear upon such issues. More particularly, it shall be the aim of the Commission :

1. To encourage the formation, in each country and in each church represented in the parent bodies, of commissions through which the consciences of Christians may be stirred and educated as to their responsibilities in the world of nations.

The influence of Christians upon international problems must be made effective mainly through individual governments and inasmuch as the relation of public opinion to official action varies, the methods of expressing this influence will vary. It must be a major purpose of the Commission to assist churches in the several lands to express their judgments on world issues to their governments.

2. To gather and appraise materials on the relations of the churches to public affairs, including the work of various churches and church councils in these fields and to make the best of this material available to its constituent churches.

Thus the Commission will draw spiritual sustenance from our Christian people. If the Commission is to be an effective body, there must be channels through which the hopes and fears of Christian people can flow into the Commission, and through it to Christians in other lands.

3. To study selected problems of international justice and world order, including economic and social questions, and to make the results of such study widely known among all the churches.

Only a limited number of carefully chosen problems can be given the thorough study required. Such study should utilise the best available thought from any quarter, should seek counsel of informed experts, and should bring to bear on the problems insights derived from Christian faith.

4. To assign specific responsibilities and studies to sub-committees or special groups, and to claim for them the assistance of persons especially expert in the problems under consideration.

Much of the Commission's most important work will have to be done through groups, smaller and more readily accessible than the Commission as a whole. Special effort should be directed to assure that such sub-committees, while necessarily limited in scope of membership, shall be as fully representative as possible.

5. To organise study conferences of leaders of different churches and nations.

Through such conferences, meeting in an atmosphere of Christian fellowship, significant Christian judgment on international issues may be reached, and the work of the churches in the several nations may be guided and advanced.

6. To call the attention of the churches to problems especially claimant upon the Christian conscience at any particular time, and to suggest ways in which Christians may act effectively upon these problems, in their respective countries and internationally.

7. To discover and declare Christian principles with direct relevance to the relations of nations, and to formulate the bearing of these principles upon immediate issues.

In preparing and issuing public declarations, the Commission should build upon the results of earlier work by the parent bodies in this field, such as the Stockholm, Jerusalem, Oxford, and Madras Conferences. In general, the character and scope of such declarations may well follow the general lines thus established. More specifically :

(a) When the World Council of Churches or the International Missionary Council as a whole is meeting, in an Assembly, conference, or committee, the Commission might recommend statements which, if adopted, would have importance as representative of Christian opinion (outside Roman Catholicism) all over the world.

(b) Since the Councils meet infrequently, the Commission on International Affairs would, in the interim, have liberty to speak in its own name, making clear that the Councils had not endorsed the statement.

(c) If occasions arise in which the officers or sub-committees of the Commission feel impelled to speak without waiting for consultation with the Commission as a whole, they should make clear that they are not committing any group other than themselves.

8. To represent the World Council of Churches and the International Missionary Council in relations with international bodies such as the United Nations and related agencies.

The Commission should maintain such contacts with these bodies as will assist in :

(*a*) the progressive development and codification of international law ;

(*b*) the encouragement of respect for and observance of human rights and fundamental freedoms ; special attention being given to the problem of religious liberty ;

(*c*) the international regulation of armaments ;

(*d*) the furtherance of international economic co-operation ;

(*e*) the acceptance by all nations of the obligation to promote to the utmost the well-being of dependent peoples, including their advance toward self-government and the development of their free political institutions ;

(*f*) the promotion of international social, cultural, educational and humanitarian enterprises.

9. To concert from time to time with other organisations holding similar objectives in the advancement of particular ends.

III

THE CHURCH AND THE DISORDER OF INTERNATIONAL SOCIETY

F. M. Van Asbeck

I. THE TASK AND ATTITUDE OF THE CHURCH

WE speak of the task of the Church, of the word of the Church, of its message, its power and weakness, and of its guilt. In the international field especially, where we are concerned with different nations and with the different churches of non-Roman Catholic creed, where we cross frontiers and denominations, the question is forced upon us : What do we mean in using the word " Church ? " In these contexts " The Church " does not mean the sum of all the existing churches, nor the *Una Sancta* itself. In the words " The Church " we express our firm belief in a new reality, which is taking form and substance in the efforts of the different churches to reach, through all divergencies of opinions and attitudes, theological and ethical, a consensus concerning the central and vital problems of the present.

That new reality, the ecumenical fellowship, compels us to reconsider and to re-think international relations, in the midst of which the Divine Message has to be proclaimed and the outlook towards the *Una Sancta* kept open. In all its preaching, in all its admonitions and warnings, the Church has to be conscious of the existence of the *Una Sancta*, transcending all the cleavages and divergencies on earth. But it would be arrogant, godless presumption to equate our ecumenical fellowship with the *Una Sancta*, as though the Kingdom of Divine Love were already present in this world.

New theological reflection leads to new concrete and practical conclusions on the relations between Church and world, and on the witness of the Church. The Church cannot keep silent upon the conclusions arising from its reconsideration of world affairs.

The world wars have shaken the conscience of the churches and roused them to a clearer perception of their task in the international sphere ; of their special responsibility for the founding and the foundations of a world order, in which all the peoples of the earth may " lead a tranquil life " (1 Tim. ii, 2). Till the first world war the Church had almost totally neglected its duty towards the international society ; and even after that pandemonium its response to the burning questions of international order, authority and liberty was at first lamentably weak. This plain default of the Church, however, can be explained, though certainly not justified, by the general conception of international questions as " *arcana imperii*," as the private preserve of the governments of the so-called sovereign states, and in particular of the Great Powers. Ordinary men, so doctrine and practice since the eighteenth century have taught us, have no legal standing in, and no concern with international relations and their law (or lack of law). They were only " objects " of that peculiar branch of law, debarred from a voice in its application, from judgment and criticism. The same passive rôle was assigned to the churches, and they acquiesced—that was their fault. The Church, then, has been unfaithful to its divine vocation of proclaiming the gospel to the powers of the world in their dealings and decisions, of exhorting and warning them. It has failed to subject the international society to the test of the Christian message; it has not risen above national conceptions, national interests, judging them all in the light of God's revelation. In so behaving the Church lost the confidence of many but, worse, it failed to bring its own unique contribution to the founding of peace and justice between the nations.

Since Oxford 1937[1] the Church has been painfully aware of opportunities missed, of tasks neglected, and of its sin against its Lord. And it cannot give more sincere proof of repentance and conversion than by applying itself now to its full task in the international field, that of proclaiming God's Holy Will for or even *against* the world of nations.

In this task the Church has to recognise its limitations : the Church is neither competent nor called to recommend concrete decisions in the international field. Individual Church-members may do so in virtue of their personal knowledge and competence, and it is their high duty to fulfil this task according to their lights. In the present time of searching for new solutions the duty of the Church towards those members is to bring them

[1] It is very important to re-read, in connection with this paper, the relevant part of the report of the Oxford Conference (*The Churches Survey their Task*, pp. 167-187).

together in order to deepen and strengthen their testimony.   As a body the Church has another, a higher, a spiritual task; that is, to put relations, situations, facts in the light of the biblical message, to throw new light upon them from that eternal source.   This is the inalienable contribution of the " *Oikumene* " towards the re-ordering of this world ; it is at the same time a task of unparalleled difficulty and magnitude : to point out the sole foundation, namely, that God, Creator of heaven and earth, is the Lord of all the nations and their governments—" the earth belongs to the Eternal, all earth holds, the world and its inhabitants " (Ps. xxiv, Moffatt translation).   He who has delivered us and who will continually deliver us from all evil, He who has given peace unto us and who requires peace from us in this world, requires fervent and continual prayer for peace and justice.   It is the Church's duty to translate the meaning of the words of Micah vi, 8 into various spheres of life, and to proclaim this message on the foundation that its Lord Jesus Christ is the real Lord of the world ; to Him ". . . full authority has been given in heaven and on earth " (Matthew xxviii, 18, Moffatt translation), and His authority calls all worldly authority, all powers, all thrones, all governments to account, and passes judgment on them by the standards of justice and mercy.   The Church, itself human and frail, can know in the light of Christ's authority the treasures of obedience and faithfulness.   It is its solemn task and responsibility to proclaim Christ's universal authority in the society of nations also and to offer its treasures to it.

In the world of nations the Church has a wider field to till than specific Church—and mission—interests.   The establishment of a real international order on the foundation of justice and law must claim a prominent place in its concern, an order for all men, irrespective of origin, race, creed, nationality or class.

Wherever this task of proclamation, of exhortation and warning is neglected, especially in the field of international relations, the highest court of appeal against worldly authority, against might and power of whatever nature and substance, collapses, and all curbs and checks on the use of power disappear. The absence of such appeal, of checks and restraints, means that there and then the way lies open to a totalitarian régime of any type—even a democratic type which may conceal a dictatorship

D

of mighty material or non-material interests. That is why freedom of creed and cult constitutes the very foundation of any legal order, including the international.

Whenever the Church speaks, it must, in order that its word be effective and practical, have a clear vision of the world, in the midst of which it speaks, and to which it addresses its word, and a clear knowledge of facts and currents, fancies and motives, secret or open. The Church must know and take into account, first, the character and the organisation of the world society to-day and the mechanism of its behaviour ; second, the actual, concrete tensions and adjustments, conflicts and co-ordinations such as : problems of transition from war to peace, the spirit and attitude of the Great Powers, the supply of primary necessities, the German problem, the poverty and weakness of Europe, the race problem, the colonial problem, the Jewish problem and Palestine, the confrontation of Christendom and Islam, protection of minorities, and a host of other problems.

2. THE CHARACTER AND ORGANISATION OF WORLD SOCIETY

When speaking of our present-day world affairs, what do we mean by advocating the establishment of an international legal order ? What is the significance and the rôle therein of national sovereignty ? What should be the relation between power and law under such an order ? What of an international authority ? All those questions need reflection and rethinking in the Church, for at every moment, in its action and in its silence, the Church will be confronted with them.

The apostle Paul (1 Cor. xiv, 33, Moffatt) makes a sharp contrast between disorder and harmony, saying that God is a God not of disorder but of harmony. In the international sphere war is in sharp contrast to peace. War means disorder, it is the very negation of a legal order. " Peace " translates in the international sphere Paul's " Harmony " ; it is the worldly aspect of harmony, for the word means the compacting or fitting together of views and interests, attitudes and behaviour into a stable whole. Peace is something very much more profound than non-violence, non-war. Peace in the international world is only present where and when men are earnestly, sincerely striving to attain and to maintain a legal order. We cannot, and we should not, in this earthly dispensation, deny the existence of opposition, of clashes of power ; but over and against them we should affirm, and surely the Church should affirm, the paramount obligation of maintaining and strengthening a legal order above states and nations, under which differences may be solved, clashes prevented, and in which power finds its right place.

Now, an " order " presupposes a permanent relationship and hierarchy, like the " orders " of animals and plants in biology. A legal order means such a relationship and hierarchy in human interests and values, determined as far as possible by an unselfish agency, following a settled method controlled by standards of justice, not by temporary and casual power-relations, in the interests of the deciding person or group. A biological " order " is purely descriptive, a legal order has to fulfil a purpose, has to give a meaning to the life of its participants, which is always and everywhere in the last resort the protection and fostering of human physical and spiritual life, in order that men may develop all the gifts God gave them, for His glory and His Kingdom. The international legal order has to fulfil this purpose in all relations which extend beyond the frontiers of national communities.

To understand the world society of to-day it is indispensable to keep in sight the following main characteristic.[1] In that society various religions, social conceptions, legal orders, ideologies, exist side by side, insulated or interrelated, some of them politically or even fundamentally disunited, connected by no common conviction ; and inseparably bound up with that pluriformity is a difference of economic systems and of standards of living.

For the world of states has not re-integrated itself into a " community " of states or nations since the mediæval " *corpus christianum* " disintegrated. It survived only as a rather loose " society," and the French appellation for the League of Nations, " Société des Nations,"[2] revealed in a striking manner its very nature. When at the end of the middle ages the " *corpus christianum* " of Europe broke up, the existing unity lost its common basis. That process went further and during the nineteenth century the society of states came to be suspended in the air of relative power. Since the nineteenth century we have

---

[1]Cf. the Oxford Report, pp. 171-174.
[2]Concerning the League of Nations, cf. the Oxford Report, p. 175.

been confronted with a new historical situation, viz., the existence side by side of isolated states, between which there is no moral or spiritual bond. Some rudiments of former conceptions survived, but less and less remained of such a common conviction regarding moral values as governs a homogeneous national community— a *pre-legal* " existential " decision (often taken unawares and so to say unconsciously) concerning the purposes of human life in society, a decision which for Christians derives from the Gospel and confronts us with the fundamental relationship between God and man, and between man and man as redeemed by Christ.

Indeed, between the states of the world in general, the essential conditions for a real " community " of nations have never been fulfilled; they lacked always and still lack the distinctive features of a true community : a pre-legal decision on its purpose and basic convictions ; the firm solidarity, transcending national interests, of purposes and attitudes and behaviour ; and, bound up with that solidarity, a binding authority. On the contrary, it has mostly been only the varying need of adjusting their parallel, or diverging, or even opposing national interests, or sometimes an acute common danger, which determined the weak inner cohesion of that society of states—notwithstanding some more or less fruitful endeavours towards a more solid structure, like some of the international administrative unions or the two Hague Courts of Arbitration and of Justice. The hierarchy of values and interests found —and still finds—its definite expression in the power of the single states or of their alliances and other combinations at any moment available, and in their potentiality in case of conflict ; it is not expressed in a principle based on moral and spiritual unity, in which power has found its right subordinate place. A solidarity, and consequently a community, in the true sense of that beautiful term, was and is found only in some of the partial or limited, regional or functional combinations of states, which live or act together on a common ground.

Looking at the world at large, we can only recognise that, since the first world war, conditions making for greater unity have deteriorated. For the superiority of the West, unquestioned up to 1914, exercised a certain levelling influence between the states of the world through the westernised upper classes of the non-European states. During the first war that superiority received a deadly blow ; new peoples came to the fore, dormant civilisations were awakened to a new life. And now after the second war, bringing strengthened nationalisms and new antagonisms in its train, the world stage is prepared for the interplay of four or five civilisations, which have practically no common ground. Within such a civilisation perhaps there will reaffirm itself or there may grow up a community of states, based upon common descent, a common creed, common conceptions, or perhaps upon a common hostility to some other group.

International society thus being still weak, there is no true authority above the states, nor even, save in the International Court of Justice, tentative beginnings of one. Such an authority would comprise—side by side with the existing governmental bodies, which are mostly exclusively composed of official representatives of the state-governments, acting generally, save in a few exceptions, under instructions from and responsible to them—bodies, which, although created by the states in a treaty or otherwise, would be composed of individual members, chosen for their personal competence and integrity, bodies which would function without any further intervention, instruction or approval by governments, as the direct organs *of the international society itself*. (Under the League of Nations, the Permanent Mandates Commission belonged to this category of supra-national organs, though acting only in an advisory capacity.) The present world society, however, shows only a juxtaposition of states and, except in the International Court, most of the international organs are composed of purely official representatives. Where the prominent rôle is played by the national state, and more particularly by the Great Powers which hold the limelight, intercourse between and co-operation of the states is carried on primarily to serve national interests. But we ought gratefully to record the growing discussion of subjects of common international interest. Nothing is gained by disguising patent facts ; even the *United Nations* constitutes only a loose *confederation*—although, especially in the cultural and social domains, a new outlook for integration of world society is opened up—for the United Nations itself does not rest upon a pre-legal decision, a common conviction of all its nations regarding moral values. It rests principally and overwhelmingly on the various, diverging, legal orders of the member-states ; it represents, itself, a political, unstable order, in which considerations of influence and power, only weakly restrained by conceptions of right and justice, define decisions and demarcate responsibilities.

This weakness of our world society manifests itself again in its law.[1] The law of the international society shows clearly the marks of a law lacking supra-national validity. It has retained the character of a private law contract between parties, although already some features of an institutional, a public rule of law are visible in the contractual form. However, institutional as over against contractual law requires the sanction of a firm authority over and above the " state parties." The states thus have the double task of implementing and executing the international rule and, at the same time, of establishing laws and maintaining law and order within their own society. Confronted with the huge problems of the international society, international law in most cases proved weak ; for in these great problems, involving the vital interests of states, governments, falling back on their national conceptions, decided according to their national views, pride, prejudices and convictions.[2]

The binding force, the power to effect order of international law has diminished rapidly since the decline of the so-called natural law of the Middle Ages and Renaissance, *pari passu* with the limitation of its sanctions to mere persuasion and self-help. The classical doctrine of international law went on to deny the binding force of that law, to destroy the subordination of sovereign states to international precepts, or propounded some formalistic theory which tried to combine fire and water, such as the formula of the self-limitation of states, which in fact is no limitation at all. The age of great uncertainty in all matters regarding international law, international authority, international obligation began. Our plight is, that even now, after two wars, we have not yet wholly overcome the fatal suggestions of the classical doctrine of international law, its insincerities, inconsistencies and uncertainties.

In consequence the sun in the solar system of world politics is still always the national state, called an independent and sovereign power and considered equal to its fifty or sixty partners. Here and there, for various political, social, economic, cultural purposes, there exist general unions and *ententes*, or regional understandings, various forms of international co-operation in special fields, closely or loosely knit. But even in the most

---

[1]Cf. the Oxford Report, pp. 174-5.
[2]Cf. the Oxford Report, p. 173.

modern mechanism for general co-operation between states, the United Nations, the national so-called sovereign state forms the foundation. It would not be otherwise possible to erect such a superstructure ; nevertheless the great central question for our generation remains this : What kind of relationships between member-states does this general organisation provide ? And can this organisation meet the growing needs of an inter-dependent world ?

The prominent rôle and unique significance of the national state finds a striking expression in the loyalty, that is the obedient subservience generally of man towards his state, his readiness for unlimited sacrifices on behalf of his state. Broadly speaking, loyalty found until the world war its highest expression and farthest extension in relation to a man's own country. His native land meant for him his social and spiritual home, a place of security as well as a source of inspiration. No such loyalty existed towards " humanity," towards his continent, nor even, save in exceptional periods, towards congenial nations. Now, the world war has given rise to a new sense of obligation, an obligation not felt towards one's native land directly, but towards the defence of human dignity. It was shown by the splendid acts of all those self-sacrificing men and women, who voluntarily enlisted against the " *hostis generis humani,*" the foe of all mankind. Ths new, but as yet undeveloped, loyalty may prove an important element in a future, more integrated, world organisation. On the other hand we should not forget conscientious objectors[1] and the problems concerning loyalty, originating from their attitude, the age-long problems of the tension between loyalty towards God and towards Cæsar.

It is this leading rôle of the national state, which in ordinary and in legal speech is indicated by the word " sovereignty." In every community and in every society and in every group of men, there must be, unless it is to crumble to pieces, a central point of authority and power, towards which in time of decision, emergency and danger, people may turn their eyes, for which they will curb their personal wills. In the international sphere this pre-eminent place is still occupied by the national states, each acting by itself or in consultation with others, in ententes, in alliances. It is one of the main functions of the United Nations to provide a room and a table, around which national representa-

[1] Cf. the Oxford Report, pp. 178-183.

tives may promote the interest of all by frankly facing the threats to law and order. One of the chief needs of the world is that this work may be done in a manner and a spirit, adequate to the interests of the world *as a whole* and not only to the particular interests of one state or another or of a certain group. But as long as an effective authority above the states has not been installed, national authority will wish—in this disunited, unintegrated world—to control, as long as possible and to the utmost degree, political influence and power as well as the obedience of its citizens. So long as no international agencies exist, deemed worthy of confidence and invested with effective authority, the normal seat of authority will remain with the national state. Such agencies do not exist at the present moment. Least of all does the Security Council of the United Nations command confidence, nor has it effective authority, being hampered by the discord of those permanent members, from whose unity its practical measures must derive their very birth and efficiency. Sovereignty should mean, then, not unlimited power used and exercised according to the *bon plaisir* of the sovereign states, but, in the absence of effective supra-national authority, employment of state-competence and power, for the benefit of the world society, according to law and justice. Again it clearly appears that our world, as its primary social and political need, demands the gradual development and growing effect of true authorities above the states.

But that original sovereignty of the national state means indeed a temptation, especially, but not only, for the great states, who combine sovereignty with power, and are thereby in a position to use their high competence not for the benefit of the society of states, for the ordering of international life, but for selfish interests to the detriment of others or of the world as a whole. Such power may be exercised and applied by military means (but that looks too brutal nowadays and entails dangerous consequences), or by economic influence and pressure, open or disguised, or by the quite modern means of terrorism and of adroit, venomous propaganda.

The world of states is a hard, impersonal world, composed of impersonal, primarily self-regarding national states, which are entrusted with a splendid, most responsible task, but in its discharge have to be restrained by their subservience to a higher society ; and in the service of higher permanent interests, they

THE CHURCH AND INTERNATIONAL SOCIETY

must co-operate in a system of law and order. This demands a
legal organisation which is more than a loose *political* co-operation
ad hoc. The world has to combine all its efforts towards the
founding and strengthening of an *institutional* organisation, based
on a *common* principle. We are far away from, and not at all
inclined to, the unitary world state, a leviathan which might
crush the smaller states, and destroy all that is valuable in the life
of all states, great and small.

That does not, however, imply that we have to sit down
quietly and be content with the present imperfect organisation
of our world, which is so poorly equipped for the handling of
common interests. Up till now, generally speaking, the regulation of international interests lies in the hands of the states directly
concerned, mostly without the concurrence of disinterested third
party judgment ; though the United Nations are in a position
to provide help if desirable, if only by means of friendly advice or
indirect pressure from other governments. But governments
they are, and as such must look first to their own national
interests, and take into account possible repercussions of an
attitude or a decision on other policies. The world still lacks
an agency which will safeguard international interests on their
own merits within the whole fabric of international life.

There lies the reason why change in inter-state law presents
itself as a distinct and difficult problem. International law in its
written form (in treaties and agreements, etc.) is for the most part
not the expression by a superior authority of the common
conscience of a community, as is national law in homogeneous
states, but—especially in treaties of limited participation, and
more particularly in so-called " political " treaties—a compromise between group-interests determined by their relative
power.[1] Change under such circumstances means a new
adjustment, to be negotiated by the parties directly interested,
possibly under some pressure. In this respect the world
needs a body higher than the single states, by which the
fortuitous pressures might be institutionalised and constitutionally
directed.

Again, the reference of international disputes to arbitration
or judicial decision depends, save under the optional clause of the
Statute of the International Court of Justice, upon the voluntary
agreement of the parties concerned.

[1] See page 54 above.

Above all, the maintenance of international peace, of the embryonic international legal order, is closely interwoven with the protection of specific interests of individual states, and so depends upon their voluntary consent. No direction and no action come from a central agency of impartial, supra-national standing. So long as no such agency, disposing of effective force to uphold decisions and maintain order, has been created, in the last resort, the Great Powers feel that these tasks are their responsibility. There lies the cause of armaments and the armaments race, the increasing burden of which is shouldered in the belief that national security must be protected by national means. In a non-integrated society of states reduction of armaments seems an almost hopeless task, because, as history teaches us, it opens up at once questions of relative power between the big states. International security calls for international protection by international means, by pooling of defence-systems and defence-instruments, or rather, by the institution of a real international defence-system, aiming at security for the world *as a whole*. The United Nations Charter contains a relatively bold approach to such an international defence-system, but its realisation depends upon a preceding growth of the sense of interdependence rising to a supra-national level. And we have learned to regard an effective method of regulating international interests as a pre-condition of such a defence-system, which implies the discovery of a method for changing the existing law along peaceful paths (to which we invited attention a moment ago), or, in current language, for the settlement of disputes of a non-legal character.

We should not, however, close our eyes to some curious features of the complementary rôle of the Great Powers in the exercise of international authority. They have often furnished some substitute, though a weak one only, for a supra-national authority, in their hegemony in the world of States. More than a century ago that substitute could be discerned in the " Concert of Europe " consisting of the five Great Powers of that time ; to-day we all know the permanent members of the Security Council, whose hegemony, however, is distracted by their discord. Nevertheless, such hegemony, if justly and responsibly and consciously exercised, could develop into a kind of virtual supra-national authority. Hand in hand with it goes pressure, one of the instruments of that very primitive authority. But Great Powers being what they are, always provide a mixture of self-interest and of wider and higher interests, in which the former predominates.

The crux of our present-day world organisation lies in the canalisation of hegemony and pressure into some institution, even in a tentative, provisional form, of a real supra-national authority. Such a reform surpasses our imagination, but, nevertheless, is the major end which we seek to attain in our quest for peace, for an international legal order.

So long as the national state is the only basic sub-structure of the society of states, it seems natural that the agencies of that society should be composed by the governments, and consist of members designated as their representatives. It seems equally necessary, that the society should acquire its own, direct, autonomous organs for the handling of its common interests.

Therefore we come back to the question touched on above : whether in the organisation of world society we ought not to try to pass, with circumspection and discipline, but with courage and imaginativeness, from the present purely *confederate* to what might be called a more *federal* stage, in all those domains where common interests must have precedence over national group interests— even if it were provisionally only between those states whose life and work rest on a common basis of moral and spiritual values. In other words, must the governmental, the " official " principle be always or nearly always followed ? Or can there be found a *useful preparation of real supra-national authority* in connecting that governmental principle with what we might call the " popular " principle of inviting qualified persons to sit on international bodies, perhaps during an initial stage only in an advisory capacity ? This was done in the former Permanent Mandates Commission, and works in connection with the Executive Committee of the Food and Agriculture Organisation, or, in quite another field, the Research Council, auxiliary to the Caribbean Commission. It seems unfortunate that a body such as the Commission on Human Rights of the Economic and Social Council of the United Nations must, because of a general decision taken by that Council in 1946, consist only of governmental representatives, although each government indeed remains free to refrain from giving instructions to its delegate on the Commission.

It has been shown in the preceding argument, how and why the present world organisation is built on group-(state-) co-operation and group-representation. But it is a common lesson of experience in all parts of the world and in all walks of life, that a purely group-organisation always shows a tendency (for example in communal representation in colonial territories) to stiffen relations between men, to obliterate those general interests which transcend the group-interests, to diminish the chance of appeals to a higher justice than that of the groups, and to enhance the power of the mighty, or to produce a series of deadlocks.

The organisation of the United Nations, its possibilities, and also the weakness inherent in its almost purely governmental structure, has already come under review several times, in passing. As the United Nations is the most notable, the highest and most far-reaching attempt of our day in the search for an international order, in our quest for peace—as was the League of Nations in the inter-war period—it deserves our closest, most earnest and objective attention, and the strong support of the Church. It is of primary importance that we should be conscious of its value, and above all of its limitations, in order neither to be unduly optimistic, nor perforce condemned to suffer a black disillusionment. The Church in particular should avoid ordinary optimism concerning this and other worldly affairs, knowing full well that man is a frail earthly vessel.

It is easy to underrate the value and importance of the United Nations when we look at the practical results it has achieved. Suppose for a moment, however, that the United Nations collapsed, our heavy loss would at once be apparent. It is, of course, too early as yet to draw up an exact balance-sheet of its achievements. Yet it is already certain that its Assembly is the most important gathering in the world for the exchange of thoughts and opinions, for reconciling interests, for the settlement of grievances and for the gradual upbuilding of an international order, precisely because it provides a forum for the nations, a meeting-place where they can learn to know each other better and thereby try to overcome their differences of basis and outlook. The Economic and Social Council, in its more limited membership, in its flexible decentralisation of business, through auxiliary commissions and the various specialised agencies, is capable of making a valuable contribution to the prevention of friction and conflict ; and the same applies to other permanent organs of the United Nations.

The attainment of satisfactory results, however, depends upon the fulfilment of two conditions : first, that governments and nations combine wholeheartedly in the earnest endeavour to make the noble preamble of the Charter a living reality instead of only another document ; and, second, that governments (until now the sole sub-structure of the Organisation) should spare no effort to draw their peoples into this international work.

What, then, are the limitations of the United Nations ? They are many.   But the principal limitations have their origin in the following causes.   Firstly, that governments and peoples, in their practical behaviour, do not as yet seem to be entirely free from antiquated conceptions and obsolete legal theories on sovereignty : the Charter of the United Nations itself cuts through the old concepts and theories in many places, but its deadly weakness lies in the comprehensive veto provisions for the Security Council, securing to the Great Powers individually the unfettered appeal to their own sovereign judgment, maintaining by this privilege the old " halo " of unlimited sovereignty, and thus weakening the political integration of our world.

The second cause of limitation is this : The United Nations has maintained, up till now, an almost exclusively governmental structure in its organs.   This structure appears, on the one hand, unavoidable in the present dispensation, because of the power-centres in the world.   On the other hand it is a brake on the successful functioning of the United Nations organs, because its purely governmental organisation makes it susceptible to all the political influences which disturb the life of the nations.

Thirdly : the quasi-universality to which the United Nations tends is at once a source of strength and a cause of weakness.   The world of nations having become a whole—still incoherent but nevertheless interrelated in several fields of action—the United Nations does indeed need that quasi-universality if practical and useful results are to be attained in those fields.   But throwing together, as it does, states of unmistakably different character, it erects at the same time a barrier to strong and united action.

The absence or deficiency of a common " ethos " is indeed the basic cause of the weakness of the United Nations.   As the members are so widely different, their differences in first principles, in outlook, in moral and spiritual convictions, are too glaring to be overlooked.   Whenever those differences are overshadowed by the practical necessities and needs of the world, taken as a whole—*primum vivere*—the organs of the United Nations, working in their governmental structure, may arrive at voluntary common decisions, taken by governments in juxtaposition, by means of reciprocal consultation, persuasion and exchange of views, but not by a common superior authority.

On the other hand, in all cases where concerted action is dependent upon the existence of common moral and spiritual convictions, i.e., on a common " ethos," the unavoidable necessity appears of confining co-operation to a smaller circle of states and nations, who adhere to the same or to congenial principles of life and work ; a co-operation less universal, but precisely for that reason much more close and intense, which may find its effective expression in the unreserved handing-over to an impartial agency of the settlement of international interests between members of the group. It will then be possible to try to form within such smaller circles common institutions which would be composed of men of expert knowledge and personal value, working independently of their governments. Such institutions would lead their own corporate life in virtue of the confidence in the members of the group, but would be independent in their day-to-day activities. The organisation of such groups of more closely associated peoples for specific purposes would seem to be all-important in the useful development of the United Nations ; and also, wherever possible, the range of such institutions, acting on their own authority and responsibility as organs auxiliary to governmental agencies, should be extended.

The question might now be asked : does all this mean that we have to strive for a " world government " ? Yes, and no. If the expression " world government " has to be taken in the sense of a unitary government of the whole world on the pattern of national governments, clearly the answer must be " No." It must be emphasised that such a Leviathan would crush us all. But if this means stressing the need for a gradual building-up of a common authority in the appropriate fields of activity, the answer should be " Yes." But we should avoid too ambitious schemes and high-flown terms such as " world government." We should be content with the unpretentious aim of a common authority to be set up in any and every field where the objectives and the moral structure of the participating states promise valuable practical results. The United Nations must always be on the watch for opportunities of strengthening a more truly federal co-operation between states in a certain group, by their common subjection to a superior authority. This would help to remove obstacles which arise from the existence of national frontiers—the stereotyped tokens of isolated national spheres.

Such institutionalised co-operation would tend to strengthen security, to prepare the way for an international legal order and unity between nations, and provide an approach towards the unity of the " *Oikumene.*"

All the preceding problems and questions are presented to our world with urgent intensity by the new weapons of mass destruction. Their discovery has again brought home to us—and this time in appalling explicitness—that the world in regard to armaments has grown into a whole, into a single scene of deadly peril for us all, that all the nations of the earth are forming now, even against their professed views and dealings, a community. And for what purpose ? What community ? Not a free, spiritual or social community for the service of peace and welfare, but an inescapable community of danger and fear.   All that their growing interdependence has not been able to impress upon them, all that their interrelation of interests in other walks of life has not succeeded in creating, the modern means of mass destruction, of blowing up this earth created by God, are bringing into existence : namely, an unorganised community of eventual death and destruction, which, however, mankind either refuses to recognise or, by reason of its inveterate conceptions and its insuperable suspicions, can only dimly perceive.

Under this modern threat all questions of sovereignty, of autonomous national defence, take the aspect of a caricature, even in the case of the big powers. Now, in 1948, there has sprung into being one supra-national common concern, far elevated above national interests and national *noli me tangere* ; and the first task and prime responsibility of our disfigured, mutilated world, lies in the sincere facing of our exact situation as it is now and the bold endeavour to remould our world institutions so that they may become adequate to our wants. That is to say, that we resolve to build up, stone upon stone but at high speed, real supra-national authorities which can be effective in parrying the imminent danger, and in ensuring co-operation in the field of defence and armaments, and eventually restore security. In this field the world has to pass at one giant stride from the present loose confederation to a closer integration, into a community—

even if it is provisionally of limited interests only—bearing more distinctly federal marks. That implies a withdrawal of national governments in favour of an international authority, representing our world as a whole in its perilous plight. Indeed, the discovery of the means of mass destruction might constitute a blessing in disguise, if it could compel us to a reform which till now has been beyond our vision, but which in these days is imposed upon our faltering wills, if we are to preserve the lives and souls of fellow-creatures, of our brothers of whom each of us in turn is the keeper.

Let us meanwhile not forget the other, the brighter side of this medal : the new discoveries in the field of nuclear energy contain at the same time a promise of new possibilities for our distracted world, possibilities which in their turn can only be put to the service of the peoples of this earth by an agency which is able to protect our common interests, regarded and handled as belonging to the world as a whole.

Now let us look back for a moment at the ground we have tried to cover. The nations are living in an exceedingly pluriform society, strongly interdependent in interests, united *under*, not yet *by* a common menace, yet always still without a common moral and spiritual basis and without adequate institutions. The sense of obligation under a common international law, elevated above the fragmentary treaty-law, remained weak. A national obligation, expressed as loyalty to a man's own state, was recognised. On the other hand, an international obligation, which in its essence is a social obligation towards a community of nations, is mostly still lacking. What is the reason for this lack of a sense of international obligation, and for the consequent weakness of international law ? It is the absence of a supra-national community. Why is it that such a community is still non-existent in the world taken as a whole ? Here we arrive at the limits of rational thinking and intellectual research. Here we are faced by a bare fact : the *concordia* on which the *pax hominum* (Augustine) must be based does not exist.

The founding and maintenance of an international legal order, i.e., of peace as the prerequisite of " harmony," depends upon the fulfilment of a *condition*, and on the other hand makes a stringent *demand* upon us. The condition is this : the existence of a community, living by a common conception of justice and human dignity. The demand : the establishment of a solid organisation, capable of dispensing law and justice according to that common conception, and of maintaining law and order. This demand can only be satisfied when the condition has been fulfilled, according to the measure (geographical and otherwise) of its realisation ; that is to say, so far as a common conviction of law and justice exists among the members of the community. Thus an international legal order will be determined by (1) the degree of integration (oneness) of the world, which is a social and spiritual fact, not dependent for its consummation upon our wills, but indeed on our hopes and prayers ; and (2) the degree of our readiness for new steps and efforts towards new designs of international authority ; these are not facts outside our will, but are directly and essentially dependent upon it.   From the extension (geographically and as to specific matters) and the intensity of that integration there will be born a community of *nations*, in which juxtaposition of *states* and co-ordination of sovereignties will no longer alone determine an essentially political structure, but, along with these, also a hierarchy of values and a common subordination of states to an authority above them.   A combination of juxtaposition and hierarchy : this is the typical feature of a federal structure.

It should be clear from this argument that a legal order above the states, which is the one and only aim of our quest for peace, is for the time being only gradually and partially attainable, and will assume different aspects in relation to different matters of common concern.   We shall not have to fight *against* war and national sovereignty, but to arm ourselves *for* a legal order above the states, for an international law with binding force, for " peace."

In matters which are not deemed of universal concern for the whole world, we shall have to strive for a legal order over those nations only which are already united by a common conviction.   The gain, even as an example, might prove to exceed all expectation.

On the other hand, in matters concerning which a common conviction has not yet grown up, the world will have to content itself with the beginnings of a purely confederate form of organisation which prevails to-day, a form which now, as always, can only be workable if the participants act in good faith and mutual respect, faithful to the plighted word, and if they can succeed in freeing themselves from greed for power and profit. This

E

may seem wishful thinking and a platonic incentive to good behaviour.   In fact it is the one and only condition for ordered life, national or international.

Slowly and gradually the conviction has gained ground that some fundamental principles of order and conduct exist even for impersonal political institutions such as the states. Among these good faith stands first.   But the most important point in this connection is not the recognition of the principle itself, it is the fixing of the means controlling the observance of the principle in the practice of states.   The final opinion on the observance of good faith ought not to be left to the exclusive judgment of the interested state or states, but should be referred to impartial, " third party " judgment.   In particular, this is true for appeals to the well-known *clausula rebus sic stantibus* (a treaty considered binding only " so long as things stand as they are "), or to the still more indefinite " law of necessity." Such impartial control amounts to creating an effective restraint on the use of power (economic, journalistic or otherwise), and the rendering of power subservient to higher justice.   It means at the same time the strengthening of solidarity, i.e., the common responsibility of states and nations for the well-being of the whole world.   But to speak of solidarity is to be driven back to the fundamental problem of the moral and spiritual unity of nations, their mutual obedience to a higher order.

3. THE CHALLENGE TO THE CHURCH

The lack of solidarity between the nations of the world to-day is the life and death challenge presented to the Church in the field of international relations.   The Church cannot remain unmoved before the spiritual disunity which nowadays looms large on the international horizon and tends to paralyse the world, and, more dangerous still, to foster the forces of war and destruction.   In the political arena there may hang an iron curtain, there may be an apparently impassable gulf between groups of nations, but in the spiritual realm this is an unbearable situation.   At such a juncture the Church must feel a deep unrest which should make it alert to prayer, thought and action. The burning question of the clash of the diverging pre-legal existential decisions[1] must never be forgotten.

[1] See pages 50-53 above.

The first duty of the Church in this respect is to look the facts squarely in the face ; it must recognise the existence of those facts and their implications, but it cannot leave the matter there. For the Church is an ecumenical fellowship, transcending all human divisions and groupings. The Church recognises only one Christian decision, above all the political or politico-spiritual decisions : that is, the duty of obedience to the Lord of the whole earth. From this starting-point the Church must follow consistently the lines of approach to the existing disunity. First, it must investigate the origins of the divergencies, their historical as well as sociological sources and backgrounds ; and to that end the churches of the world must listen to each other in true fellowship, as servants of one Truth. Secondly : from that true knowledge and Christian understanding the churches should search for points of contact, for lines of communication between the different world conceptions. There is no time to lose, and the work demands a long, strenuous, tough effort. The Church is not a disinterested onlooker : the whole work of the Church in the domain entrusted to it, i.e., the " Oikumene," is dependent for its progress or failure upon the results of this effort.

All this may seem rather facile verbiage in a conference paper, or only a veiled proof of the unavowed but nevertheless all too real embarrassment of the Church. It may be considered unduly and falsely optimistic, or even as " sounding brass " ; but when we look closely at this task of understanding and uniting, we cannot fail to be impressed by its magnitude as well as by our seeming audacity, remembering our human frailty and limitations. It is, however, the task par excellence in the international world, and if the Church does not undertake it with haste and devotion, we shall be regarded as unprofitable servants.

In undertaking this task, the Church must clear itself from all bias, all uncritical assumptions, all unconscious leanings towards traditional conceptions and superstitions, and all contemptuous self-righteousness ; and this applies to all churches, each in its own field.

The point of contact between the several churches is, now as ever, the consciousness of mutual responsibility. We are all threatened by the danger that Matthew xxv is not a real, a stirring force in our lives. All that happens in the West is part of the life of the East, and vice versa, and all suffering, all privations there are the direct concern of the churches here : where one member of Christ suffers, all the others suffer with him. In the political sphere it may be that when something happens behind an iron curtain there, or a silk curtain here, the rest of the world may become resigned or lose interest, but the Church can never accept an attitude of aloofness.

By seeking to know, to understand, to clarify, to reassemble under common obedience to the higher commands of Christ, the Church must remain active and alert, must maintain spiritual contacts, foster ecumenical unity, heal wounds and console. It is clear that the first and essential condition is that all the churches should enjoy liberty for their individual confession or creed, for common understanding, for unhindered intercourse with one another, because they are all enlisted in the *militia Christi*, a unity of mankind beyond politics, breaking through the idolatry of nation, race or class.

In so living and acting, the Church would form a new " front " of spiritual solidarity, in which it would express its consciousness, in the first place, of the value of dignified human existence, and then above all, of a life of *purpose*, destined to fulfil the Lord's commandments. In practical terms, this means that the Church must take a clear stand for the disinherited, for the weak, the downtrodden, all over the world, i.e., must work for social justice in its different forms, for social security as a pre-requisite to true human life. As Christians we must give a clear demonstration of solidarity and justice, both within the Church's walls and outside, in national and international life. The indispensable witness of the Church, by which it will be judged in the eyes of the world, is to defend that solidarity and justice.

4. THE WORD OF THE CHURCH

The disorder of the world, then, seems due to two causes, and therefore we look on it as fate and guilt. The one cause lies in the profound differences of civilisation, insight, outlook, purpose. This seems to be due to fate ; but looking more deeply into Holy Writ, we begin to perceive in it many sinful aspects of a secularised world. The other cause of present disorder lies in greed for power and profit, as they manifest themselves in a self-righteous sovereignty or an equally arrogant nationalism, both striving for their own ends regardless of other people's interests and claims, and of higher justice ; or in tendencies towards economic monopoly, anti-social exploitation of the weak, whether weak social groups or of weak peoples. There is no real, enduring cure for this all-pervading disease of group egoism but a return to obedience to God's commandments, and, in the worldly sphere, the building of a just social and economic and political organisation, based on good faith and mutual respect, both within the states and in the international world of states. Christians have, as statesmen or as private individuals, the duty to show to the world the leaven of their faith in their private lives and in their public offices, and in their dealings with other groups and nations, to devote themselves to the cause of " peace " in all its manifold aspects, to convince the world of their sincerity, and to learn from other nations, where these seem to have progressed farther than their own on the path of social justice in the broadest sense of the word.

It is amidst this disorder of world society, due to lack of coherence and egoism, that the Church has to speak its word. Though international in outward appearance, being planted in different national soils and living in different surroundings, the Church is doomed to failure if its life remains confined to its different national embodiments. For in the Church, in contrast to any other agency, is *the* real supra-national community, a community not created by man, but by God's intervention in this worldly dispensation ; having within its purview the " whole earth and all it holds " and charged with the care of man, a creature after God's image. *Oikumene* means something which is radically different from the world of states and of nations, and the *ecumenical* work transcends by the call of the Church's Master all human *international* co-operation.[1] The ecumenical leaven should revolutionise the international world. That means that, as the *Corpus Christi*, the Church has first of all to put its own house in order, so that in its form and appearance it may be obedient to the call of its Master.

In obedience to Him the Church must proclaim that the state is not an end in itself, nor does it establish its own law, but it is God's instrument for the establishment and maintenance of a legal order in this world, a legal order both for *national* life and for *international* life, for there are no watertight compartments. The sole foundation of world society, which has already been

[1] Cf. the Oxford Report, pp. 168-169.

mentioned (viz., that God is the Lord of all nations ; that Jesus Christ has been given full authority in heaven and on earth), leaves no room whatever for self-righteous sovereignty : all authority exists by the grace of God. The state has to maintain order for the protection of human life and dignity; the Church's duty is to point out to the state, when necessary, this prime responsibility. And secondly, the Church has to put all existing law, all existing situations, to the test of justice.

Instead of appealing to national sovereignty as binding together the loose rights of any individual state, all states, however divergent in outlook, must arrive at a common recognition of their duties, tasks and responsibilities, for the protection of basic principles of law and justice, of human rights and fundamental liberties. It is the function of the state to ensure a tolerable realisation of these basic principles in any society, national or international. They are to maintain the external expression of the belief that man as a human being has a dignity, being delivered by Christ from sin and decay. The Church must preach the fore-ordained Kingdom of God among men. It must point out that human rights and other basic principles can never be equated with the reign of Divine love and of man's responsibility before God ; but it must insist that without those basic principles of public and private behaviour declared and guaranteed, demonic forces are free to obstruct the penetration of God's commandments into human life. There will never be a Christian state ; still less, a Christian " United Nations." But the Church must exhort governments and ordinary men to found a society on justice and law, national as well as international. The administration of justice in this world calls for independent, conscientious, responsible persons, to whom the task of maintaining justice and order can safely be entrusted. Justice here on earth takes its deepest meaning from the observance of God's commandments in this shattered world. The Church must continually bear this in mind, as part of its apostolic and missionary task.

From all this it will have become clear that the Church cannot plead for one definite political system, for in every one of them lies the danger of the demonism of power. The Church must, however, denounce the irreconcilable antagonism between any state, or class, or any other totalitarian system, and justice. The Church must protest with all its might against the destruction of human dignity and freedom and genuine solidarity. Apart from this, it can only show a preference for that system which leaves the way open for man to obey the call of Christ, and which gives the best protection for man to live and act as a responsible person in his family, in his community, above all in his Church. The first and last word of the Church should be responsibility, and it must therefore defend such systems as recognise the real public responsibility of a government. Only under such a system, coupled with an independent judiciary, is the way open to a tolerable protection of fundamental liberties, i.e., those liberties under which the relationship between God and man is not destroyed or restricted.

In the world of states likewise, that system has a claim to the Church's preference which promises the best chances for nations to live and act as responsible communities under a rule of law. It must be emphasised that the over-accentuation of the national sovereignty of the isolated state, such as we witnessed often in the past, and which still occurs in our interrelated world, is fraught with the deadly danger of lawlessness. The history of the last century has abundantly taught us this, especially in a world like that of to-day, in which states and nations have grown so markedly interdependent.

The Church is, therefore, entitled to say, and indeed must stress, that some form of federative co-operation between the states of the world is a demand of the Christian conscience. This co-operation must do justice of that growing interdependence, and is a pre-condition of that international order which is our declared ultimate aim. The Christian conscience demands this above all, for the realisation of the ecumenical fellowship (*cf.* page 47) which is our starting-point and our goal.

If Christ is the " *Kurios*," the Church must urge the establishment of an international legal order. But the Church as a body is neither called on nor entitled to indicate exact legal ways leading towards the end in view, nor to make pronouncements concerning the organisation of such an order and the form of its institutions. The task of the Church is to awaken the consciences of men in and outside its precincts to the urgent necessity of such an order, supported by authority ; to foster the recognition of such an order and authority ; and to see that that great work be undertaken and duly accomplished with all possible energy.

In other fields too the Church has kindred tasks to accomplish.

International disorder originates partly in disorders within national frontiers. In its preaching of love to our neighbour the Church should insist that the community must open to all its members, within the national states as well as in the international sphere, the possibility of work which has a purpose and a meaning, and that the community should provide social security for its members. Again, in those fields the Church must plead for the protection of fundamental rights and freedoms of man as a responsible person. The social and economic anarchy of the world in several respects, a characteristic feature of our world, which is one of the forms of disowning Christ's message, must be overcome. This means that the Church should urge the duty of all who wield economic power to serve the world as a whole and to be accountable for its stewardship. If the Christian principles of justice, service, stewardship and responsibility are earnestly observed, the disintegration of world society might be attacked at its roots.

The highest task of the Church still remains to call man to repentance and conversion, to a sincere denial of hatred and egoism, and to lead in prayer and supplication *ut omnes unum sint* (" that all may be one ").

The Church of Jesus Christ, a community which transcends all differences of nations and states, races and cultures, classes and groups ; the embodiment of a once mercifully given, suprahuman reality created not by men, must posit Augustine's maxim : *Pax hominum ordinata concordia* (" Peace among men is the tranquillity of order "). When churches and nations obediently exert all their forces for the attainment of such a concord, then they on their side accomplish all which is within their power, in order that God's mercy may deliver us from all our evils and distresses, and that He may fulfil His design for this world.

IV

CHRISTIAN RESPONSIBILITY IN OUR DIVIDED WORLD

It is necessary in this chapter to set together two distinct viewpoints, for it is only by a careful consideration of all the factors involved that the light of truth may be brought to bear upon the tensions of the present world situation.

(a) THE CHRISTIAN CITIZEN IN A CHANGING WORLD

John Foster Dulles

FOREWORD

THIS paper is written by a layman who has been active in the field of international affairs. It is primarily an action paper, not a theological paper. It accepts, explicitly or implicitly, basic Christian beliefs and suggests how, in the actual situation, they may impose on Christian citizens a duty of practical conduct.

There is no thought that the Church should endorse the conclusions reached or the lines of action suggested. The writer is, indeed, one who believes that the Church ought not to make authoritative pronouncements with respect to detailed action in political, economic or social fields. Practical political action is not often a subject for authoritative moral judgments of universal scope. Those who act in the political field must deal with the possible, not with the ideal ; they must try to get the relatively good, the lesser evil ; they cannot, without frustration, reject whatever is not wholly good ; they cannot be satisfied with proclaimed ends, but must deal with actual means. Those necessities prevail conspicuously in the international field where tradition, national interest and group loyalty have accumulated to an unusual degree. They place limits on what is practically possible ; they introduce error into every human judgment ; they increase the ever-present risk that men will see as " right " that which is self-serving.

73

Facts such as those mentioned require that the churches should exercise great caution in dealing with international political matters.   They should not seem to put the seal of God's approval upon that which, at best, may be expedient, but which cannot wholly reflect God's will.

It does not, however, follow that Christian faith and Christian political action are unrelated.   All citizens have to act in relation to political matters—inaction being only a form of action, a clearing of the way for others who do act.   Also, Christian citizens, when they act, will try to be guided by Christian insight and Christian inspiration.   Political institutions moulded by those who take a Christian view of the nature of man will be different from those moulded by atheists.   What the churches elect to say will have political consequences.   What they elect to keep silent about will also have political consequences.   So the churches, too, have a relationship to practical politics that is inescapable.

Since that is so, it seems that the churches ought to know what are the problems which Christian citizens face.   "Thy word is a lamp unto my feet and a light unto my path."   But the churches cannot throw the light of the Word upon the Christians' paths unless they know where those paths lie and what are the obstacles that need to be illumined lest the Christian pilgrim stumble and fall.   It is useful, no doubt, for Christian citizens to be inspired by the vision of a distant, heavenly scene.   But also it is useful to have light upon the way.

Obviously, Christian citizens throughout the world do not all face identical problems or have identical duties.   No single presentation can adequately inform the churches.   There are, in the world, many paths for Christians, all leading toward a central point, the doing of God's will on earth.   Some paths lead from the East, some from the West ; some from the North, some from the South.   Each of these paths has obstacles of its own.   In turn, these obstacles constantly shift.   What is described now may be irrelevant by to-morrow.   Despite the fact that the scene is world-wide and shifting, the churches should seek to keep informed.   Otherwise, they cannot keep each way illuminated with shafts of the divine light.

This paper seeks to show, in relation to international affairs, what is the political path which some Christians have to tread, what they see as the obstacles ahead, and how they think they can, perhaps, overcome these obstacles and wrest the initiative from forces of evil, ignorance and despair which exist in every land and which seem to be conspiring to overwhelm mankind with awful disaster.

The writer recognises, quite frankly, that the path he describes is a path which leads from the West. He knows full well that that way differs from other ways. These, too, should be known, for the Church concedes no priority or privilege to any nation, race or class.

As the churches come to know better the practical problems which Christian citizens have to face and the lines of action in which they may become engaged, the churches in turn will be better able to minister to the actual needs. They will be better able to show, to each and to all, that Christ is indeed the Way, the Truth and the Life. As Christ is so revealed, He will draw all men unto Him, and that supreme loyalty will provide the unifying force which otherwise men seek in vain.

I. THE INEVITABILITY OF CHANGE

The basic political and social fact that citizens must face up to is the fact of change. Life and change are inseparable. Human beings constantly change. So, too, do human societies. There are always some who unthinkingly wish that they could stop change and freeze a moment into eternity. That cannot be and, indeed, we should not want it to be. If it happened, it would mean an end and the replacement of life with death.

Christians do not regret the inevitability of change. Rather, they see in it a cause for rejoicing. Some religions see man as bound to a wheel which turns and on the turning of which he can exert no influence. As a result of that assumption, it follows, for them that the ideal mental state is one of indifference and renunciation of hopes and efforts which can end only in frustration. The Christian believes that he can do something about change to determine its character and, accordingly, he looks upon the inevitability of change as something that provides opportunity. That opportunity has a dual aspect. Outwardly, there is the opportunity to make the world more nearly one in which God's will is done on earth as it is in heaven. Inwardly, there is the opportunity for personal growth and development which comes out of grappling with situations and trying to mould them.

When there is change, something that *is* disappears and something that *was not* appears. Also, whenever there is change there is a means, a force, that brings change to pass. The Christian seeks the disappearance of that which he deems imperfect. But the disappearance of something imperfect is not, of itself, sufficient to make change good. If that were so, all change, by whatever means, would be good, for everything is to some extent imperfect and there cannot be change without the disappearance of some imperfection. The Christian tries to appraise change not merely in terms of what disappears, but also in terms of what replaces that which disappears. This appraisal involves an appraisal of means as well as ends, for the means by which change is accomplished makes an indelible impression upon the result and becomes, indeed, a part of the result.

For Christians, the great social task is to deal with the forces that make *some* change imperative so that (*a*) these forces will make their principal impact on what can be and will be replaced by something better ; (*b*) the forces for change will leave relatively immune what at the moment cannot be replaced by something better ; and (*c*) the forces for change will not themselves be evil and un-Christian in character.

2. THERE IS NEED THAT CHANGE BE INSTITUTIONALISED

Political leaders who have, or want, power, usually talk much alike as to the social ends they seek.   They all propose to increase the sum total of human happiness. The manifestos of communism, nazism and democracy have much in common. Many people pick their leaders simply on the basis of their promises and on the basis of the zeal which they seem to manifest. Sometimes the very violence with which leaders would seek their ends seems a recommendation, as being a proof of zeal.

The Christian citizens will consider not only the social ends which are professed in words, but also those elements which, we have seen, make up the nature of change. They will inquire into whether the changes proposed will replace something imperfect by something better ; will leave immune what cannot be improved and will avoid means which are evil. They have learned that the actual result will probably be determined more by the means than by the professions of long-range ends. Also, they know that a choice of violent means may not indicate honest zeal, but a lust for the increased power which comes to political leaders whenever violent means are sanctioned.

Difference of opinion about means is often the critical difference. Christians prefer means of the kind which, they believe, Christ taught. They are not inclined to look with approval upon means of violence and coercion. They have seen that, over the ages, war, revolution and terrorism have been repeatedly invoked for noble ends. But change brought about in that way is hurried and it usually gets out of control. It crushes blindly what happens to lie in its path. At times it inspires fine and sacrificial qualities, but also it develops in men hatred of fellowman, vengefulness, hypocrisy, cruelty and disregard of truth. History seems to show that when these evil qualities are invoked to produce good ends, in fact they vitiate or postpone the professed ends. Change sought by methods of force, violence and coercion seldom produces lasting, good results. The Oxford Conference of 1937 said :

" Wars, the occasions of war, and all situations which conceal the fact of conflict under the guise of outward peace, are marks of a world to which the church is charged to proclaim the gospel of redemption. War involves compulsory enmity, diabolical outrage against human personality, and a wanton distortion of the truth. War is a particular demonstration of the power of sin in this world and a defiance of the righteousness of God as revealed in Jesus Christ and Him crucified. No justification of war must be allowed to conceal or minimise this fact."

Some Christians believe that the use of violence is of itself so un-Christian that it should never under any circumstances be resorted to. Most Christian citizens, it seems, do not accept that view. The vast majority appear to believe that while they ought not themselves to initiate the use of force as a means, once force is invoked by others to do injustice and to impose conditions violative of the moral law and of the Christian conception of the nature of man, then to use force to prevent those results may be the lesser of two evils. Christians would generally agree that methods of change other than violence are to be preferred because violence, unless it be the dispassionate force of police power under law, almost always generates un-Christian qualities which cancel out, or at least greatly dilute, the value of the changes which violence brings about.

If force is discarded as the accepted means of change, then there have to be established procedures and political organisations for the purpose of making peaceful change. Such procedures have, to a considerable extent, been established within states, but they are lacking in the international field. There, as elsewhere, history teaches the inevitability of change. If one examines an historical atlas and looks at the political arrangement of the world 100 years ago, 200 years ago and so forth, one cannot but be impressed by the magnitude of the changes that have occurred. Most of these changes have been effected by war or the threat of war. Each war brought about the disappearance of something that was imperfect. Often it involved the doing away of power in some men and nations which had become disproportionate to their ability or readiness to use that power for the general welfare. In that sense, the change was good. But, also, the method of violence has done terrible things to the hearts of men. It has not brought individuals to greater love of God and neighbour in accordance with the great Commandments. Indeed, the result has been, on the whole, quite the contrary. The prestige of Christianity in the world has been gravely impaired by the frequency with which the so-called Christian nations have used violence as a method of international change. Furthermore, the hatred, falsification, cruelty and injustice incident to each war has, we can see in retrospect, done much to provoke new war and all the evil that that entails.

3. INSTITUTIONS FOR CHANGE REQUIRE DECIDING WHO CONTROLS

Christian citizens can readily conclude, as a generalisation, that there ought to be political institutions which will enable international change to take place in a peaceful way. But that conclusion is not, of itself, very significant. It cannot have any practical consequence unless also there is another decision, namely, whose judgment will determine the timing and the nature of peaceful change. Change *ought* to be based upon reflection and deliberate choice, not upon accident and force, of course. But *whose* reflection and choice are to be controlling?

That is a hard question. Within nations there is no uniform answer. In the international field few have attempted seriously to answer it and those few are not in agreement. Uncertainty, disagreement and competition about that largely explain why, in the international field, change has so far been left mostly to accident and violence.

It used to be widely held that political decisions should be made by rulers who were not responsible to their people. To-day, it is generally agreed, at least in theory, that it is better that men should be self-governing through some representative process which they control. But that theory is seldom carried out in practice, even within nations. In many countries of the world power is exercised by dictators. Of these, there are many types. Some are men who, loving power, have taken it and make no attempt to rationalise their action. Often, by written con-stitution, their government is a " republic " or " democracy." Some dictators are benevolent, taking power only to tide over a real or imagined crisis. Some exercise dictatorial power in order, professedly, to train the masses and discipline them into a common mould which, it is thought, ought to precede self-govern-ment. Such purposeful dictatorships are often termed " totali-tarian."

There are other countries where the peoples do in fact, through representative processes, exercise a very large measure of influence upon the choices that are made as to change. These societies customarily describe themselves as " free societies." Some call them " responsible societies " or " self-disciplined societies." We use the phrase " free societies " because it has wider popular use, although we recognise, and hereafter emphasise, that there is interdependence between freedom and self-discipline and sense of responsibility. We also recognise that even in the so-called " free societies " there are usually some who are, in fact, excluded from equal opportunity to participate in the deliberative process which determines when and how change shall be effected.

In no country is there a " pure " democracy in the sense that all of the people have equal and direct participation in all of the deliberations which determine change. Also, in no country are dictatorships so absolute that those who possess the governmental power wholly disregard what they sense to be the wishes of the people. Even so, the organisation of the different nations shows that there are great and momentous differences, both in theory and in practice, as to whose choice should determine change. These differences are a great obstacle to institutionalising change at the international level. Therefore, the matter deserves further consideration.

4. FORMS OF GOVERNMENT COMPATIBLE WITH CHRISTIAN IDEALS

Christians tend to favour the free society of self-discipline. That is probably because Christians think of man primarily in terms of the individual and his relations to God and to fellow man. It is only individuals who have souls to be saved and God, it seems, is not concerned with nations, races and classes, *as such*. He is concerned with individual human beings. Christians, who believe that, want a political society which, recognising the value and the sacredness of individual personality, gives the individual the opportunity to develop in accordance with the dictates of his own conscience and reason, and also puts on him a responsibility to exercise freedom with regard for the welfare of fellow men.

Christians believe that for one man to possess arbitrary power over his fellow men is an un-Christian relationship. It usually corrupts him who rules and it tends to debase those who are ruled, if in fact they acquiesce in being ruled.

Furthermore, Christians believe that civil laws, made by men, should, so far as possible, reflect the moral law. We believe that there is implanted in every individual a potential awareness of right and wrong and that under favouring conditions the composite of such individual judgments will reflect the moral law better than the judgments of absolute and self-perpetuating rulers. Also, as a practical matter, unless laws reflect and codify the moral judgments of those subject to them, they are not apt for long to be enforceable.

For such reasons, Christians tend to prefer the free society. But also they recognise that peaceful and selective change is not assured merely by giving people a right of suffrage. The voice of the people is not always the voice of God. It is easy to arouse masses for destruction without regard to the problem of replacement. Mob psychology is seldom conducive to selective change and it does not in fact represent individual reflection and choice.

A free society, if it is to effect peaceful and selective change, must be a society where, in addition to the right to vote, the people possess and use personal freedoms and access to information and the opportunity to exchange and propagate thoughts and beliefs so that there is, on an individual basis, genuine reflection and sober choice of minds and spirits which are both free and developed by use and self-discipline. There is also need of tolerance, particularly in the sense that political power may not be used to promote any particular creed.

The free society may at times of emergency, such as the emergency created by war, grant one man or a few men very extraordinary, even dictatorial, powers. But the people will reserve effectively the opportunity to end these powers when the occasion for them has passed.

Economically, a free society does not have to be a *laissez faire* society. There are some who profess to believe that only a *laissez faire* society adequately encourages individual development. There are, however, few who to-day would put that belief wholly into practice. In all states, even those most dedicated to " free enterprise," there is governmental control of at least some of the tools of production, such as railways and public utilities, which are endowed with a special public interest. In most countries, there are important collective and co-operative enterprises. It would seem that there is no inherent incompatibility between the Christian view of the nature of man and the practice of economic communism or state socialism. Communism, in the sense of " from each according to his abilities, to each according to his needs," was early Christian practice.

In the modern world, particularly where there is industrialisation, there is much interdependence and necessity for co-operation. In part, this necessity can be met by individual knowledge of how, in a complicated society, individual acts affect others. To that knowledge there needs to be added self-control and sense of duty to fellow man, so that individuals will voluntarily refrain from acts which they see have injurious consequences more than offsetting the benefits to self. But even where the people are possessed of much self-control and sense of duty, there may have to be added public controls and centralised direction to promote the equitable distribution of goods in short supply and to insure co-operative and co-ordinated action on a scale adequate to the needs of our complicated economies.

One may have different judgments as to what economic

F

structure is best adapted to modern conditions and as to the kind of incentive which is required to insure needed productivity. There are times and conditions when the most effective appeal is to self-interest.   There are other times and conditions when the greatest appeal may be to men's sacrificial spirit.   The Christian Church seeks constantly to make men's motives more lofty, and to invoke concern for others rather than for self.   Christians believe that those that are strong ought to bear the infirmities of the weak, and not to please themselves.   But there are few who fully heed that injunction.   Christian citizens, in seeking to organise society, have to take account of what men *are*, not what the Church thinks they ought to be.

From the Christian viewpoint, the essential is political and economic conditions which will help, and not stifle, growth by the individual in wisdom and stature and in favour with God and man.   We want conditions which, in so far as practical, will, in fact, exalt the dignity of man.   The essential in this respect is the content, not the form.   The conditions which best assure that will doubtless vary from time to time and from place to place.

It is not possible to attach the Christian label to any particular political or economic organisation or system to the exclusion of all others.   It is not possible to say that " free enterprise " is Christian and socialism un-Christian—or *vice versa*. It is not possible to say that a popular representative system of government is Christian, or temporary dictatorship inherently un-Christian.   It is, however, possible to condemn as un-Christian societies which are organised in disregard of the Christian view of the nature of man.   This would include those which are totalitarian in the sense that they recognise the right of some men to seek to bring the thoughts, beliefs and practices of others into conformity with their will, by processes of coercion.

It could be argued that if Christians really believe that the truth is uniquely revealed by God through Jesus Christ, they ought to seek an organisation of the state which would make it possible to use every power, including police power, to compel acceptance of that truth and the liquidation of heretics and non-conformers.

There have been times when that viewpoint prevailed. Christianity, over its two thousand years, has had many experiences and has learned much.   It has learned that when Christians use political power, or any coercive or artificial means, to give special advantage to their distinctive sect, the outcome is apt to be an ugly thing. We reject methods which, history seems to teach, pervert Christianity. If we reject totalitarianism for ourselves, we, *a fortiori*, reject it for others. Believing that our own faith cannot remain pure when coupled with methods of intolerance, we also believe that no faith can enter into that partnership without corruption.

5. PEACEFUL CHANGE IS POSSIBLE

Practical experience seems to show that where the people have a considerable degree of self-discipline, where they recognise duty to fellow men and where they have considerable education, then they can operate political processes which make for change which is peaceful and selective. In the western democracies, the political institutions have to a great extent been influenced by Christianity. (By Christianity we do not mean clericalism which may be an impediment to peaceful and selective change.) In these countries, conditions approximating to those of a free society have on the whole existed for 150 years or more. During that period, social and economic change has been so immense that conditions in any one of these countries to-day would completely bewilder those who lived there a hundred or fifty years ago.

The changes have, in the main, been peaceful changes. There has been little coercion, terrorism or civil war. The conspicuous apparent exception is the United States' war of eighty-five years ago, called in the North the " war of the Rebellion," but in the South the " war between the States." It was, in essence, more international than civil war. The basic issue was whether certain sovereign states had, by prior compact of union, given up the right to resume full sovereignty.

The social changes effected by free political processes have in the main tended to increase the opportunity of the individual to develop according to the dictates of his conscience and reason. Slavery has been abolished. There has been a definite trend away from treating labourers as animals or machines are treated. Women have been freed from grave disabilities. Economically, individual initiative, experimental and competitive, has produced great richness. The " industrial revolution," while it has brought evils, has shown men how, with less physical effort, they can produce much more. Infant mortality has been greatly reduced, health generally improved, and the span of life lengthened. Education is general and the development of spiritual life has been kept free of political inhibitions. Graduated income taxes and death duties effect a very considerable distribution of production in accordance with need.

To say these things is not to be self-righteous or complacent. There are many great blots and many deficiencies. One notable blot is the persistence in the United States of a considerable, though diminishing, measure of race discrimination. There persist inequalities of many kinds, economic, social and political. There is no assurance that ways have been found to prevent the cyclical breakdown of production process and the vast misery consequent therein. By no means is God's will done as it is in heaven. To be satisfied would be un-Christian.

But it is not un-Christian to point out that where political institutions show evidence of Christian influence, the result is good fruit. If that were not so, one could doubt that Christianity did in fact reflect God's ultimate revelation to man. Christ said : " By their fruits shall ye know them."

It seems, both on the basis of theoretical reasoning and on the basis of practical experience, that peaceful and selective change can be assured under the conditions of a free society of self-discipline. There is no comparable evidence to show that under a despotic or totalitarian form of society there can be sustained change that is peaceful and selective and which progressively increases the opportunities for individual growth.

6. WORLD SHORTAGE OF FREE SOCIETIES WITH TESTED POLITICAL INSTITUTIONS

There are not in the world many societies which have tested political mechanisms whereby decisions reflect the choice and reflection of the people as a whole. That, in the main, is not because such institutions are not wanted, but because various conditions have militated against their realisation. Many peoples have been long in colonial dependency. Some, like the peoples of India and Pakistan and certain Arab states, are only now moving from dependency to full independence. Some, like the peoples of China and Indonesia, are in chaos and strife. Some, like the Germans, Japanese and Italians, are still under, or just emerging from, the military control of the victors. Some live under constitutions which, in words, vest sovereignty in the people ; but they are, in fact, ruled by a small group which perpetuates itself in power by force, subject to change by periodic revolution. Some live under " dictatorships of the proletariat."

These facts are significant because they affect the practicability of developing internationally processes of change which will be peaceful and selective. It means that there do not exist, on a world-wide scale, tested institutions of political liberty and that there is an absence of the foundation needed for building a world structure which has political power to legislate change. The creation of a World State involves a mechanism of power and the selection of individuals to direct it. If the power is to be sufficient to make possible change which is adequate to replace violent change, there must, somewhere, be large discretionary authority. But it would not be possible to-day to assure that the discretion would come from peoples who were free, and morally and intellectually trained for the use of political freedom.

Theoretically, it is possible to devise a world representative system so " weighted " in favour of the societies of tested freedom that their representatives would have the preponderant voice. The others, who are the majority, would never consent to those few societies being accorded world supremacy. They would, in a sense, be justified. For while the free societies have shown good capacity to govern themselves, they have not shown the same good capacity to govern others, of different races and cultures. It would not advance us to recreate and extend the colonial system under the guise of " world government."

To-day, any world-wide system for institutionalising change would inevitably be despotic. Either it would vest arbitrary power in the persons of a few individual officials, or it would vest great power in the small fraction of the human race who have tested political processes for reflecting the individual choice.

The great majority of the world's population will not, and should not, agree to be ruled by the " free societies." The " free societies " will not, and should not, go back under despotism.

This impasse is a source of great peril. It leaves international change to be effected largely by force and coercion. It does so at a time when the means for corrupting men's souls and destroying their bodies have grown far beyond anything that the world has ever known. Thus, Christian citizens can feel that each, according to his means, has a duty to act to increase the possibility of world political unity and processes for peaceful change. That does not mean that Christian citizens will treat unity as the all-sufficient end, to which they should sacrifice what to them seem justice, righteousness and human dignity. They will seek the conditions for unity with the urgency of those who know that great disaster impends and with the practicability of those who know that such disasters cannot be averted merely by the incantation of fine words.

7. THE DEVELOPMENT OF FREE SOCIETIES

If peaceful change requires deciding whose judgment is to prevail, and if the judgment of a free, disciplined, society is the only reliable and generally acceptable judgment, then the extension of free societies throughout the world is prerequisite to a world-wide institutionalising of change. Many Christian citizens see that as the great long-range political task. Its accomplishment would make it possible to set up and operate in a non-despotic way international mechanisms for peaceful change. That task has two aspects :

(a) It is first necessary to preserve and improve free societies where they now exist. Free societies are delicate plants. To grow them is a long, hard task and, once they are grown, they are in constant danger of withering away. The post-war climate has been particularly hard on free societies. The cumulative result of two world wars is grave economic distress coupled with great human weariness and disillusionment. Under these conditions, men have a longing to be taken care of. Also, the economic margin for survival has been reduced to a point where centralised planning has seemed necessary. To men who are preoccupied with the struggle for the basic, material needs of life for their families, bread may be of more compelling and immediate importance than civil rights and freedoms. Such conditions lead to giving great power to a few men.

Delegation of power does not, of itself, necessarily mean an abandonment of freedom. It may be an exercise of freedom to meet an emergency and the people may retain both the legal right and the practical political mechanisms for ending the delegation when the emergency has passed. As we have noted, free societies usually give dictatorial powers in time of great emergency, such as war, and it has been shown that they can withstand temporary dictatorship of this kind. Nevertheless, there is always grave risk in conferring dictatorial power because such power can readily become self-perpetuating.

To preserve the characteristics of a free society within the areas where it now measurably prevails will itself be a difficult task. It will require vigilance and dedication by Christians as citizens. That dedication should not be merely in the interest of *preservation*, but of *improvement*. Only effort motivated by the creative urge can generate the needed energy and enthusiasm. Struggles are seldom won merely by a defensive strategy.

(*b*) New free societies must be developed, and this can be done and should be done rapidly wherever the necessary human foundation exists. Fortunately, much has been done, through varied channels, to create those foundations. The Christian churches have played, in this, a great part. The Christian missionary movement has had a great world-wide influence in developing in men a sense of duty to fellow man. Also, Christian schools and colleges have stimulated education throughout the world. On the moral and educational foundations developed over past generations, much is now being done to erect free political institutions.

Until recently, nearly one-third of the world's population were the subject peoples of the " free societies." Within the last three years, free institutions have been set up in India, Pakistan, Burma, Ceylon, the Philippine Islands and certain of the Arab states. A large measure of autonomy is envisaged for Indonesia. The total number of peoples thus acquiring political freedom represents about one-quarter of the population of the world and could more than double the total population of the free societies. That is an amazing and encouraging occurrence which should confound the pessimists and inspirit the disillusioned.

Of course, it is not certain that all of these new political entities will, in fact, maintain societies of freedom in the full sense. In part, the present development represents a great experiment. In many of the areas momentous and difficult decisions remain to be made, and there is not yet the kind and degree of individual moral and intellectual development which would easily assure a peaceful outcome. There will be need of sympathetic understanding, material aid, and scientific and technical assistance from the older societies of freedom.

There remain dependent colonial areas which can be developed toward self-government and free institutions. The colonial powers, by the United Nations Charter, have pledged themselves to seek that development; and to aid in attaining the result there has been created the Trusteeship Council.

It should be remembered in this connection that political wisdom generally comes only with practical experience. If people are to be held in guardianship until they have fully developed all the qualities desired, there will be an indefinite prolongation of guardianship. It is better to err on the side of giving freedom prematurely than to withhold it until there is demonstrated proof of ability to use it wisely. To learn by self-experience is apt to involve much suffering. But few learn adequately from the experience of others.

There is in China nearly one-fifth of the human race. Some Chinese leaders have, in recent years, sought to replace despotism with free political institutions. But progress has been slow. The people are materially impoverished and only a few have book-learning. They have had to undergo a war and occupation longer than that of the European continental allies. Individualism, in terms of the family, is perhaps excessive and a sense of community too restricted. But the people still possess richly the qualities which will enable them to make a great addition to foundations of political liberty.

During the last century there developed a sense of fellowship between the Chinese people and the peoples of the West, largely because of the activities of Christian missionaries, educators and doctors. Now, more than ever, such activities need to be continued and, indeed, intensified.

There is a great responsibility toward the vanquished peoples of Germany, Japan and Italy. The victors have made themselves the government of Germany ; they, in fact, direct the government of Japan and will largely influence the post-war development of Italy. The peoples of these countries have education and personal morality in large measure. It ought to be possible for them to develop into free societies. That is a task of great difficulty because of the evil war has bred. But it is a task of unique importance.

A survey of the globe shows that it is possible for upwards of three-quarters of the human race to develop peacefully and quickly—say, within one or two generations—the use of free political institutions. No doubt there would be many inadequacies, as indeed there always are. But it is possible to foresee conditions under which there would be obtainable, from most of the peoples of the earth, judgments which reflect the thinking, on an individual basis, of minds and spirits which are free and developed by political experience and self-discipline. On that foundation it would be possible to establish, internationally, procedures for peaceful change which would not be despotic, but which would reflect that moral sense which, we believe, is potential in every human being.

The programme suggested has a particular appeal to Christians because it is a peaceful programme to which the Christian churches can make a great contribution. There can be parallel effort by the churches and Christian citizens.

The free society cannot be equated with a Christian society and it is possible to have free societies whose institutions are predominantly influenced by non-Christian religions. But the Christian faith especially emphasises those qualities of self-control and love of neighbour which are needed for the good operation of a free society. So, Christian citizens could feel that to extend free societies was a great long-range effort to which they could worthily dedicate themselves and seek to dedicate their nations. Thereby they would be laying the indispensable foundation for world institutions for peaceful and selective change. Those engaged in that effort could feel that they were making the world more nearly one where God's will would be done, and they would be responsive to the appeal of the masses that a way be found to save them and their children from the death, the misery, the starvation of body and soul which recurrent violence now wreaks upon man.

8. CONFLICT OF PROGRAMME WITH SOVIET PROGRAMME[1]

The programme which we suggest is one that, if vigorously espoused, could enlist great support throughout the world. In the countries to which we referred in the preceding section, both

[1] Unless otherwise indicated, quotations are from J. Stalin's *Problems of Leninism,* Moscow, 1940. This volume is currently circulated by official Soviet agencies as an authoritative expression of present-day Soviet doctrine.

the people and their leaders predominantly want peaceful evolution as free societies. There are, of course, everywhere some who put their primary reliance upon means of violence, but in the countries referred to even those do not dare openly to advocate force as an ideal method. In these countries there is freedom for citizens to advocate the use of political processes which are peaceful rather than violent. Our programme would not, however, receive co-operation from the Soviet Communist Party and those in the world who are guided by, or subjected to, its dogma. The reason is not so much difference of opinion between Soviet and non-Soviet leaders as to the final ends to be sought, as difference of opinion as to the means by which those ends can be achieved.

The programme we suggest is one for peaceful evolution toward conditions which will make possible the world-wide institutionalising of change. The emphasis is on *peace*, both as end and means. The Soviet Communist Party does not believe in such peaceful evolution. It believes that only by violence and coercion can it secure its desired ends.

The difference about means creates a great gulf between Soviet practices and the practices of those not dominated by Soviet Communist philosophy. These differences in practice are especially important in the realm of international affairs and they cannot be ignored by those who, as citizens, have to take a stand on the international issues of our time. It makes it necessary to compare theory with theory and practice with practice and not to judge on the basis of comparing the theory of some with the practices of others.

The long-range social ends which Soviet leaders profess to seek are in many respects similar to the ends which Christian citizens seek. As a matter of political organisation, Soviet doctrine does not look upon its " dictatorship of the proletariat " as the final best result. Such dictatorship is to be a preliminary phase which will gradually wither away in favour of a condition where the people are self-governing. Soviet dictatorship is " preparing the ground for the withering away of the State, which is one of the basic elements of the future stateless Communist System " (p. 38).

Economically, Soviet leaders seek " a much higher productivity of labour " (p. 295), " the abolition of exploitation of man by man " (Constitution, Article 4), and ultimately the distribution of the production of labour in accordance with the formula " from each according to his abilities, to each according to his needs " (p. 570).

Socially, Communist doctrine envisages " the equality of the rights of citizens of the U.S.S.R., irrespective of their nationality or race, in all spheres of economic, state, cultural, social and political life " (Constitution, Article 123).

In its foreign policy, the Soviet Union is " the most internationalist of all state organisations " and seeks the amalgamation of all " into a single state union " (p. 37). It seeks for colonies the right " to complete secession " and " independent existence as states " (p. 51).

There is nothing in these long-term ends irreconcilable with what Christians seek. Indeed, most of those ends—and more— have been sought by Christians long before there was any Communist Party. Christians seek to develop in individuals such a love of fellow man and such capacity for self-control and self-sacrifice as to reduce to a minimum the need for the State as a dictating authority. As we have noted, the early Christians " had all things common . . . and parted them to all men as every man had need " (Acts ii, 44, 45). Christians have long taught and sought the equal dignity and worth of the human personality without regard to race, nationality, colour, class or sex. They have sought for colonial peoples self-government or independence as rapidly as circumstances might permit. Internationally, they have been the most ardent supporters of plans for world organisation.

There is, we can see, much in common as regards ultimate social ends. But even as to these there is a difference in emphasis between Soviet and Christian thinking. Soviet thinking proceeds from a materialistic premise, whereas Christian thinking proceeds from a spiritual premise. Soviet leaders hold that " the material life of society . . . is . . . primary, and its spiritual life secondary," being merely a " reflection " of material life (p. 601). Christians believe that material and social conditions on earth are primarily important as creating the conditions needed for spiritual development. Christians believe in a moral law which derives from God and which establishes eternal standards of right and wrong. Soviet leaders do not believe in such concepts as " eternal justice " (p. 595).

These differences are important because they lead to the

differences as to means. Where political institutions and
practices reflect a materialistic philosophy, they readily subordinate the individual to some group, which may be nation,
race or class. The individual who seems to get in the way of
the chosen group may be treated ruthlessly and liquidated, or
forced to conform, without such treatment involving a violation
of any professed belief. It takes a spiritual approach to measure joy in terms of "one sinner that repenteth, more than
over ninety and nine just persons, which need no repentance."
To those who hold the materialist philosophy of Marx, Engels,
Lenin and Stalin it seems permissible to treat the welfare of a
particular class as the ultimate end and to use means which will
promote that end irrespective of the effect of those means upon
the dignity and sacredness of the individual human personality.
Many of the long-term social ends professedly sought by Soviet
leadership are equally sought by Christian citizens, but the
spiritual philosophy of Christianity requires the rejection of means
which can logically be accepted by those who have a materialistic
philosophy.

Soviet leaders assert that the desired ends cannot be achieved
peacefully and should not be sought peacefully. "Force is the
midwife of every old society pregnant with a new one" (Karl
Marx's *Capital*). "Up to a certain period the development of
the productive forces and the changes in the realm of the relations
of production proceed spontaneously, independently of the will
of men. But that is so only up to a certain moment, until the
new and developing productive forces have reached a proper
state of maturity. After the new productive forces have matured,
the existing relations of production and their upholders—the
ruling classes—become that 'insuperable' obstacle which can
only be removed by the conscious action of the new classes, by
the forcible acts of these classes, by revolution" (p. 617).

"Can such a radical transformation of the old bourgeois
order be achieved without a violent revolution, without the
dictatorship of the proletariat?

"Obviously not. To think that such a revolution can be
carried out peacefully, within the framework of bourgeois
democracy, which is adapted to the rule of the bourgeoisie, means
that one has either gone out of one's mind and lost normal human
understanding, or has grossly and openly repudiated the
proletarian revolution" (p. 126).

This belief that the desired results are to be sought only by violence, not by peaceful evolution, is not just theory. It reflects itself in the whole structure of Soviet society, and in its policies, domestic and foreign.

Internally, there is the militaristic pattern that is typical of a state of war. Absolute power rests with the heads of the Soviet Communist Party, which functions as a war-time general staff. " The proletariat needs the Party first of all as its General Staff, which it must have for the successful seizure of power " (p. 79). The Soviet proletariat is considered as " the shock brigade of the world proletariat " (p. 538). The Party itself operates under " iron discipline." " The achievement and maintenance of the dictatorship of the proletariat is impossible without a Party which is strong by reason of its solidarity and iron discipline. . . . The parties of the Communist Internationale, which base their activities on the task of achieving and consolidating the dictatorships of the proletariat, cannot afford to be " liberal " or to permit freedom of factions. The Party represents unity of will, which precludes all factionalism and division of authority in the Party " (pp. 81, 82). This internal unity is achieved by periodic purges in the course of which it is necessary " to handle some of these comrades roughly. But that cannot be helped " (p. 542).

The Soviet State is one of the tools of the Party. " The Party exercises the dictatorship of the proletariat. However, it exercises it not directly but with the help of the trade unions, and through the Soviet and their ramifications . . . not a single important political or organisational question is decided by our Soviet and other mass organisations without guiding directions from the Party " (pp. 134,135). The State, in turn, under such guiding direction from the Party, is a militant organisation. " The State is a machine in the hands of the ruling class for suppressing the resistance of its class enemies. . . . The dictatorship of the proletariat is the rule—unrestricted by law and based on force—of the proletariat over the bourgeoisie. . . . The dictatorship of the proletariat cannot be ' complete ' democracy, democracy for all, for the rich as well as for the poor " (pp. 32, 33).

Under this form of organisation, individuality is suppressed. In the field of politics and even of literature and the arts, there is coercion to think and act along uniform Party lines and there is coercion to eliminate any elements that might be discordant.

In its foreign policy, the Soviet Union shows its adherence

to the theory that the ends which it seeks can only be achieved by violent means. As regards the colonial areas, it seeks independence through revolution rather than through peaceful evolution. This is perhaps the fundamental reason why the Soviet Union has so long refused to sit upon the United Nations Trusteeship Council which is charged with promoting the peaceful evolution of dependent peoples toward independence or self-government. It prefers to seek " revolutionary alliance with the liberation movement of the colonies and dependent countries " (p. 52). In non-colonial areas there is penetration, secret and open, designed to bring into key positions those who accept the iron discipline of the Party and, as conditions seem opportune, resort is had to such methods as political strikes, sabotage, terrorism and guerrilla warfare. The Party has well-organised schools to train personnel for such tasks. These tactics have shown themselves in China, Korea, the Baltic States, Greece, Hungary, Bulgaria, Roumania, Poland, Czechoslovakia, Germany, France, Italy and elsewhere. It is not suggested that whenever there is violence in any of these areas the Soviet is wholly responsible for it. In some of the areas internal conditions are of such a nature as themselves to be promotive of unrest. But the Soviet Communist Party openly encourages and seeks to exploit conditions of violence.

The Soviet Union is a member of the United Nations and that membership can be harmonised with the policies of the Soviet Communist Party. The first purpose of the United Nations is " to maintain international peace and security." That is an end to which the Party can subscribe because war is not a preferred method of the Party. The violence and coercion which it invokes are the violence and coercion of internal struggle, the struggle to get the " police power " and then to use it for liquidating the " class enemies." Wherever the processes of the United Nations seem to stand in the way of Soviet efforts to promote such violent effort, the Soviet Union stands aloof. It has boycotted most of the specialised agencies of the United Nations designed to promote peacefully the economic, social and cultural well-being of the members. It has boycotted the Commissions on Greece and Korea which are designed to maintain the integrity of these states as against revolutionary penetration from the Soviet Union or other states dominated by Communist Parties. It refused to sit on the " Little Assembly " as well as on the Trusteeship Council, which is designed to promote peace-fully the evolution of colonial peoples to self-government or independence.

The Party doctrines to which we have referred are intensively taught to all Party members and are fanatically accepted. There is ample evidence to show that Soviet policy in fact reflects those doctrines and reflects the view that the changes desired cannot be effected peacefully and that " a ' peaceful ' path of develop-ment " is possible only " in the remote future, if the proletariat is victorious in the most important capitalist countries " (p. 35).

We also see that this dependence upon methods of violence brings with it much the same " compulsory enmity, diabolical outrages against the human personality, and a wanton distortion of the truth " which have led Christians to oppose " wars, the occasion of war, and all situations which conceal the fact of conflict under the guise of outward peace " (Oxford Conference, *supra*).

Since the formation of the Soviet Union there has been a constant effort to portray the Union as surrounded by vicious and rapacious enemies. " We must remember that we are surrounded by people, classes and governments who openly express their intense hatred for us. We must remember that we are at all times but a hair's breadth from every manner of invasion " (p. 157, Lenin). There has been constant effort to arouse hatred toward so-called " bourgeois " or " imperialist " peoples, and notably the British and Americans. " Let not our hatred of our foes grow cold " (*Pravda*, January, 1948). Normal social intercourse is looked upon as partaking of treason ; inter-marriage is forbidden.

It is taught that the nature of so-called imperialist or bourgeois countries is such that they must attack the Soviet Union and that " the existence of the Soviet Republic side by side with imperialist states for a long time is unthinkable. One or the other must triumph in the end. And before that end supervenes, a series of frightful collisions between the Soviet Republic and the bourgeois states will be inevitable " (p. 156, Lenin).

The militaristic regimentation within the Soviet Union involves many outrages against the human personality. These are reflected by frequent violent purges, by terrorism through secret police and by political concentration camps containing millions of persons.

Soviet propaganda by press and radio makes little effort to base itself on fact. It fabricates freely. Where facts are given, they are usually so given as to create an impression that is far from truth. That, of course, also happens elsewhere, but in a free society there is opportunity to combat falsehood by challenge and contradiction.

Because the Soviet party relies on means of violence, coercion, hatred and falsehood, the good ends it seeks do not, in fact, arrive—as is usual under such circumstances.

At a time when individual political responsibility has been greatly increasing in the world generally, it has contracted within the Soviet zones of influence ; and within the Soviet Union itself the leaders seem to contemplate indefinite postponement of that " withering away," that " atrophy," of dictatorship and that increase of individual self-rule which is one of the proclaimed ends (pp. 656-662).

At a time when economic inequalities have been levelling off in the capitalistic, free enterprise, countries, the Soviet state has found it necessary to reject the idea of " equalisation " and " levelling the requirements and the individual lives of the members of society " (p. 521). Increasing reliance is placed upon the stimulus of individual reward and self-gain (p. 363). Marxism, it is now taught, " is an enemy of equalisation " (p. 521). The workers get " payment for their work in accordance with its quantity and quality " and in accordance with the principle " he who does not work, neither shall he eat " (Constitution, Arts. 118, 12). There is indefinite postponement of the " higher phase " when there will be distribution " to each according to his needs " (pp. 569-570). Money, it is true, is not the primary means to power and special privilege. But other means are widely prevalent.

At a time when earnest and effective efforts are being made to achieve equality without regard to race or class, the Soviet Party intensifies class warfare and its " classless " society is relegated to the indefinite future because, it is said, the struggle of the " new class " against the " bourgeoisie " is not a " fleeting period," but an " entire historical era, replete with civil wars and external conflicts " (pp. 30, 31).

At a time when the Western democracies, notably Great Britain, were peacefully bringing political independence to upwards of 500,000,000 people, Soviet leaders, the great talkers about the right of peoples to "independent existence as states" (p. 51), have not themselves produced any freedom for any people, but the Soviet Union has been annexationist.

At a time when the other Great Powers became increasingly disposed to increase the authority of the United Nations, Soviet leaders, while professing to seek a "single state union" (p. 37) have refused even to discuss moving toward that result by some diminution of the "veto" power within the Security Council.

It is not contended that Soviet communism is wholly bad. We have seen that all change has elements of good because everything that is is imperfect. Certainly, there was so much imperfection under the Czars that any change from that could readily work some improvement. Also, Soviet leaders do not rely wholly or continuously on means of violence and there have been some good, peaceful developments, notably in the field of education. Also, the very fact that there is a Soviet challenge has had a stimulating effect upon the Western democracies which, for their own good, needed the spur of competition.

Unfortunately, however, it seems basic in Soviet doctrine that there is now no "peaceful path of development." During the thirty years since the October Revolution, the emphasis, both in doctrine and in practice, has been on violent and coercive revolution, with results which confirm what history has so often taught, that good ends are not readily achieved by means of violence, terrorism, hatred and falsity such as the Soviet Party advocates and uses. Those who adopt these methods give an impression of great zeal and of great concern for their Cause. What they do attracts great attention just because it is violent, whereas peaceful change usually attracts little attention. But close analysis usually shows that when change is sought to be wrought by violence, the sense of progress, while exhilarating, is illusory.

So it is that while there is no irreconcilable conflict between the ultimate social ends which are professedly sought by Soviet communists and those ends which Christian citizens seek, there is great difference as to the means which should be used. That difference derives both from the different philosophical and moral premises and from conflicting judgments as to the kind of means that, in fact, can be relied on to produce the desired ends.

G

9. PEACEFUL RECONCILIATION OF PROGRAMME WITH
SOVIET PROGRAMME

The Soviet reliance on change by force and violence constitutes a serious obstacle athwart our suggested programme.
Soviet influence is considerable and it is now favoured by external
conditions.   World War II created a vacuum of power in many
areas.   Of the eight so-called " Great Powers," three—Italy,
Germany and Japan—have been engulfed by the disaster of
defeat.   Three—United Kingdom, France and China—have
been enfeebled by the struggle for victory.   Therefore, there is
about the Soviet Union a power vacuum into which it has
already moved to bring some three hundred million people,
representing about fifteen nationalities, under the dominant
influence of the dictatorship of the proletariat and its revolutionary
theories and practices.

Even more important than this fact of political vacuum is
the fact that there has developed in the world much of a moral
vacuum.   The so-called western or Christian civilisation has
long accepted most of the social ends now professed by the Soviet
Communist Party and, indeed, its goals have been even more
advanced.   But of recent years, it has seemed to be half-hearted
and lacking in fervour or sense of urgency.   The result has been
that many people have unthinkingly compared the idealised
purposes and theories of the Soviet programme with the worst
practices of western nations.   Others, eager for quick results,
uncritical of means, have been attracted to the Soviet programme by the very violence of its means, which have seemed a
proof of zeal.   The fact that Christian citizens tend to favour
non-violent means is taken as proof that they lack zeal.   The
consequent degree of following attracted by the Soviet dynamic
programme has encouraged Soviet leaders to entertain great
expectations of realising their particular " one world."   Their
ambitions have mounted so that there is indeed grave danger of
that " series of frightful collisions between the Soviet Republic
and the bourgeois states " which Lenin and Stalin have forecast
as inevitable.

Christians must dedicate themselves to prevent such developments.   There are in the main two ways of doing so.

First, Christians must reject, and see to it that their nations
reject, the Soviet thesis of the inevitability of violent conflict and

they must not imitate Soviet leadership by placing reliance on violent means.

Secondly, Christians must see to it that their nations demonstrate that peaceful methods can realise the goals which we all espouse.

There is disturbing evidence that the so-called " free societies " are themselves tending to adopt those features of Soviet procedure which Christians particularly condemn. In the United States great emphasis is being placed upon achieving military supremacy and military counsels are more influential than has normally been the case in that republic. Some portions of the American Press are stirring up emotional hatred against the Soviet Union and there is some distortion of truth, principally through the exaggeration of what is true but of minor importance.

It is no doubt desirable that the free societies should be resolute and strong. Also, it is important that the members of free societies should understand the true nature of the Soviet programme so that they do not abet it mistakenly. Also, there is no good in concealing the fact that the Soviet programme is dangerous. Whenever any particular group sets out to dominate the world and to do so by methods of violence, coercion and terrorism, a tense situation is bound to result. No doubt Soviet leaders do not want major war, although we must recall that Lenin has stated, and Stalin has repeated, that " if the ruling class, the proletariat, wants to hold sway, it must prove its capacity to do so by military organisation also " (p. 156, Lenin). But even if, as we believe, Soviet leaders now look upon their methods of internal penetration as more effective than international war, still the situation is risky. It requires a very nice judgment to use force precisely to the degree which will gain the maximum without precipitating actual war. Such an effort also assumes, on the part of others, a degree of self-control which we hope and pray exists, but which is not a certainty. Thus peace is at the risk of incidents or miscalculations. The free societies need to face up to that reality. But also they must strive to exercise iron self-control, being determined not themselves to use force to crush the Soviet experiment. They may not like the Soviet experiment in state socialism and its dynamic world-wide programme, but they must recognise that a free world is a world of difference and that any society has a right to experiment and compete. Marshal Stalin claimed that the results of the Soviet first Five Year Plan proved that " the working-class is as able to build the new as to destroy the old " (p. 439) and that they have confounded the claim of capitalism as the " best of all societies " (p. 440). If, in fact, the Soviet system of state socialism can peacefully confound capitalism, it is entitled to the opportunity to do so. Unhappily, the Soviet does not rely primarily upon such methods of peaceful competition and comparison. But the Soviet methods, while they are in part methods which Christians will generally reject, are so far at least methods short of war and Christian citizens of the free societies must make a supreme effort to do all that lies within their power to keep it so and to see that their nations use peaceful responses which are available and which can preserve and extend the system of free societies.

The most important response to the Soviet challenge will be in effecting peacefully the reforms which Soviet leaders contend can only be effected by violent means. We must by actual demonstration disprove Stalin's dictum that " one must be a revolutionary, not a reformist " (p. 597).

The western democracies won their prestige in the world through their great peaceful accomplishments. The industrial revolution, the concept of " liberty, equality and fraternity " and the experiments in political freedom created world-wide confidence in the dynamic and life-giving quality of their institutions. But for long now, these democracies have faced no serious competition. The quality of their effort has deteriorated and they have, to a considerable extent, been coasting with a momentum that is waning. Many do not like it that a challenge has now arisen. Many would prefer peace which is a condition of tranquillity or stagnation, where all threat and challenge are removed and where men can feel that they can safely relax. Some are inclined to the view that unless we get that kind of peace, we do not have peace at all, and an irresponsible few talk of using force to crush the challenger. That is folly. Those of us who are of the western peoples face the task of mental adjustment to a dynamic peace where there is competition. We need to make it clear to ourselves and we need to make it clear to proponents of other systems that we welcome a world in which there is peaceful competition. Above all, we need to make it clear that we can peacefully, through reform, bring about results which all men want and which they will be apt to seek by the violent methods which the Soviet sponsors unless we can prove that they can be achieved by peaceful means.

Whenever a system is challenged, there is a tendency to rally to support the system " as is." The world becomes divided between those who would maintain the *status quo* and those who would change the *status quo*. As we have seen, those who would sustain the *status quo* inevitably are defeated. And almost inevitably the issue is resolved by violence. The result may not be the particular changes desired by the dynamic powers, but equally, it does not maintain the status which their opponents sought to preserve. So it is that in the face of Soviet challenge we must not rally to the defence of our institutions just as they are, but we must seek even more ardently to make them better than they now are.

In fact, much progress has been made along this line. We have already referred to the action of Great Britain in bringing about five hundred millions of colonial dependent peoples peacefully to self-government. That has been the most effective way to demonstrate that the achievement of self-government by dependent peoples was not dependent upon a Soviet " revolutionary alliance " (p. 52) and that it is possible to achieve by peaceful means results which the Soviet leaders profess to want but which they have said could only be achieved by violent means.

The " free societies " have also made considerable progress in achieving an economy whereby production is on the basis of ability and distribution on the basis of need. The steeply graduated income and estate taxes which now prevail generally in " capitalistic " countries take largely from those who have ability to accumulate and to an increasing extent this is being distributed to those in need, in the form of social security programmes. These countries are in fact much closer to the so-called " higher phase " of communism than is the Soviet Union itself.

Socially, the great blot on the escutcheon of the democracies is the discrimination against coloured persons practised by much of the white population of the United States. Here, however, the problem is recognised and great efforts are being made to deal with it. It is not possible by legislative fiat to eradicate social prejudices, the origins of which go back hundreds of years. There is, however, a vast change which is in peaceful process.

The danger is that those who face the Soviet challenge will feel they must defend themselves on every count. There is some evidence that the Soviet challenge is, to an extent, having that natural result. Christians must stand strong against that, recognising the imperfection of every system and of every nation, not identifying righteousness with anything that is, but constantly striving to prove that the evils that exist can be eradicated by peaceful means.

That demonstration is already gathering momentum, and as that momentum grows, the Soviet menace will become innocuous and Soviet leaders themselves will probably abandon, or at least indefinitely postpone, their efforts to produce change by violent means. Probably they will not do so as a matter of conviction, for the conception of violent change is deeply ingrained. But they can be expected to alter their tactics as soon as there will no longer be available to them in the different countries of the world sufficient support for successful revolutionary measures. Soviet leaders are realists. They do not consider that violence must be continuous or that it should be recklessly undertaken. Their aim is to strike " at the decisive point, at the decisive moment " (p. 63, Lenin). There is not uninterrupted attack and there may at times be strategic retreat. " They have to realise—and the revolutionary class is taught to realise by its own bitter experience—that victory is impossible unless they have learned both how to attack and how to retreat properly " (p. 65, Lenin). " The object of this strategy is to gain time " (p. 65). There must be a " selection of the moment for the decisive blow " (p. 64).

So it is that while Soviet leaders believe in violent means, they do not believe in continuing violence and they do not believe in violence being precipitated until the moment comes when " all the class forces hostile to us have . . . exposed . . . their practical bankruptcy " (p. 64, Lenin).

The years between the Soviet revolution and World War II involved a very large exposure of practical bankruptcy on the part of non-communist nations. During that period the " free societies," at least, were not at their best. Soviet leaders have encountered weaknesses which have afforded them great opportunities and given them great encouragement. Within recent years that situation has begun to change. There have been some great constructive developments. To some of these we have alluded. It is possible to push forward along these lines and it is imperative that this should be done.

It is regrettable that the Soviet Communist Party and those that follow its guiding directions will not co-operate in a world programme to develop peacefully conditions needed for peaceful change. But that non-co-operation need not operate as a veto. If, through fear or morbid fascination, the free societies do nothing, then they do indeed make inevitable those violent revolutionary processes, those frightful collisions, which Soviet leadership would precipitate as its means to its ends.

The Soviet challenge loses its potency once the free societies show a capacity for constructive action. As we have said, the challenge, in its present phase, seems not a militaristic challenge, like that of Hitler, Mussolini and the Japanese war lords. It is a call to revolution. If the non-communist societies, faced by that challenge, stand still and do nothing, for fear of offending Soviet leadership, they are lost. If they quietly move ahead, showing a practical capacity to achieve peacefully the things which Soviet leaders say can come only after an " entire historical era " of violence, then those talkers will quickly be rated as " incorrigible windbags "—to use Stalin's expression (p. 533).

It is important that there be these peaceful developments both domestically and internationally. We have already outlined what might be the grand, over-all, international programme. But such a long-range programme is not enough to meet the present need because it does not contain enough possibility to register quickly decisive results and thus to create general recognition of the capacity of the free societies. Intermediate programmes are needed, where successes can be registered, prestige gained and momentum acquired. We shall go on to consider what might be some of these intermediate programmes.

10. INTERMEDIATE STEPS AT PRESENT PRACTICABLE

It is not necessary to stand still and do nothing internationally until there has been laid the world-wide foundation for a free world society. There is much which can be done, to-day and to-morrow. There are already two great assets with which to work. One is the great and all-pervading force of the moral law. A second is the existence of an organisation—the United Nations—

which brings together in public association most of the nations of the world. On the basis of these two facts, many intermediate successes can be achieved.

Exposure to Moral Judgment

The moral law has universal influence. There are some who deny its existence and who try to educate men to ignore it. It is never immediately and universally effective. But still there is general, world-wide agreement about " right " and " wrong " in their broad outlines. That fact is of immense importance, for it makes it possible to use moral force for peace and justice at a time when there cannot yet be an adequate political mechanism.

Moral power can be a powerful force in the world. That is not a mere pious hope. It is the judgment of every realist throughout history. It was Napoleon who said that " in war, moral considerations make up three-fourths of the game." It was Admiral Mahan who said that physical force was useful only " to give moral ideas time to take root."

Allied leaders during both the First and Second World Wars did much to consolidate and marshal world sentiment to ensure Germany's defeat. They did that through great statements of aims, such as the Fourteen Points and the Atlantic Charter, which appealed to the moral conscience of the world. It is possible also to frame issues and organise moral power in the interest of peace.

The United Nations is a political machine which even now can be used to make moral power work during peace to preserve peace. That is largely due to Christian influence.

Many thought that world organisation should be primarily a military organisation to carry out the will of the Great Powers. That was, indeed, the conception which dominated the representatives of the Soviet Union, Great Britain and the United States when they met at Dumbarton Oaks in the summer of 1944 to make a first draft of the Charter. But our church people did not think much of an organisation which would be primarily military and which would depend chiefly on physical force. So they worked hard to make their point of view prevail. It did largely prevail at the San Francisco Conference of 1945, thanks in great part to the small nations, which did not want to be placed permanently under the military dictatorship of the three big Powers.

So, the San Francisco Conference radically changed the plan of Dumbarton Oaks. It emphasised the United Nations General Assembly as a place where the representatives of all states, big and little, would meet and discuss any problems of international relations, and where even the great nations could be required to subject their conduct to the judgment of world opinion.

The United Nations has now been functioning for over two years. Many are disappointed with the results. They would like the United Nations to be able to dictate and enforce the particular results which they want. As we have seen, the United Nations cannot now be that kind of an organisation. However, it has revealed great possibilities. Of course, it has not settled everything. Indeed, the international situation is gravely troubled. But the United Nations has shown that it need not be a mere spectator. It can do something. It can call every nation's international acts to the bar of public opinion, with confidence that that will have healthy practical consequences.

We have seen how, in time of war, the public verdict of right and wrong exercises a powerful effect. The United Nations has begun to show how, in time of peace, public opinion can exercise a powerful effect. At the San Francisco Conference and at the subsequent Assemblies of the United Nations political leaders from many lands have presented views on many matters. Always the speakers were obviously conscious of the fact that their audience included the representatives of many million people who possessed great power and who were primarily swayed by moral considerations. Every speaker presented his case with regard to what he thought was world opinion and he tried to get its backing. Almost always the different governments presented their positions otherwise than they would have done had they been meeting in secret and not subject to informed world opinion. That is a fact of great moment. It does not make future war impossible. It can make war less likely.

Things equal to the same thing are equal to each other. If world opinion can bring the foreign policies of the different nations toward harmony with the world's moral judgment, then those policies will automatically move toward harmony with each other.

It ought to be normal that major international policies which create fear or resentment anywhere should be subjected to the scrutiny of the Assembly.

The United Nations Charter provides that the Assembly may discuss any situation, regardless of origin, which it deems likely to impair friendly relations among nations. Thus, the Assembly can act as the " town meeting of the world," as was the design. If any nation is afraid to have its international policies discussed, that is good proof that they ought to be discussed. In the Assembly the sponsors of questioned policies would explain them and welcome an expression of the confidence of the Assembly. The verdict would not have any legal consequences. There may not be immediate and clear-cut compliance with it, but an unfavourable judgment would to some degree influence the future of the condemned policy and make more likely its modification or abandonment. No nation, however strong, will lightly defy a verdict which seems to reflect the informed and aroused moral judgment of mankind.

Soviet dictatorship is sensitive to public opinion. It is by no means stupid enough to think that it can prevail merely by force. At home it can, within limits, make public opinion what it will. But only within limits. The Party recognises that it must " properly express what the people are conscious of " and that this is a " necessary condition " (p. 152). Stalin says that the Soviet Union joined the League of Nations in 1934 because it recognised that the possibility of exposure would deter wrongdoers. " . . . despite its weakness the League might nevertheless serve as a place where aggressors can be exposed " (p. 628). The Soviet representatives, more than any others, have used the United Nations as a forum for appealing to public opinion. They recognise that, in the outer world, where police power and control of news are not at their command, Soviet foreign policy cannot prevail unless it can bring people generally to believe in its rightness.

So, while the United Nations cannot to-day be converted into a mechanism directed by a few persons having power to rule the nations, it can be used to subject national acts to the test of moral judgment. Moral power arises from the most humble to reach the most mighty. It works inexorably, even though slowly. It will not suit the impatient. But it can achieve solid results. The important thing is that the United Nations be used for purposes for which it is adapted and not be discredited by attempted use for purposes for which it is ill adapted.

Some relatively minor changes would serve greatly to increase the capacity of the United Nations to serve as a medium for focusing world opinion upon national acts. There should be a permanent organ of the United Nations able, at all times, quickly to bring to light the facts necessary for world opinion to form an intelligent judgment. The Security Council logically should do that. But its freedom to investigate is limited by the Permanent Members' right of veto. If this cannot be changed, then it may be that the General Assembly could undertake this task, perhaps through its " Interim Committee " or " Little Assembly " so as to assure at least what Stalin referred to as " exposure."

Social and Economic Agencies

The United Nations is not designed merely to deal with political problems. It is also designed to promote human welfare. One of the great conceptions embodied in the Charter was that the unity gained in war could be preserved in peace if the war allies went on together to combat the social, economic and physical enemies of mankind. So the Charter branded intolerance, repression, injustice, disease and economic want as the common enemies of the morrow, just as Nazi Germany and Imperialist Japan were the common enemies of the day. It proposed that the united nations stay united to wage war against these evils.

These possibilities of the United Nations have not, as yet, been adequately developed. Commissions and specialised agencies are at work, but they have not yet had time to achieve any dramatic successes and, indeed, their work has largely been lost sight of because political controversy in the Assembly and Security Council has seemed more exciting, more news-worthy and more important. The economic and social tasks of the United Nations should be brought into proper perspective and pushed with effort comparable to that invested in the political phase of United Nations work.

International Bill of Rights

One of the most important of these social tasks of the United Nations is the bringing into force of an agreed international Bill of Rights. The United Nations Charter itself, by its preamble, affirms faith in fundamental human rights and in the dignity and worth of the human person. One of its basic purposes is to achieve international co-operation in promoting and encouraging respect for human rights and for fundamental freedoms for all. Provision is made in the Charter for a commission for the promotion of human rights, which Commission has now been established. It ought to be possible through this Commission to bring about increased acceptance of a Bill of Rights. This, if done, would greatly facilitate the building of the foundation required for transforming the United Nations itself into a more effective political instrumentality. This important subject is being dealt with in another chapter.[1]

Functional Agencies

A further important area of usefulness lies in the development of functional agencies to carry out agreed policies. The United Nations itself, under present conditions, cannot legislate generally. There are, however, some matters as to which a policy could be voluntarily agreed upon between all or most of the member states. Then these agreed policies could be entrusted to some functional agency to carry out. One of the proposals regarding atomic energy illustrates this type of procedure. The fact that that particular proposal has not yet been accepted, does not show that the functional approach is itself unsuitable. The functional approach is the easiest and most painless method of breaking down, or at least breaking through, national boundaries. It does not involve any blanket delegation of power which could be used despotically. It is merely a means of achieving, on an international basis, a concrete result sought by different nations.

In the United States, the State of New York and the State of New Jersey have, through a treaty consented to by the Federal Congress, created the Port of New York Authority, which develops the sea and air facilities of the New York Harbour area. It finances its own projects. It serves an end which is greatly in the interest of the people of both states and it does so by means and methods which are so inconspicuous that few citizens of either state are aware of the fact that they have made a very large surrender of sovereignty to an inter-state body.

[1] See Chapter V. " Freedom of Religion and related Human Rights," by O. Frederick Nolde.

Functional agencies, to advance mutually desired ends, can be set up under the auspices of the United Nations in agreement with the member states or such of them as are concerned. The operations of the agencies within the agreed scope of their authority could be free of any veto power.

It is particularly important that atomic energy should be brought under world rule. There exists a moral basis for such rule because all of the governments have expressed the view that there should be effective means to assure that this new power should be used constructively for man's welfare and not destructively for, perhaps, the extermination of mankind. The United Nations Assembly, as its first important act, voted unanimously to establish a commission to accomplish this result. However, nearly two and a half years have since elapsed and differences as to the means of control have created an impasse. Meanwhile, the knowledge of how to use atomic energy for destruction is doubtless growing and competent persons say that the monopoly of know-how may be broken in the near future. A situation of great gravity would arise if behind the present ideological differences there lay the menace of atomic weapons. It would be particularly grave if these weapons were held by persons who espouse the use of violent means to achieve their ends. Civilisation is drifting dangerously toward the edge of an awful precipice. To save it may require that atomic energy should, on a world-wide basis, be promptly brought under international control.

Regional Agencies

The United Nations Charter provides for regional agencies and agencies for collective self-defence. Through such agencies, international organisation can be developed more rapidly than on a world-wide scale. Inevitably, world-wide development is the slowest ; local development is quicker. Political institutions have developed from cities and principalities to counties and states and finally to great aggregations of states, like the Soviet Union and the United States, bound together by a federal system, and the British Commonwealth, bound together by loose agreement and common loyalties which have become traditional. The Pan-American defence system is a striking illustration of how groups of nations may unite on the basis of common interest and common trust.

Steps toward political, economic and monetary unity are being taken by many nations of Europe. This is a good development. A Europe divided into a score or more of separate unconnected sovereignties can never again be a healthful and peaceful part of the world. To substitute unity and strength for disunity and weakness is precisely the kind of positive action of which the free societies must prove themselves capable.

It is axiomatic that world government is the last step and the most difficult step to take. It is easier to develop political mechanisms on a less than universal basis than on a universal basis. By doing that, men can increase somewhat the possibilities of peaceful and selective change on an international basis. If, for example, ten nations can find a common political mechanism, they should not be prevented from doing so merely because sixty nations cannot do the same thing. It would be as logical to say that the states of the Soviet Union or of the United States should not have come together politically because that unity could not be achieved on a world-wide basis. Regional pacts and arrangements for collective self-defence are expressly authorised by the Charter of the United Nations (Articles 51, 52). They should be encouraged, subject only to the qualification that they should be genuinely based upon legitimate common interests ; should in no sense be a military alliance directed against any other state ; should sincerely seek to maintain and promote universality through the United Nations. To-day there are in the world a series of international groupings. There is the Soviet Union and its several associated states. There is the British Commonwealth. There is the Arab League. There is the Pan-American system. Such groupings can be steps toward the universal world order which is the goal of our long-range programme.

.   .   .   .   .

We could go on indefinitely in this vein. We have, however, said enough to indicate that, with a moral law of universal scope and with the United Nations as a place to bring together national acts and world-wide judgments, important intermediate results can be achieved. There is much to be done on a less than universal basis, within the framework of the Charter. Nations and peoples can do much to help each other. Such efforts do not take the place of our long-range programme, because they do not constitute a conscious, planned effort to create, on a world-wide basis, the conditions prerequisite to a general institutionalising of change. But interim measures can gain the time and the prestige needed for successful development of a long-range programme.

What seems urgent—and possible—is to revive in men a sense of moving peacefully toward a state of greater perfection. Many have been beaten and broken in spirit by the violence of the forces that have been loose in the world for now upward of a decade. They temporarily placed hope—perhaps undue hope—in the United Nations. But that hope has largely gone and there is despairing acceptance of the idea that continuing violence is inevitable for an entire historical era.

That is a dangerous mood. It can, perhaps, be broken by acts which, even in a small way, show the possibility of peaceful change. Let us, therefore, not despise what is presently possible, knowing that out of small things can come a rebirth of faith and hope, and that out of faith and hope can come great things, far beyond any that are here portrayed.

CONCLUSION

The Rôle of the Christian Church

Many will feel that the programmes here outlined are quite inadequate ; and those who feel that way may be quite right. Certainly our suggestions seem unimaginative and stodgy in comparison with many programmes, particularly the Soviet programme for achieving its ideal single world state by means of world-wide proletariat revolution. We have tried to write under a self-imposed ordinance, namely, to propose only what we felt might *practically* be achieved by *peaceful* means and without the sacrifice of hard-won human rights. No doubt, even within this limitation, there are better prospects than are here portrayed. But no programme which is both practical and peaceful will seem as exciting and dramatic as a programme which is purely imaginative or violent.

Leaders who invoke violence attract a fanatical following because they seem to know what they want and to be determined to get it. They give an impression of being right just because they seem willing to risk much to achieve their goals. Many seem to feel that " truth " is whatever people are willing to fight and die for, and that unless people advocate killing and dying, they must be doubtful in their own minds. So it is that ways of violence often become exalted and ways of peace are often depreciated.

It would be easy to arouse the so-called " free societies " of the Western " Christian " civilisation to initiate a great crusade, a holy war. Their programme could be expressed in many fine-sounding slogans, such as the " smashing of atheistic despotism " and the " removal of the last remaining obstacle to indispensable world government." Such a programme would evoke great enthusiasm and many fine sacrificial qualities. Many would gladly fight and die for such ends.

We reject any such procedure because of our profound conviction that its violence would end in utter frustration. We consider that such a procedure would be as irreconcilable with Christianity as is the violent procedure which Soviet leaders advocate and that in either case the procedure would produce results quite different from those sought.

We are fully conscious of the fact that peaceful and practical programmes will seem to many to evidence a lack of zeal and to conceal a desire selfishly to preserve the evils of the *status quo*. That appraisal, in our opinion, can be and should be changed. Christians should, we believe, appraise more highly than they seem to do the self-control, the self-discipline and the respect for human dignity required to make change by peaceful means. The Christian churches could, we think, find the way to make peaceful efforts seem more inspirational and be more sacrificial. It is a tragedy that inspiration and sacrifice in large volume seem to be evoked only by ways of violence. If the Christian churches could change that, then, indeed, they would help the Christian citizen along his way.

We have not outlined tasks which could be participated in only by Christians because, we believe, that if Christians advance a political programme which only Christians can support, they logically must contemplate a monopoly of power and privilege on behalf of their particular sect. That, we have made clear, would, in our opinion, vitiate the programme. But the task which we have outlined is a task which should arouse the Christian churches to a sense of special responsibility.

What is the need? The need is for men and women who

can see what now is and what can be. Christ put particular emphasis on vision and light. He taught men to see truly and to avoid the hatred, hypocrisy and selfishness which blind men or warp their visions. If Christian churches do not produce the needed vision, what can we expect but that mankind will stumble.

The need is for men who have the peacefulness which comes to those who are possessed by the Christian spirit of love ; who have the power which comes to those who pray, repent and are transformed and who have the dedication of those who leave all to follow Him.

The need is for more effective political use of moral power. The moral law, happily, is a universal law. But Christians believe that, through Christ, the moral law has been revealed with unique clarity. The Christian churches ought, therefore, to be especially qualified to help men to form moral judgments which are discerning and to focus them at the time and place where they can be effective.

The need is for full use of the present great possibilities of the United Nations. It was Christians most of all who wanted a world organisation which would depend primarily on moral rather than physical power. They have it. Now it is up to the churches to generate the moral power required to make the organisation work.

The need is to build the foundation for a more adequate world organisation. A world of free societies could be that foundation, and free society depends, in turn, on individuals who exemplify Christian qualities of self-control and of human brotherhood, and who treat freedom, not as licence, but as occasion for voluntary co-operation for the common good. So, again, the Christian churches have the great responsibility.

The need is for effort on a world-wide scale. The Christian Church is a world-wide institution. Consequently, the individual Christian may exert his influence not only as a citizen but also as member of a church which in its corporate life has a contribution to make. The Church demonstrates in its own life the achievement of community out of various races, nationalities and communions. It develops a common ethos. Its missionary movement constantly extends the fellowship of those who share the same loyalties and purposes. Its ecumenical movement deepens and consolidates that fellowship. Its programme of relief and reconstruction restores hope to the despairing and reconciles

H

those who have been enemies. The Commission of the Churches on International Affairs is beginning to give stimulus and leadership to the more direct impact of the churches on the current problems of relations between the nations. Thus the churches themselves in many ways can help build the bases for world order.

So it is that, as we analyse the need, Christian responsibility emerges as an inescapable fact. It is a fact that ought to have practical consequences. The potentialities of Christian influence are great, but the present weight of Christian impact is wholly inadequate. If, in the international field, Christians are to play their clearly indicated part, their churches must have better organisation, more unity of action and put more emphasis on Christianity as a world religion. That, we pray, will come from the Amsterdam Assembly and the final realisation of the World Council of Churches.

(b) OUR RESPONSIBILITY IN THE POST-WAR WORLD

Joseph L. Hromadka

I. THE PERSPECTIVE OF HISTORY

Because of these abnormal times, the Church of Christ has to deal with the basic issues of our present international life both with extreme caution and with courageous clarity. We are living, three years after the end of World War II, on volcanic ground, pregnant with destructive explosions and earthquakes. The old international order is gone. No great issue has been solved, not one area of our earth has achieved stability and security. In the history of the human race it is a unique, unprecedented situation. Never in the past has the *whole* of the world been shaken so profoundly as during the last thirty years. Since the last war the magnitude of the international crisis has manifested itself with such terrific and inescapable pressure that every thoughtful person feels the proximity of an avalanche which at the mere echo of a loud voice may bury what has been left of our civilisation and spiritual heritage. This is why we should approach any big problem of our present international life with extreme caution.

However, for the same reason we urgently need a courageous clarity of mind. Much of our present confusion and perilous tension is due to our lack of understanding of what is actually going on among the peoples and nations of the world. Everywhere we observe frustration and impatience, distrust and fear, and everywhere we sense the danger of an explosion because of an inadequate understanding of the magnitude and dimensions of the international catastrophe. Each one of us knows of instances when human impatience and anger killed a seriously sick man, and when the same impatience and anger had originated and grown because the people around the patient had been unaware of the gravity of his illness. From my own experience I can say that both the most irritated and sanguine critics of the international situation, and of " the other side " in particular, have lacked a clear vision of the nature and the abysmal depth of the contemporaneous crisis. The simple truth is that the rapid changes of history are transcending our normal categories, that, lacking imagination and vision, we are unable to grasp the meaning of the present turmoil and so become either disillusioned and cynical, or angry and hostile towards the nations and the men who seem to thwart our plans so wantonly. Hence it is essential that once again we try to understand courageously and clearly the basic nature and issues of contemporaneous history. Courageously, that is—to go beyond our pleasant and popular clichés, to break through our accepted conventions, and to abandon ideas which are already out of date. We lack courage, but we likewise lack clarity which resists and withstands the intoxicating haze of comfortable simplifications.

How far we are from the days of thirty years ago when the progressive, freedom-loving men were stirred by the great idea of " making the world safe for democracy ! " Ever since those days of " a new spring " many events have taken place which have unveiled the weaknesses and frailties of the modern, free, civilised society ! Then, we earnestly believed that the great ideas of a free, autonomous, self-determining humanity might be adequate to meet the issues of the modern era, not only to destroy the shackles of the feudal, autocratic, monarchical régimes, but also to build up a new Temple of human freedom and justice. We failed to overcome the fatal consequences of World War I and to establish a new, better, durable order on the ruins of the old. The basic issue of our times, both in national and international life, is far more than freedom and democracy. It goes beyond the categories of capitalism and socialism, liberalism and communism, even beyond what we call the alternative of " a free society or a totalitarian system," the alternative of the democratic, free West or the communistic, regulated, controlled East. The whole of the civilised human race is sick, and none is justified to claim a monopoly of means and medicines for the cure of the disintegrated international order. We are living in a crisis that is more than a crisis of democracy and freedom, of liberalism or humanism. What is at stake is much more than modern civilisation and free society. The ultimate principles and axioms of truth, justice, human personality, love, and the organic moral fellowship of men are at stake. Modern man, both in the West and in the East, has lost a real understanding of the supreme authority and the supreme court of appeal to which all men, all nations and races, ought to subordinate themselves in order to understand one another and to discover a common ground on which to start the construction of a new and better order.

2. THE PERSPECTIVE OF THE BIBLICAL MESSAGE

A right historical perspective is needed if we wish to have a right insight into the main issues of our international struggle. This is not enough. As members of the Church of Christ we need a still more adequate vantage point, the perspective of faith. The faith we mean is the certainty of the real presence of the Crucified and Risen Lord in the midst of our present misery and calamity. The place of the Church is beyond all human, political, national and cultural divisions and hostile groupings, beyond all hatreds, fears, suspicions, political devices and platforms of the post-war world. This is by no means to minimise the importance and validity of social, political and international ideals or aspirations. The Church of Christ may be non-political, but she is not indifferent to the problem of bringing order into a chaotic human society. Even he who knows the main *motifs* of the history of our civilisation is not in a position to assess the profound political contributions the Church, as such, has made to the structure of our society. She is not neutral in the struggle between freedom and slavery, justice and lawlessness, order and chaos, civil rights and tyranny. And yet, the Church has a peculiar mission : to go down, to the very abyss, where men as miserable sinners stand before their Lord, and where men commit clumsy blunders and make inescapable personal and political decisions. This is exactly where the prophets and apostles have sent her. The Lord of holiness, justice and mercy has descended from the heaven of heavens into the darkest valley of human corruption and sin, and has broken the bondage of guilt and death exactly where the power of godlessness and destructive evil seemed to triumph invincibly over Christ and His Kingdom. The Church can live only in the presence of her Lord. This means that she has to stand where He stands, and to do what He has done, to identify herself with human helplessness and need.

The present moment of history makes us more responsive to the mystery of the Biblical Testimony, or—at least—it opens our eyes to the fact, so often previously hidden, that the power of sin and confusion, both in the personal and political realm, transcends our capacity to cope with the catastrophic situation. The whole human race has been shaken out of its complacency, and the world's ruins reveal our helplessness. We have been awakened to *what* we are and *where* we are. " They are all gone aside, they are all together become filthy : there is none that doeth good, no, not one " (Psalm xiv, 3 ; Rom. iii, 12). This is not to proclaim a morbid relativism and to deny a real, specific responsibility on the part of individual nations or groups for the catastrophe in which we live ; this is rather to warn us against any effort to identify the Church of Christ with a definite political cause or to use her against any international *bloc*. Here we are : victors and vanquished, " Western " democrats and " Eastern " socialists and communists, citizens of the European-American civilisation as well as heirs of Eastern, Asiatic cultural tradition, different in race and education, but all of us united in common misery and sin, as well as in faith and ultimate loyalty to the Crucified and Risen Lord. Are we ?

Deep as is the difference in the measure of our responsibility for the destruction of the old international peace and order, and for the terrific losses in life and material welfare, we have to look at the contemporaneous international situation from the perspective of our common guilt and suffering on the one hand, and, on the other, of the real presence in our midst of the Crucified.

It is not so easy. Each one of us has been influenced and formed by his particular national heritage and political ideology. Consciously or unconsciously, we justify our political prejudices and concepts on the ground of our own national traditions, being rarely able to draw a clear line between the Biblical message of justice and freedom and the political ideas we share. Furthermore, being under the spell of our national political aspirations, we are historically and psychologically handicapped in our effort to understand other nations and the ways in which they have socially and politically organised the life of society. A Western democrat believes in his brand of democratic methods and processes and is easily impatient or irritated when a nation chooses another way of political action and organisation. There is nothing more important than to be aware of one's own political weakness and shortcomings, and—simultaneously—to look at other nations from the perspective of their historical past and against their social background. Before we engage in controversy and struggle let us understand one another and approach the basic issues in a spirit of self-control and constructive co-operation. If we meet one another as poor sinners equally responsible for the days to come, and if we listen to the word of the Living Lord, present in our midst in His holy compassion and mercy, then we may do something essential for the new order of peace and justice, justice and peace.

3. THE NEW HISTORICAL SITUATION

Let us, again, consider the dimensions of the historical changes and the magnitude of what has to be done. The heavy burden of the restoration of the international order and co-operation has been shifted on to the shoulders of two new Powers which, until 1941, were only in a loose way responsible for the maintenance of world trade and international peace. The American nation and the Soviet people are newcomers, just entering the stage of world architects. Neither of them has undergone an adequate test as to its skill and ability to lead other nations along the lines of peaceful collaboration. This is to a certain extent a fortunate situation. Both the American nation and the Soviet Commonwealth (the Federal Union of Soviet Republics), being comparatively young and new, are unfettered by a petrified political tradition and diplomatic routine, and may approach the big issues of our time with that freshness of mind and courage of imagination which help us to grasp the real, vital needs of the human race and to throw overboard all obsolete inhibitions and outdated, paralysing fears. The peoples of the U.S.A. and the U.S.S.R. have very much in common : they are numerically big, rich in territory and in actual (America) or potential (the Soviet nation) material treasures. Both of them are technically minded, eager to learn, to invent, to organise, and no obstacles will stop them. A European citizen looking at the American West and the Soviet East cannot help being impressed by a touch of titanic dynamism in these two new powerful organisers of the new world. Whereas the old European nations were oppressed by an age-long tradition in politics, social culture and way of life, the two great victors and leading nations of the present era are relatively free and unshackled, and may face the heavy task of the new human order with boldness and a genuine understanding of what the *present* moment demands.

However, the same profound historical change which has pushed the two new Powers into the forefront of international life is causing peculiar anxiety and uneasiness—a mood very different from that after World War I. The present political upheaval itself is a revolution unprecedented in the political history of humanity. The British Empire in the process of liquidation, the breakdown of French power, the dismal fall of Germany, the throes of Indian national independence, the civil war in China, the end of the last feudal tradition in Central Europe and in the Balkans—who can grasp the meaning and the potential consequences of these almost volcanic revolutionary changes ? Let us repeat : We are living in the midst of an international revolution unsurpassed in human history. If we are scared by the very word " revolution," we had better get readjusted to it lest we fail to cope with the abysmal problems pressing us to the wall ! All is fluid, nothing is stable and secure, political life resembles burning lava from a volcano, threatening our dwellings and our treasures. Are the Americans and the Soviet people capable of dealing adequately with the scope and nature of the change, and with what ought to be built on the débris of yesterday ? None of us can possibly make any prediction. There are, naturally, men and women who are terrified by the advance of the Soviet power—unknown, unpredictable, sometimes ruthless and brutal, sometimes irresistible on account of its deep appeal to the mind of common men. There are, however, millions of those who are depressed by the growing military power, economic wealth, and atomic energy in the hands of the American nation, all the more as it is so well protected by two oceans and by very good neighbours. Many of us are inclined to take the present position of the U.S.A. for granted, as a reassuring safeguard and stronghold of what we call Christian civilisation : The United States as the projection of the Western Christian tradition and of humanism with its emphasis upon the dignity of man, the sacredness of conscience, freedom of human personality, civil rights, habeas corpus, tolerance and political self-determination ![1]

And yet, we must not ignore the fact, that the U.S.A. has become the wealthiest nation in the world and that for many millions, not only in the East, it is a symbol of the power of money, and has—rightly or wrongly—ceased to be looked upon as the Promised Land of freedom, progress and happiness. A large section of humanity is afraid of America, of the demonic temptations of money, capital and wealth. This should be considered. What matters in the realm of the international struggle is not only brute, tangible facts, but also moods and sentiments, fears and hopes, prejudices and sympathies.

Here we are, standing at the dividing line of two eras of history, between the Western world, with all its noble tradition, represented by the American people, and on the other hand, the " Eurasiatic " East represented by the Soviet Union, claiming for the first time in history an equal share in the leadership of the world. Now these two giants, instead of co-operating in the construction of a peaceful order, find themselves in a situation of growing mutual distrust and dislike. This is a terrifying situation. The breakdown of the Versailles peace of 1919 was, in a large measure, due to the disunity of the victors. They won the war, signed the peace treaty, and then disbanded without any consistently united effort to organise the peace. We well know that a lack of a reasonable unity among the present victorious Powers might result in a similar international chaos or vacuum, and that one hasty step and panicky action might cause a

---

[1]Nobody who has come in touch with the American people in churches, colleges, universities and many other institutions would be ready to deny that America is in many ways a stronghold of what is dear to any freedom-loving man.

catastrophe of unimaginable dimensions. It is the conviction of the present writer that the situation, though far from being satisfactory and reassuring, is not desperate and that the sinister predictions of an approaching armed conflict of the great victorious Powers only aggravate the main problems of our time, and slow down the process of healing post-war mankind. It is the great mission of Christians in all countries to keep the rival fronts in close touch with each other, and not to allow a petrification of the international *blocs* that would make further discussion and debate impossible. So long as the two " sides " speak to one another, so long as they revile each other, the situation is not beyond repair. Let us talk together ! Do not let us give up ! Do not let us abdicate ! This is not a time for black despair and hopeless resignation ; this is a time of great opportunity. As we walk at the edge of the deep abyss do not let us be paralysed by fear, but let us combat our dizziness in a spirit of faith and hope !

4. THE PROBLEM OF THE WEST

The people of what we call " the Eastern *bloc* " (including Central, South-Eastern and Eastern Europe) have a deep respect for the traditions of life of the European (and American) West. The breakdown of Western civilisation would be a tragedy that would affect all the great values the " Eastern " man loves and adores. The subordination of man to the God-Creator and Saviour, Who is the God of grace and justice and the Lord of history, guiding it to the ultimate victory of truth and merciful justice ; the subordination of human instincts and passions to the clarity of intellect and to the majesty of an awakened conscience ; the norm of justice as superior to power ; love as the transforming force of social life ; the freedom of a responsible personality as against the claims of any human authority to rule the human soul—all these principles have been the underlying *motifs* of Western history, often betrayed and corrupted, and yet invincible and re-emerging as long as there have arisen groups of men and women who believed in them and were ready to work and die for them. The people of the East, whether they tend more to the right or to the left, would shudder, should those great ideas and norms cease to be the leaven of our personal and public life.

There are, however, some warning questions to which a citizen of the West should listen, and take into serious consideration.

1. The prestige of the West, during the years 1919-1940, was greatly shaken and has not recovered. Let us not speak of the Spenglerian prognosis of the " Decline of the West " : It was based on a philosophy of history that proved to be philosophically and politically fallacious and was invalidated by the events of the last ten years. However, the fact that the Western orbit of the world failed to organise and maintain the peace of 1919 cannot be disputed and disposed of lightheartedly. The authority of the Western democratic powers after the Armistice of 1918 was enormous, especially in Central Europe and in the Balkans. A united, socially and politically courageous policy in regard to the post-war world might have been able to cope with the situation. The social and moral aspirations of the masses, aroused by the Russian revolution of 1917, might have been guided into more or less normal channels of human progress if (I apologise for the " if " !) the Western nations had shown a far-sighted understanding of the downtrodden and oppressed peasants and workers of the Central and South-Eastern areas of Europe. The atmosphere of anxiety and fear lest the Soviet revolution should seize the masses of the European nations paralysed the energy of the victors and contributed to their disunity, which eventually resulted in the political decay of Central and Western Europe. The democratic nations were losing their moral prestige, as well as their political influence, until the integrating and creative power of democracy faded away. The fascist and national-socialist movements were indirectly, and in a measure also directly, strengthened by the moral and political vacuum created by the failure of the democratic victors to organise the world.

2. Hence millions of European citizens are doubtful whether the " free democracies " of the West are qualified to meet the needs of the present era, and to organise effectively a new order on the basis of real social justice and equal opportunity. Serious misgivings exist as to the ability of Western democracy to safeguard the progress of a genuine political and national liberty, let alone social security. Is not a material, economic interest on the part of " big " industries and financial concerns looming behind all the high-sounding slogans of " a free democracy," behind all the efforts to protect " individual freedom," " free enterprise " against any control by government, society and state ?

The blind or bankrupt leniency of the liberal democratic governments towards the reactionary régimes which one by one swept away the political life of Europe and after 1920 reinstated the old, seemingly vanquished elements of feudal conservativism in their old positions, has made the common man of Europe rather suspicious of the political tendencies prevailing at present in some leading Western states.

The vigorous and, at times, brutal reactions of the radical movements in Poland, Hungary, Roumania, Bulgaria, Yugoslavia, and also in Italy and France, against the local elements responsible for the pre-war régimes, cannot be interpreted solely as a Soviet machination. They have grown out of indigenous needs and memories. Their dynamism is proportionate to the blunders and failures both of the respective national régimes of the pre-war era and the leading Western democratic powers of Europe. It is essential to keep in mind the historical background of the countries which are undergoing the process of a total social and political transformation. The Soviet Government and the communistic parties may have taken advantage of the failures of the past for their own ends. However, the easy simplification with which many people in the West have been trying to interpret the present events in the Balkans and Central Europe as a sinister Soviet or communistic expansion might fatally blind our eyes and deafen our ears to what is actually going on in those areas. This is not at all to justify or to condone the methods and individual acts of the present rulers in the countries under consideration. This is just to remind ourselves of the failures of the democratic régimes during the Balkan, Austrian, Abyssinian, Spanish and Munich crises in the thirties of our century. Only in this way can we correctly understand the violent resentment on the part of the new politically advancing elements in many European countries against any effort made by " the West " to assist, in the name of formal democracy, the classes and individuals responsible for the previous régimes. There exists a grave danger that the Western democracies are—justly or wrongly—identified with social and political reaction, and that they will lose all political and moral authority. The shadows of Spain and Munich have not disappeared ; on the contrary, they loom as a portentous omen on the horizon.

3. How far are the Western democracies *morally*, intellectually, and spiritually capable and competent to deal with the

basic needs of our era? This is a question not to be lightly dismissed. The sentiments of anti-Soviet, anti-communistic fear, suspicion and hysteria as they prevail, and seem to be cultivated, behind the official " Western " policy of the present day, seem to reflect an ominous lack of moral and spiritual vigour. What the peoples of Europe, in general, and of Germany, Central and South-Eastern Europe in particular, badly need is a spiritual, intellectual, moral power to cope with their national, political, cultural issues. The " West," as it makes itself known, and the many adherents in European countries of the " Western orientation " are united merely in their negative, hostile attitude to the Soviet Union and communism—and are depressingly weak in their positive, spiritual and intellectual convictions and faith. What is it that the Western man really believes in? What are his basic convictions? What is it that he would be willing to live and die for? The fear and anxiety of a Maginot-line mentality which tries to preserve the old treasures and values instead of creating new ones are not strong enough to meet the challenge of the present day. They reveal a spirit of self-defence. The people who are afraid and uncertain about what they believe or what they ought to establish, are under a constant temptation to yield to a political or social reaction, or to an urge to stop the morally and socially justifiable process of history. They will yield to the peril of being destroyed by the explosive elements accumulated by blindness and weakness, instead of shaping and forming the fluid lava of the present spiritual and social life. From my own experience I know of many instances—even in my own country—where the non-communistic groups have failed, precisely because of their lack of common convictions, and of a united, morally and politically dynamic programme ; whereas the communists know what they want, are well disciplined, and are hard-working people.

Hence, what is urgently needed is an earnest self-examination by the people of the West about their essential heritage and mission. Let me repeat over and over again : all Europeans, Eastern not less than Western, would be terribly impoverished, intellectually, morally and politically, if the " West " should break down under its own weariness, exhaustion and lack of vision. The "East" of Europe, in its present stage of history and way of life, is lacking in many of the great values and achievements of Western civilisation. The destiny and mission of " Mother

Europe " are tied up with the achievements and the heritage of Western Catholicism, the Reformation, the Renaissance, the Enlightenment and Democratic Humanism. If the West should waste its treasures through a lack of faith, through spiritual indifference and self-complacency, an atmosphere of a graveyard would, for a long time, deprive the whole European orbit (the East included) of its inward resilience and creativity. The struggle for human dignity, for the sacredness of human personality and for a responsible freedom, without which our life would become bleak and miserable, would be carried on under very difficult conditions and circumstances.

Everybody who knows through personal contact the real civilisation of Western nations cannot help being impressed by its refinement, decency, tolerance, by its respect for human freedom and individual welfare. However, one cannot be unaware of the growing spiritual weariness, of the hollowness of so many " Western " ideas and institutions. Why is it that it is just those so-called Westerners, in many countries on the border-line between the Western and Eastern orbit of Europe, who indulge in complaining and grumbling without a real understanding of the historical moment, and without a vigorous and constructive plan for the future ? The West is losing ground in many European countries not only on account of a tremendous pressure on the part of radical socialism but also because of its own lack of faith and courageous realism. The Western idea of freedom, liberty and democracy is too formal, too unrelated to the basic issues and realities of the present times.

Yes, indeed, the " West " should refrain from blaming one-sidedly the aggressive socialist and communist groups, and examine its own mind, and the reasons why so many Western concepts and institutions have been losing the power to attract the imagination of the masses. A formal democratic process is not an end in itself, hence a formal freedom of thought, expression and speech is not an end in itself. The masses of common men are interested in the goal and the purpose to which human freedom and free institutions ought to be dedicated. The baffling historical changes during the last ten years have shaken the very foundations of the old civilisation and way of life. The destruction of both material and spiritual treasures is such that many nations and countries, primarily in the most devastated areas, are facing the almost insurmountable task of reorganising disintegrated society and of building up more adequate forms of social and economic life. Something new is in the making. Much of the old way of life has got to be given up ; many of our ideas and categories which our fathers took for granted have to be reconsidered, reshaped, re-defined.

Facing the present situation of destruction and devastation (primarily within the area of Soviet influence) many people have come to realise that what really matters is not primarily political freedom, but a well-thought-out, reliable plan of a new society based on social justice, human dignity, enduring peace. At the danger of repetition let us once more remind ourselves of new or renewed efforts to preserve the *status quo*, the privileges of decaying classes and groups, to stop the progress of history and to destroy what the common people have most longed for. There exists a shrewd, subtle tendency to protect and to preserve the racially, financially and socially privileged groups and parties under the pretext of freedom and formal democracy.

There are peoples whose situation may be compared to a flood inundating and destroying villages and towns, to a fire, sweeping across a city, to a volcanic eruption covering with dust and debris vast areas of a country. Millions of dead are heaped on the ground. How can we under these conditions expect a normally functioning democratic process ? In such a situation, what matters is to help the people, to disarm wrongdoers, to assist, to save, to establish dams, to extinguish fire, to organise reconstruction, not to thrive on individual freedom or on freedom of reporting. In certain circumstances discipline, service, responsibility, self-control, self-dedication are superior to freedom and human rights !

The re-examination of Western ideas against the background of what has been, morally and spiritually as well as politically and socially, the most dynamic *motif* of Western history is needed precisely at the present time. We do not advocate an attitude of compromise and " appeasement " ; we advocate an effort to revitalise what has been the creative genius of French, British and American democracy, and of civilisation. Anyone who is ready to study the legacy of the best architects of Western civilisation will more adequately understand the real process of history within the " Eastern orbit," and avoid a misleading, abstract over-simplification of some of the present policies in the

" East," dictatorship, totalitarianism, Soviet aggression. Such a simplification may partly be justified ; the dangers of dictatorship and totalitarianism are not absent. But it is wrong, and erects a barrier between nations, if it blinds human eyes to the historical urgency of the social and political transformation of the " Eastern " nations, releasing many inward creative forces which for centuries have been kept under the deadening pressure of old institutions and privileges. How difficult it is to ascertain a real fact, the real issue of an event, to understand it rightly, to report it truthfully and to interpret it with a relative correctness ! You may compile a good report of many true facts ; and yet it may be a pitifully false picture if you ignore, miss or misconstrue what is the living kernel of a historical process, and if you push more or less irrelevant details into the foreground.

The living, unfettered Word of God and the fire behind the most creative manifestations of our history may help us to get closer and more understandingly to the heart of things in Central and Eastern Europe, and to realise that a real advance of social and political democracy may proceed through channels and détours which defy our preconceived ideas and institutions, and yet, correspond to the real substance of the present history of those countries more adequately than what used to be the pattern universally accepted by all advanced, civilised nations.

A new, careful study of the basic issues of the Reformation in the light of the Biblical message has helped the Church of Christ (in recent years) to resume her vital mission and to break the shackles of a sterile confessionalism as well as of morbid ecclesiasticism and bourgeois secularism. A new insight into the very foundations of Western civilisation may do the same : it may overcome the weakness of our democratic formalism, which has lost its substance and has become a tool of privileges and vested interests ; it may open our eyes to the aspirations of nations and masses which in a clumsy, awkward, harsh and crude way are trying to arrive at a nobler place under the sun. I see all the potential dangers of the " Eastern " form of social and political progress. But we will not be able to challenge and overcome them unless we see, and sympathetically understand, the longing of the " Eastern " masses for more human dignity, social equality, cultural progress, and for a fair share in the political responsibility for the new world order.

5. THE PROBLEMS OF THE EAST (THE SOVIET ISSUE)

Essential as it is to examine one's own spiritual and political outlook it is not enough.   There is another urgent matter we have to face : to know, to understand and to interpret—as adequately as possible—the situation within the " Eastern orbit " of the present world, the orbit which has become one of the two main pillars of any future international order.   We must not stop where our statesmen and diplomats have stopped.   Even if our political representatives should arrive at the conclusion that further discussions and negotiations are useless, we have to go beyond the political concepts and diplomatic divisions. Here, again, let us keep in mind that the present issues cannot be reduced to an easy, inviting formula.   Western man, separated by the barriers of history, geography, and mental processes from the Soviet world, is tempted not only by propaganda but also by the many acts behind the " Iron Curtain," to interpret the ideological and political structure of the Soviet system as another manifestation of modern totalitarianism.   For many a Western Christian, the issue of the Soviet Union is— in its essential nature—identical with, or analogous to, the issue of Hitler-Germany.   Nazism and Sovietism may, they say, differ on minor points, but are identical in their ideological and practical effort to subordinate man, his dignity, responsible freedom and integrity, to an earthly idol, be it race and blood or social class and state, which has usurped the throne of a divine Absolute and deprives the individual soul of any free, moral, cultural, or spiritual self-determination.   Hence, they say, the attitude of " Western man " towards the Soviet orbit cannot be other than that of an uncompromising hostility : The Soviet system based on the philosophy of communism, *e.g.*, dialectical materialism, is the incarnation of an anti-Christian religion.   The spirit of communism and its fanatical self-expression reveal the fact that here we have to do not with a merely political platform and system, but with a false, godless religion, with a pseudo-religion, against which we must fight without fear or compromise.   This is, broadly speaking, the attitude of a vast multitude of Western men towards the " East."

It is here, however, that I wish to make a distinction of paramount importance.   The phenomenon of communism is in its essential structure different from that of nazism. Communism does not adhere to any metaphysic that would elevate an earthly reality (be it the class of the proletariat or the ultimate classless society) to the plane of an Absolute. The philosophy of nazism is based on the concept of the Nordic race and blood as undefiled manifestations of the Absolute spirit of the Universe and as the metaphysically ultimate source of truth, justice and real life. The philosophy of communism (in its Marxian or Leninian and Stalinian version) moves within the plane of history, uninterested in what is beyond history. Its atheism is rather a practical reaction against the forces of the pre-socialistic society than a positive, philosophically essential tenet. In many ways, we may say, the classic theory of communism (as has often been pointed out) is a secularised Christian theology, often furiously anti-Church ; but it insists that communism has done for the poor what the Church should have done, but which she has transformed into a liturgical, mystical, opiate. Communistic atheism is, in a large measure, rather a tool and weapon of an anti-bourgeois or anti-feudal political propaganda than a distinctive faith and metaphysic. It is more agnostic than positively metaphysical. Its dynamism and its religious sentiment are, to be sure, a substitute for religion, but its vigour is due to an engrossing, fascinating idea of a society in which man will be free of all external greed, mammon and material tyranny, and in which a fellowship of real human beings in mutual sympathy, love and goodwill would be established.

We must not forget that what we call communism, which is one of the expressions of an age-long struggle against social exploitation and insecurity, has always had two aspects : one more formal, philosophical, revolting against the official *Weltanschauung* of the feudal and bourgeois society (*e.g.*, dialectical, historical materialism), and the other, more material (in its very essence idealistic), struggling for a social system in which all class differences would fade away, the demonic, tyrannical power of money and private property would be crushed, and all men and women would be united on the same ground of human dignity, freedom and love. The tenet of dictatorship is there, too, and has played a tremendous rôle in the days of revolution and civil war and in the transition era of socialistic reconstruction. It has produced many unnecessary hardships, and has caused much anxiety, hatred and violent hostility. One of the most

I

serious shortcomings of the present communistic leaders in various countries has been the emphasis they have laid upon dictatorship at the expense of the positive idea of a classless, socialistic community. Millions of common men and intellectuals would be awakened to the real issues of our time and other millions would be morally disarmed if the leaders of the new régimes in Europe would point more convincingly to what the end and the goal of the present social struggle actually are.

As we now approach the " problem " of the Soviet Union, let me remind the reader of a distinction to be made between the concepts (categories) of communism, the Soviet régime and the Russian people (including all the other nationalities of the Soviet area). No matter how closely associated they may be they are not identical. The Soviet Revolution of 1917 prevailed under the leadership of the Bolshevik Social Democratic Party, and its Commander-in-Chief, Vladimir Lenin. For many historical reasons, not to be dealt with here, it was they who were able to reorganise the disintegrated and chaotic Russian Empire. The philosophy of dialectical, economic materialism proved to be efficient to concentrate the new ruling class upon the main issue : to transform the feudal, and, as far as it existed, bourgeois society into a socialistic system. However, the philosophy of communism and the Bolshevik (now communistic) Party on the one hand, and the Soviet system, on the other, are not identical terms. If a comparison is in order, the issue with which we have to do is similar to that in France after the Revolution of 1789. The philosophy prevailing in the revolutionary days may have inspired the leaders and the masses to act, to overthrow the " ancien régime," but it was not necessarily and essentially connected with the structure of republican, revolutionary France. The same is true of the Russian situation. Russian political and cultural history since 1917, to be sure, cannot be understood without the impact of the Marxian-Leninian philosophy and without the leadership of the Bolshevik (communistic) Party. Sociologically and politically, the general chaos in the vast area between Poland and the Pacific Ocean was, after the breakdown of the old régime, of such dimension that only a very vigorous, disciplined political group and a distinct philosophy could have gradually checked the anti-revolutionary and other disruptive tendencies, and restored an organic unity out of a totally atomised and disintegrated national life.

The present strict, and, at times, harsh régime under the guidance of the communistic élite, which may, in a way, be compared to a monastic order, can be adequately understood and appraised only against the background of Russian history, the revolutionary era, the civil war of 1918-1922, and the many interventions by foreign Powers. The vast empire, without any genuine democratic tradition, held together by the absolute power of the Tsars and integrated by the politico-religious myth of the emperor wielding the sceptre of a divinely inspired autocracy, fell to pieces and was for a long time threatened by innumerable perils from within and from without. If we objectively, and with fairness, consider the backwardness of the masses, the relatively swift reorganisation of the territory, the defeat of internal and external enemies, and the stupendous transformation of the old social system into a new, socialistic, collectivistic structure of society, we cannot help being impressed by the enormous energy, skill and organising ingenuity of the ruling party. This is not to be understood as a consent to the very ideas and methods applied by the Revolution ; this is just to emphasise the absurdity of the various ways in which the Soviet situation has been criticised and condemned by applying abstract political yardsticks or by comparing it with the democratic institutions and processes originated, grown and perfected under an utterly different historical sky. What I have in mind is to interpret the dictatorial régime of the Soviet system as a historical necessity in a country consisting of multiple ethnic, and in part culturally backward elements, and in a nation which for many reasons had not been privileged to enjoy political liberties and popular education.

There is another aspect of the Soviet régime. Communistic philosophers and statesmen stress the temporary, transitory nature of the socialistic, proletarian dictatorship. They reject the nazistic and fascistic idea of a dictator as a permanent embodiment of the divine majesty of the race (nazism) or of state sovereignty (fascism). They entirely reject the idea of a personal dictatorship and maintain the necessity of the collective dictatorship of the proletarian class. It does not exclude—as the Soviet experience bears out—a unique dictatorial prestige and position of a revolutionary leader (Lenin, Stalin) or of a political group (the Politbureau of the Communistic Party in U.S.S.R.). Further, the demonic temptation of power and the lust for power, are a constant danger that the temporary rulers may perpetuate and unduly enlarge their uncontrolled authority. In the Soviet Union, the leader of the state attracts, for historical reasons, a reverence and loyalty which in Western countries is historically impossible and sociologically unnecessary. However, we may say that the very idea of communism in regard to dictatorship differs essentially from that of nazism. The more advanced the socialistic structure the less dictatorial power is needed, until—in a fully developed and safeguarded collectivistic, classless economy—all dictatorship will fade away. The Marxist theory of the state and of a perfect classless society may be false. It certainly is false. But the fact remains that communism, in spite of its idea or practice of dictatorship, is not principally absolutist and totalitarian. It tends—in its philosophy—towards a total liberation of the individual man.

I do not believe (how could I ?) that the communist ideology will, eventually and permanently, be capable of integrating the new, post-revolutionary, society, into a living body of material trust, free responsibility and service, and thus be able to preserve the fruits of the social revolution, unless it appeals to that in man which transcends the material process of history. Even a classless society cannot exist without the testimony of divine judgment, the eternal law of justice and forgiveness. Nevertheless, my point at this juncture is this : communism reflects, in a very secularised form, in spite of its materialism and dictatorship, the Christian longing for the fellowship of full and responsible love.

The Soviet, collectivistic structure of human society can exist without the philosophy of dialectical materialism. As a matter of fact, the vast majority of Soviet citizens, in towns, villages, plants, " kolkhozes," literature and art, are neither party members nor philosophically communist. The Marxian-Leninian ideology has penetrated into all realms of the social and cultural activity. However, after the new social and political order has been thoroughly rooted and entrenched and adequately secured, and after the 180 millions of Soviet citizens have been educated and come of age, the official ideology will undoubtedly undergo—as it actually is undergoing—a process of transformation from within.

6. COMMUNISM AND RUSSIAN HISTORY

That transformation may be expected also for another reason. The Leninian philosophy of dialectical materialism and the Soviet revolution carried out a unique, possibly unprecedented change and break in the history of Russia and of the whole world. Yet both of them had been only to a certain extent an import from the outside Western world. (Socialism and communism were originally Western movements !) Vladimir Lenin was a genuine Russian intellectual, a son of the Russian soil, formed and shaped by the Russian moral, spiritual and intellectual tradition. The history of *Russian* communism as well as Sovietism is scarcely intelligible without the history of the specifically Russian social and literary movements going as far back as 1825 ; possibly as far as the era of Peter the Great. The deep love for the " insulted and injured," for the miserable peasant (muzhik), for the " scum " of human society, for workers, petty artisans, in a word, for the under-dog of human society, is one of the most creative, impressive and revolutionary tendencies in the life of Russian intelligentsia and in the literary work of all the great Russian writers of the nineteenth century : Byelinski, Gogol, Tolstoy, Goncharov, Dostoyevski, Tchekhov, Gorki. The Soviet Revolution was a culmination of the long preceding struggle. The suffering and the missionary expeditions of thousands and thousands of Russian intellectuals whose social passion, warm love and self-sacrificing sympathy for the exploited is unsurpassed in the history of our civilisation, are products of this Revolution. Just as Karl Marx insisted that the masses of German workers were heirs of the great German philosophers and writers, so the leaders of the Russian revolution insisted on raising the oppressed and despised working classes to a high level of literary education and to a sense of their historical destiny.

If you happen to visit the Soviet Union you may observe a feverish educational process to combat as fast as possible cultural backwardness and illiteracy. Looking at Russia from outside, you have the impression that Soviet life is reduced to the great social and economic experiment of collectivisation under a strict political and police control. Looking from inside you see another process in full swing : a process of education in schools, theatres, centres of culture, music halls, galleries, exhibitions, museums— a process through which the knowledge of Russian history, of the great classic Russian literature and art are becoming the property and enjoyment of millions. What the non-Russian nationalities and ethnic groups in the Caucasus, Siberia and elsewhere have acquired through the revolutionary transformation of the Russian Empire, only the days to come will reveal in a fully conclusive way. The Revolution had not this end in itself. It was planned and carried out as a violent assault upon the old régime. In a large measure, however, it was a process of liberation, through which the " common man " or " proletarian " could become a citizen, with all rights and honours, and through which all the dormant, fettered moral and cultural forces of the Russian people could be released and developed.

The Russian classics are being read and re-read. Alexander Pushkin, Lev N. Tolstoy, M. Gorki (and many others, Gogol and Dostoyevski included) are obligatory reading in schools and universities.

Soviet literature and art have to consider the rather primitive and naïve taste of the advancing masses, and the writers are over and over again warned by the political leaders not to forget the education and integration of the national life, and not to yield to a refined and decadent " l'art pour l'art." Any cynical or pessimistic interpretation of life and history is frowned upon; and over-critical literary comments on what is going on in national life are severely criticised, unless they have a constructive attitude to the national process of recovery and rehabilitation.

This is not to be ignored or underestimated. The unique accomplishments of Russian authors both in literary form and spiritual content are a living factor in the life of a growing number of Soviet citizens. To-day, tens of millions of them read them with passion and hunger, whereas thirty years ago only a thin layer of the Russian nation was able to read, enjoy and appreciate the profound wealth of knowledge, wisdom, human understanding accumulated by the long procession of Russian writers who, being almost perfect interpreters of the Russian mind, have become moral and spiritual teachers of all nations. With the elimination of illiteracy country folk and townspeople, intelligentsia and common men read them alike. All the classics severely criticised the sins and evils they had discovered and uncovered in the life of the ruling classes as well as of the so-called lower strata. Some of them confronted what was the best and the worst in the West with what was the best and the worst in the

East and created an atmosphere of human sympathy, understanding and brotherhood which is as yet forming and shaping
the soul of nations. Our knowledge of man, of his depth both in
corruption and heavenly aspirations, is deeper and broader than
it was before the Russian classics were written. A reverence for
the sanctity of the human soul was, in them, organically associated
with a thorough study of Russian national life, of its blessings and
perils, its grandeur and corruption. A tender love of man never
ceases to breathe through their writings, even if the author had
descended into the deepest depth of human misery and sin or
if he had been confronted with the most repulsive aspects of
Russian society. There is no sign of cynical disillusionment,
pessimism, decadent nihilism or moral abdication in the pages
of those writers who once made Russian literature a creative
element in world civilisation. Behind all the critical analysis
in the Russian classics the reader finds an affirmative, constructive manifestation of human compassion, and a deep longing
for truth and the salvation of mankind.

Now, the works of the Russian classical writers are the regular
food and nourishment of Soviet students and citizens. Within
the framework of the present social and economic experiment a
rich stream of moral and spiritual inspiration is flowing into
the minds and hearts of the Soviet people. Neither dialectical
materialism nor the dictatorship of the proletariat gives an
adequate key to open the door of a real understanding of what is
going on in the vast spaces of Russia. Nobody can possibly
foretell the future of Eastern civilisation. In many ways its
process differs from the general trend of Western history. We
must not measure it with the criteria derived from the heritage of
Western feudalism, the Reformation, the Renaissance and liberalism. The Russian past had its " driving force," its highlights and
patterns, its own creative *motifs* and aspirations. All these *motifs*
and aspirations are working like leaven behind the revolutionary
ideas and methods of Marxian communism in general and of
Russian sovietism in particular.

There was a time when the leaders and ideologists of the
Soviet revolution tried to interpret the Christian past as a
combination of pre-scientific mythology, clerical fraud and
gross superstition, or merely as a by-product of the social structure
and economic development of Russian society. From the
moment, however, that a systematic construction of the new

national community started, a new understanding of the Christian Church and her history was initiated. Historical materialism notwithstanding, all the contributions of Christian moral standards, thought, practical life and institutions of the past have been interpreted with a new spirit of appreciation, evaluation and affirmative appraisal.

Nazism was increasingly hostile to the Christian heritage of German history, treated it as a poisonous infection which had penetrated from outside into the healthy body of an originally pure, unpolluted Nordic race. The Nazi ideologists elaborated a thorough philosophy of German history (*völkische Geschichtsphilosophie*) interpreting the German historical process as a continuous struggle between the original genuine German spirit (*Blut, Boden, Ehre, Kraft, Macht*) on the one hand, and the Jewish-Christian element (and Latin legalism) on the other. All the great figures of German history (Frederick II, Luther, Frederick the Great, Bismarck, Hitler, and many others) were put into the gallery of heroes on account of their vigorous effort to extricate the German soul from the shackles of Jewish-Christian spiritual slavery, and to free it from the poison of Christian faith. The Soviet historians, thinkers, and even the political leaders have adopted an increasingly appreciative attitude to the contribution of Christianity, and point to its " progressive " spirit. The noble Christian doctrine of man, with its emphasis on the family, its deep sympathy for the poor, downtrodden, miserable members of human society, its commandment of love for man, faith and hope with regard to the end and goal of history, its self-denying efforts during the era of foreign domination (" Tartar Yoke ")—all this has been acknowledged as a vital, dynamic and forward-driving factor of social justice, equality and brotherhood.

Family life is cultivated, and the sexual morality of the Soviet young men and young women is, in my judgment, cleaner than in my own country and in many Western democracies. The post-revolutionary moral libertinism affected only a thin stratum of intellectuals and of some " proletarian " snobs who had—in the days of turbulent events and of new, undigested ideas—lost their heads and got confused in their hearts. Since the beginning of the tremendous constructive project of collectivisation and national reorganisation all merely negative, disintegrating ideas (*e.g.*, atheism and anti-religious propaganda) have either been side-tracked or are at least unpopular. Everything that would weaken the working morale or foster sexual anarchy (*e.g.*, the ideals of sexual promiscuity) is vigorously denounced and combated.

I am not competent to deal with the present status of the Church in the Eastern area of Europe. However, some few words on the Church problem must be added. A Western observer is not in a position to judge whether the Eastern Orthodox Church or any other Church in the Soviet Union has enough real spiritual and intellectual vigour to enable it to be a real force in the spiritual regeneration and moral growth of the people. We have no right to question the formal freedom of the Church to perform her purely religious duties, to conduct public worship, to train her clergy, and to educate her children. Furthermore, the churches have undergone a great test and have shown their capacity to assist the people in the days of crisis and destruction, to give comfort and hope in suffering and at the moment of death, and to become a unifying force in the national life. The government and the Communist Party have paid a high tribute to the Church for her great services during the recent war (1941-1945).

However, it is not quite clear to what extent she is free to raise her prophetic voice on great or small issues in public, political, educational and moral life. We are not in a position to assess her active, formative contribution to the inward growth of the moral and spiritual structure of the men and women responsible for the present state of affairs in the Soviet Union. The education of the adepts of the Party (pioneers, komsomols) is based on an entirely non-religious philosophy. The official doctrine is that of Marxian (or Leninist) materialism. The Church seems to stand on the fringe of the national life. And yet, she does stand, praising God and pointing to the glory of the Triune God and to the real presence of the God-Man, Jesus Christ. She is not the only channel of the potential spiritual regeneration of the nation, but she is one element which testifies to the fact that a nation organised on a revolutionary, materialist philosophy cannot permanently live and maintain her human rights and responsible freedom without looking to the Lord of history who speaks the Word of judgment and forgiveness.

One point more should be added. Shortly after the victory of the Revolution, the Church was tragically shaken to her foundations and almost collapsed : partly, because she was so intrinsically associated with the very structure of the pre-revolutionary society, partly, because the atheistic, anti-religious elements of the Communist movement tried to liquidate, in a rather primitive way, all religious activities and institutions. Long before Marxism, Russian atheism had assumed a rather religious fervour. " The protest and revolt against God " was a kind of humanistic evangelism preaching the destruction of the evil cæsaro-papistic system and the establishment of a new, socially free and politically just Russia. The tens of thousands of Christian victims who, during the revolutionary era, suffered persecution or death were only partly " Confessors " (martyrs) ; partly they were just victims of the revolutionary upheaval, confused about the real meaning of the historical events, allied with the " White " (anti-red) counter-revolution, and finally liquidated with the old régime. But the Church survived the collapse of the Tsarist empire. She came to realise that her existence did not depend on the old social system. She survived in her orthodox, historical structure. All the efforts to organise another Church that would adjust her doctrine, liturgy and morals to the new ideology failed almost completely. " The Living Church," a sort of modernistic, theologically humanistic religious body, disappeared, after an initial success and advance, like snow in springtime. It withered away in spite of the backing it had indirectly received from the victorious régime.

This is a great lesson for the present time. Only a Church that understands the meaning of the times, and knows *where* to fight, and *what weapon* to use, is in a position to carry on. Social and political systems may come and go. But the message of the Living God, of the Incarnate Word, the Crucified and Risen Lord, and the Creator Spirit, abides for ever.

7. CONCLUSION

This is the situation within the " Eastern orbit," and in its relation to the West, as it looks to the present writer :

1. The Soviet problem must not be reduced to the issue of dictatorship and totalitarianism, although this forms part of it.

2. The categories of communism, the Soviet system, and Soviet Russia are not identical.

3. The Soviet leaders have long memories and cannot forget

all the efforts (if not the intrigues) which came from the West to thwart the Revolution, to overthrow the Soviet government, to isolate it after it was established, and to give moral support to the anti-Soviet, anti-socialist régimes.

4. The terrific destruction of Soviet territory and the enormous losses in human life (who knows how many millions of the Soviet people perished ?) during the German-Soviet war of 1941-1945 have made the Soviet régime and the Soviet people sensitive to any sign or indication of an anti-Soviet policy of " encirclement " and isolation. What has frequently been interpreted as Soviet expansion, or as a revived Russian nationalistic imperialism may be rather a manifestation of self-protection and self-defence.

5. The strength of the Soviet system is a guarantee against the potential dangers of a new international chaos and anarchy. Who can say what the weakening or the destruction of the present Russian régime would imply ? How dismal the situation of Eastern Europe and Asia, as well as that of Central and Western Europe, would become if the process of reconstruction and con-solidation within the Soviet area were stopped or paralysed ! The Western democracies are neither morally nor politically capable of coping with the crisis that would follow a critical weakening of the Soviet Union.

6. The Soviet system cannot be transplanted into a country of a different historical, moral and cultural tradition. It is rooted, and has organically grown, in the soil tilled and cultivated by the Russian people, the Russian Church, and the Russian intelligentsia.

7. The same system, however, would be gravely affected if the noble tradition of Western civilisation were seriously wounded from outside, or if it withered from within on account of its moral and spiritual decay. The Soviet social and political ideal came into existence under the influence of great Western philosophers, political writers and of the dynamic Western religious history. What would become of the noble Soviet social ideal and goal, if the Western struggle for the dignity of responsible man under the authority of the eternally valid norms of justice, truth, chastity and love ended in despair, cynical pessimism, spiritual indifference and frustration ?

8. It is exactly here that the West should concentrate its

creative ambition. The West will never attract the better elements of the post-war world (in Europe, Asia and elsewhere) by
insisting upon the old capitalistic emphasis on " free enterprise,"
" profit-motives," and " private property," or by talking about
comfort or the atomic bomb. It can preserve, revitalise and hand
over the great heritage of Western civilisation to non-Western man
on one condition : if it adheres to what the creative genius of
European and American history has created along the lines of
political, intellectual and social progress. Under the present
historical conditions of a terrific disorganisation of European
society classic capitalism would utterly fail and break down.
Freedom and political liberties without social security and
without a new, more organic, fellowship of man are, to-day,
meaningless. And a real organic fellowship of mutual trust and
confidence is fatally weak without a deep faith, warm convictions
and an ardent hope. The anti-Soviet and anti-communistic
fear in the West is partly due to the fact that the official Western
society does not seem to trust the deepest ideas of Western
history, or has lost its burning convictions and hopes.

We have dealt with the " Eastern orbit " as positively as
possible, since there is little opportunity to look at it from the
angle of the Eastern nations or from the perspective of Eastern
(European) civilisation. We are, however, not unaware of grave
dangers inherent in the ideological, historical and political
structure of the system prevailing in the area behind what is
called the " Iron Curtain."

First, the very fact of the tremendous power in the hands of
the present rulers within that area arouses serious misgivings
and well-grounded apprehensions. It is the first time in history
that the people of the present Soviet territory have proved so
strong and have crushed their enemy so completely. Unlike the
period after the first victorious Patriotic War (1812-1815), the
present Russia is able to appeal to the radical, progressive,
revolutionary elements in the whole world, and thus greatly to
strengthen her position. It is the combination of her military
victories, the enormous integration of her political organisation and her revolutionary dynamism that makes her present
advance so formidable and, in a way, even awe-inspiring.
Moreover, the other nations are not without a suspicion that
behind the Soviet social revolutionary aspiration looms a revived
nationalistic expansion of the old Russian Empire. No matter

which of the two historical patterns, revolutionary socialism or Russian nationalism, is stronger and more aggressive, the combination of both may prove to be a terrific temptation to try to dominate the world, and precipitate a fresh historical catastrophe.

Second, the philosophy of historical materialism which denies all the norms, criteria and standards beyond the process of history, reducing man to a mere by-product of his social and economic environment, may—if unresisted and unchallenged—break down moral inhibitions and self-control, and let loose the purely animal passions of envy, hatred, greed and self-assertion. The Church of Christ will have to dig her trenches and establish her walls of testimony at the farthest outskirts of human life in order to shape and form an unshakable framework of moral norms, judicial laws, social standards, without which a new barbarism would sweep across the world ; all the more since the Western spiritual weariness and the fruits of liberalistic indifference have brought about a grave peril of moral decay and cultural disintegration in the realm of the whole civilised community.

Third, it is doubtful whether the revolutionary tradition and Marxian materialism are capable of protecting the sacredness of human personality and freedom. Likewise many honest men are sometimes disturbed at the way in which the representatives of the Eastern régimes deal with political minorities and adversaries, both at home and at international conferences. Instead of carrying conviction they engage too much in propaganda and assault. They may be, here and there, right. The other groups have often done almost nothing to understand Eastern problems and have attempted, in a subtle way, to deprive the Soviet people of the fruits of victory. The Western man is, consciously or unconsciously, self-righteous, and takes his own privileged place in the world for granted ; any advance on the part of the European Easterner arouses in him fear and righteous indignation. And yet, the Eastern people would win much support from the best truly liberal and Christian groups in the West, if they used less noisy propaganda and spoke with a genuine accent of truth, sincerity and honesty.

9. Let us once more appeal to the leaders of the Soviet community and of the communistic parties to rely less on the violent methods of agitation, threat, deportation, trials and police control, and to arouse in man his noblest sentiments of sympathy for the poor, the weak, the helpless and the miserable,

to awaken him to what is after all the core of socialistic humanism.

10. The problem of Germany cannot possibly be solved without a genuine co-operation of the West and the East, a co-operation on the basis of what is best in both of them. If the German people try—shrewdly, cunningly or stupidly—to play one power against the other and to ally themselves with the seemingly stronger side, they will bring final destruction upon themselves as well as upon the whole of Europe. This is not a time for intrigue or malicious revenge, it is a time for earnest responsibility and for a realistic, sober, wise, sincere desire for co-operation.

This is a time for hope and for new beginnings. Nothing is lost, and much can be gained and achieved, if all faithful members of the Church rally in the spirit of unqualified loyalty where the Crucified and Risen Lord is waiting, and if they, in humility and penitence, try to break through the present divisions of the world and speak to one another with undiminished boldness and truth. We cannot make any predictions, but our courage and hope may pave a new highway for reconciliation and peace.

V

FREEDOM OF RELIGION AND RELATED HUMAN RIGHTS

O. Frederick Nolde

Source material for this chapter has been contributed by :—F. Bednar, W. Y. Chen, George D. Kelsey, S. A. Morrison, B. L. Rallia Ram, Alberto Rembao, Emory Ross. The author has himself represented the Churches, through the Commission of the Churches on International Affairs, at meetings of the Commission on Human Rights of the Economic and Social Council of the United Nations. A synopsis of contents is provided to facilitate reference.

SYNOPSIS

INTRODUCTION

THE tensions which agitate present-day society, both domestic and international, threaten the exercise of human rights and freedoms. Under the necessities of war, people in every free community yielded to their governments individual rights which in times of peace they were disposed to guard with jealous care. Efforts to recapture the enjoyment of personal freedoms encounter varying obstacles. Where disrupted economies have followed the devastation of war, the preservation of life has made unavoidable the continuation and, at times, the strengthening of government controls. The inability of the major victorious powers to adjust their differences has cast a shadow over every land. Without measurable assurance of a peaceful world, the traditionally free countries are reluctant to return to their accustomed ways of freedom. Totalitarian governments do little to liberalise their domestic practice and, in fact, seek to extend their view of society to foreign lands.

RENEWED EMPHASIS ON HUMAN RIGHTS

The forces which threaten human liberty have not passed unheeded. Nor has the recognition of them stopped with an awakened desire to reclaim what has been lost. It has stimulated the resolve to interpret man's rights more inclusively and to seek their realisation more universally. With mounting insistence, social and economic rights are being added to classical freedoms such as speech, religion and association. The ultimate goal of observance embraces all men everywhere, without distinction of race, sex, language, or religion.

The renewed and expanded effort in behalf of human rights is not equally vigorous at all points. This is readily understandable. In many instances, an inevitable fatigue has dulled the edge of man's inclination to struggle. Where people suffer from economic insufficiency, they are prone to devote their energies to prior needs. Where their actions are circumscribed by political controls, they submit to a situation which is for the moment unavoidable. Notwithstanding the vast numbers whose struggle has been limited by inclination or circumstance, a sufficient voice has been raised to justify the contention that man's effort to promote respect for human rights stands as an encouraging symbol in our chaotic world.

CHRISTIAN ACTIVITY

Christians, as individuals and through the churches, have played an important part in shaping the current emphasis upon the rights of man. In some instances, their activity has been stimulated by immediate exposure to actual or threatened denial of freedom. Under conditions where it was possible to continue their exercise of human rights, they were prompted to action by the adversities encountered in other lands and by the prospect that their own liberties might thereby be endangered.

It should be recognised that those Christians who suffered curtailment of spiritual freedom at the hands of their own government were placed in a particularly difficult situation. Under national socialism in Germany, issues were not always clarified. Disturbing contradictions appeared in the effort to reconcile opposition to government with loyalty to land and people. Protests raised under such circumstances merit the appreciation of defenders of liberty everywhere. That appreciation must stand even though the voices raised were limited in number and the response to them ineffectual. " They helped to cross Hitler's purpose at a very decisive point by making it possible for free Protestant Christianity, despite all the cunning assaults against it, to survive in Germany and retain all its power of germination. . . . In this one field the National Socialist system met a force which it was able to suppress but not to break."[1]

The struggle of the churches in the occupied countries gave spiritual depth to a resistance that often moved at political and social levels. Aims were variously defined. Procedures were fashioned as the need dictated. In summarising their purpose, a group of prominent churchmen in Norway stated : " We fight this battle so that we may work free and unrestrained. Unrestrained outwardly by the State's illegal encroachment, and free inwardly with a clear conscience before the Church's Master and His Sacred Word."[2] In the Netherlands, the churches resisted especially the effort of the occupying powers to confine religion to a purely spiritual realm. By every means in their power they expressed opposition to " the way in which the three main foundations of our people which are rooted in the Christian

---

[1] Karl Barth, " The Protestant Churches in Europe," *Foreign Affairs*, XXI (1943), 267.
[2] Bjarne Hoye and Trygve M. Ager, *The Fight of the Norwegian Church Against Nazism*, p. 134. (Manifesto of July, 1942).

K

Faith are being attacked, namely justice, charity, and freedom of conscience and conviction."[1]

In virtually every part of the world, Christians have become alert and active in their defence of the freedom which finds its only sure foundation in spiritual liberty. In lands where new constitutions were in process of drafting, as in India and Italy, the benefit of Christian insights was made available. Where internal difficulties followed the chaos of war, as in China and Korea, movements toward stability have been accompanied by the insistent demand for the recognition of human rights. In Latin America and in Africa, issues of long standing have taken on a new meaning and have been met with an increasingly vigorous attack by Christians. Illustrations are inadequate to convey a true picture of the noble struggle for freedom which has been waged in many lands in face of opposition and persecution.

It is safe to say that Christians in countries which remained relatively free were greatly stimulated by the struggle in lands where freedom was denied. Animated by the sufferings of their fellow Christians and by the desire to safeguard their own liberties, they addressed themselves primarily to long-range plans whereby international action could become effective in the future protection of human rights and freedoms.

THE BASIS FOR CHRISTIAN ACTIVITY

Christians have a valid concern that all human rights—civil, social and economic—should be respected everywhere. As the world comes to be more closely knit together, their sympathy is extended to people in any land where the denial of freedom brings suffering or distress. Christians believe that respect for human rights is essential to world order. When human rights are denied, man's conscience cannot operate adequately in criticism or commendation of national and international policies. The Christian recognises the commission to preach the Gospel of Jesus Christ to the uttermost parts of the world. This commission can, and, if there is no other way, must be obeyed in face of opposition and persecution. Nevertheless, when conditions favourable to the exercise of human rights exist, men are in a

---

[1] W. A. Visser 't Hooft, *The Struggle of the Dutch Church*, p. 46. (Declaration Against the Attempt to Enforce a Philosophy of Life, April, 1942.)

better position to hear the Gospel and freely to decide what their response shall be.

Underlying the motives which prompt Christian action to promote the observance of human rights is the Christian conception of man in relation to his fellow men and to God. This conception is rooted in Christian faith and represents the justification for Christian effort to secure man's freedom in society. It is to be clearly distinguished from the form which the churches use as they seek to bring governments, both national and international, to an assumption of legitimate responsibility in safeguarding human rights. There are three presuppositions which, from the Christian point of view, substantiate the claim that man has the right to freedom, particularly to freedom of religion.

First, *the Christian conception of man's freedom is derived from the faith that man is made in the image of God.* This contention embraces the view of natural law but goes beyond it. Man is a rational being and is entitled to everything that is essential to the reasonable development of his personality. There is a moral law which must be observed as man seeks his own development and which requires full consideration of the equal rights of others. When viewed solely from the standpoint of natural law, the moral law is perceived by intuition and experience. While this mode of perception is not disavowed, the Christian also reckons with the fact of revelation, and therefore finds in the historical reality of Jesus Christ a distinctive basis for man's freedom.

Second, *the dignity which is claimed for man is attested by the demonstration of God's love for him in Jesus Christ.* The conception of man's worth and potentiality reaches its highest point in the understanding of God's redemptive act in history. More than empirical or intuitive grounds are here provided for the contention that man has fundamental rights. God's estimate of man's value in his sight undergirds the contention. A divine appraisal therefore substantiates and magnifies what is claimed for man on the basis of natural law.

Third, *the right of every man to freedom is imperative in order that he may be in a position to respond to the calling wherewith God has called him.* The Christian sees in the life, death and resurrection of Jesus Christ more than a demonstration of God's estimate of man. A purpose is clearly to be fulfilled thereby. In order that man may be in a position to respond to God's call, that is, to seek his fullest growth in the light of the Gospel, he must be free to hear that truth proclaimed and, to the degree of his acceptance of it, give full expression in all contacts of life.

A JURIDICAL APPROACH

Many Christian scholars have developed theological presuppositions for man's rights and freedoms. Unquestionably, further study is needed in order that the Christian position may be clearly and convincingly advanced. Analyses of this kind will more appropriately find place in other volumes of this study series. At the present time, there is immediate and urgent need for the development of the Christian view on human rights in terms which will apply to all men and which can be used in representations to national and international political authorities. The study here projected has this need particularly in view.[1] It places the problem of Christian responsibility for the recognition of human rights in the framework of international affairs. It proceeds on the assumption that agreements thus far reached by Christians are sufficient to permit the churches now to take a united stand before the nations and peoples of the world. The churches can make their contribution to the promotion of respect for human rights only if they draw from distinctively Christian presuppositions the principles which will be universally applicable

[1] *Comment.* Reactions which were offered in the process of critical reading revealed two points of view with respect to the manner in which the issues of human rights should be approached by the churches at the present time. One view recognised that Christians must make their position clear to the world, but claimed that there was a prior need to study further the distinctively Christian conception of man and society. This position was advanced in only a small percentage of the responses. The other view accepted the value of further study but, at the same time, saw the immediate demand upon Christians to set forth their conception of human rights in terms which would apply to all men and which could be used in representations to political authorities.

The prescribed limits of the present study made it impossible to develop both approaches. Fully recognising the need for continuing theological study, the author reached his decision to devote this paper to a " juridical " consideration of human rights, particularly of religious liberty, on grounds of immediate world needs. The nations are in process of drafting an International Bill of Human Rights. Peace treaties, as well as bilateral and multilateral treaties of various kinds, are being written. Procedures must be fashioned to cope with violations of human rights. Education for freedom and responsibility is urgently required. If the churches have anything to offer for the solution of these current issues, they must speak now and what they say must be relevant to the immediate situation. The adequacy of the functional analysis—as projected in Part III of this Study and more concisely set forth in the first part of the Conclusion—must be tested by the question : Does the Christian view of man and society, to the extent that it has been defined, permit the claim that the rights and freedoms therein declared represent a goal which should be sought for all men everywhere in their exercise of religious liberty ?

and which can be reasonably expected to find endorsement by men of goodwill everywhere.

While the churches have a concern for all human rights, they hold a special interest and may claim a special competence in regard to those rights which will enable man's conscience to operate effectively in personal and social experience. Concentration upon a peculiar interest and competence of the churches does not limit Christian activity to the promotion of a narrowly conceived religious freedom. On the one hand, man is free to live by conscience only when certain related rights and freedoms are respected. On the other hand, freedom of conscience in society is imperative in order that man may pursue his effort to secure further freedom for himself and for all men.

The concentration thus suggested provides a legitimate focus for Christian action in promoting the observance of all human rights. It does not exclude other concerns. In emphasising the fundamental importance of conscience, its enlightenment and its expression, the churches will be in a position to adjust their efforts with fidelity to an evangelical conception of life.

The interpretation here given of the special interest and competence of the churches establishes the general limits under which the following analyses are projected. Religious liberty will be viewed in the context of all human rights. Upon each succeeding generation rests a continuing, two-fold responsibility : (1) to clarify the meaning of religious freedom ; and (2) to seek conditions of human relationship which will be favourable to the exercise of religious freedom.

The observance of religious liberty must be sought in the stream of life. Any contribution which is to be made through Christian instrumentality must therefore reckon with conditions which mark the current world scene. Part I will describe the present status in man's effort to make religious freedom a reality. Since detailed description will be impossible, attention will be centred upon (1) the nature and extent of the responsibility which the United Nations is assuming in promoting respect for human rights ; and (2) the form in which problems of human rights persist in national settings.

As the churches seek to fashion their most effective contribution, they should take full advantage of earlier studies and conclusions. Part II will assemble and analyse (1) the positions taken in ecumenical conferences, particularly Oxford and

Madras, and (2) actions under the auspices of national church groups during and immediately following the war.

On the dual background of prevailing world conditions and a fruitful Christian inheritance, the churches must determine the requirements which should be met in order that religious freedom may be realised in the society of our generation. Section III will view these requirements in terms of (1) man as an individual ; (2) the religious group ; and (3) the responsibility of government.

There is urgent need for the churches to fashion a procedure for ecumenical action in promoting the observance of religious freedom. The Conclusion will present in condensed form, as a basis for study and discussion (1) A Declaration on Religious Liberty ; and (2) Responsibility of the Churches in their Life and Work.

I. RELIGIOUS LIBERTY AND THE CURRENT SCENE

Clear understanding of the forces and conditions in contemporaneous society which may promote or curtail the exercise of religious liberty is a prerequisite to intelligent and effective action by the churches. Distinctive marks of the prevailing trend in international and in national approaches to the rights of man must be clearly identified. Complete analysis is here impossible. Emphasis will be laid on the manifest tendency to regard the protection of human rights as an international responsibility and on the persistence of varying problems in typical national settings.

1. HUMAN RIGHTS AND THE UNITED NATIONS

The authority to recognise or deny man's rights and freedoms has traditionally been vested in national states. When human rights were violated in any country, a foreign government felt justified in intervening mainly to protect its nationals. In scattered instances, friendly representations have been made to protest against extreme violations on grounds of common humanity.

On the background of traditional concept and practice, the advance toward an unprecedented recognition of international responsibility for the wellbeing of man may be ranked with the most significant achievements in to-day's history. Provisions to safeguard human rights through the United Nations have been developed during the formative period of its existence. These hold the possibility of revolutionising the method whereby man's rights may be secured to him within his own society. An understanding of these provisions is highly important. If the application of them should cease for a time and their effectiveness become temporarily lost, the record of what man sought thereby to achieve ought to be preserved as a stimulus to succeeding generations. If more extensive opportunities for international co-operation appear, a knowledge of the early developments will make for more adequate support by the churches. At all events, any effort of Christian people to promote the enjoyment of religious liberty must reckon with the purposes and projected activities of the United Nations.

The Charter of the United Nations

The Dumbarton Oaks Proposals for the Charter of a world organisation contained only one brief and subordinate reference to human rights and fundamental freedoms. In the period between October, 1944, when the Proposals were made public, and April, 1945, when the Conference on World Organisation was convened at San Francisco, strong popular sentiment was aroused to remedy this defect. Christians in a number of countries were active in their effort to secure in the final draft of the Charter more adequate provisions to safeguard human rights. Church leaders in at least four countries which were to be represented at San Francisco petitioned their national delegations to support the establishment of a Commission on Human Rights. Consultants to the United States delegation were sent by the Federal Council of the Churches of Christ in America and by the Foreign Missions Conference of North America. These consultants had effective opportunity, in formal conferences and in personal contacts, to reaffirm the convictions which Christians had expressed. An international Christian influence played a determining part in achieving the more extensive provisions for human rights and fundamental freedoms which ultimately found their way into the Charter.

The Preamble of the Charter, written in the name of the peoples of the United Nations, expresses determination to " reaffirm faith in fundamental human rights, in the dignity and worth of the human person, in the equal rights of men and women, and of nations large and small." One of the major purposes of the organisation shall be " to achieve international co-operation . . . in promoting and encouraging respect for human rights and fundamental freedoms for all without distinction as to race, sex, language, or religion " (Art. 1, Sec. 3). The Charter relates this purpose to the functions and powers of the General Assembly (Art. 13, Sec. 1, B), of the Economic and Social Council (Art. 62, Sec. 2), and lists it among the basic objectives of the International Trusteeship System (Art. 76, Sec. c). The Economic and Social Council is required " to set up commissions in economic and social fields and *for the promotion of human rights* " (Art. 68).

Commission on Human Rights

The fact that the establishment of a Commission on Human Rights is mandatory evidently centres in it a primary responsibility for " promoting and encouraging respect for human rights and fundamental freedoms." Accordingly, Christian leaders in a number of countries encouraged the prompt establishment of this Commission and sought to point out important responsibilities which the Commission could rightfully assume. Their efforts were attended by considerable success.

The Commission on Human Rights is composed of one representative from each of eighteen members of the United Nations to be selected by the Council. Representation shall be by nations, but each nation may determine whether or not its representatives shall be instructed. The Commission is authorised to call in *ad hoc* working groups of non-governmental experts in specialised fields or individual experts. Members of the United Nations are invited to establish information groups or local human rights committees within their respective countries to collaborate with them in the field of human rights. By subsequent action, two sub-commissions have been authorised, one on Freedom of Information and the Press, the other on Prevention of Discrimination and Protection of Minorities. A Commission on the Status of Women has been established.

The work of the Human Rights Commission shall be directed toward submitting proposals, recommendations and reports to the Council regarding : (*a*) an international bill of rights ; (*b*) international declarations or conventions on civil liberties, freedom of information and similar matters ; (*c*) the protection of minorities ; (*d*) the prevention of discrimination on grounds of race, sex, language, or religion ; (*e*) any other matter concerning human rights. Closely related to this work are arrangements for documentation, including a year book on law and usage concerned with human rights, the human rights activities of other United Nations organs, the bearing of war trial decisions on human rights, and the related activities by specialised agencies and non-governmental organisations. The Commission is further authorised to submit suggestions regarding ways and means for promoting human rights and fundamental freedoms with a view to securing the co-operation of other appropriate organs. It was agreed to accept as a general principle that international treaties involving basic human rights, including to the fullest extent treaties of peace, shall conform to the fundamental standards relative to such rights set forth in the Charter.

The Commission held its first session in 1947 and, among the various assignments accepted in its terms of reference, gave prominent place to the preparation of an International Bill of Human Rights. In June, a drafting Committee prepared working papers on a Declaration and a Convention. The Second Session of the Commission, convened at Geneva in December, agreed that the International Bill should contain two parts. The Declaration is to be a statement of principles or goals the enforcement of which must depend primarily upon the moral obligation accepted by the member states. The Covenant is intended to be a more precise document in the form of a treaty and enforcement measures will apply only to the countries which ratify the Covenant by their constitutional processes.

The texts of the Declaration and Convention as approved by the Commission, together with suggestions for implementation or enforcement, have been sent to the Member States for their reactions, and to the Economic and Social Council. Following consideration by the Commission at its third session in May, 1948, they will go—if acceptable at that time—to the Economic and Social Council, and, if approved by the Council, will be recommended to the General Assembly. According to present indications, the Declaration can be finally adopted by a two-thirds vote. The Covenant, after approval by the General Assembly, must be submitted to the Member States and will become effective only after a sufficient number of them have ratified it. The completion of this process, with respect to the

Declaration and the Covenant, may require a longer time than anticipated. Many conflicting points of view must still be reconciled and acceptable machinery for effective action devised. In a preliminary discussion on the rights and freedoms to be included in an International Bill, the Russian delegate objected to the following either because they were not necessary, were too broad, required further definition, or conflicted with national laws : right to life and personal liberty, right to petition the United Nations, non-retro-activity of penal laws, right of asylum, right of property and prohibition of unlawful expropriation, freedom of movement (migration), and freedom to resist oppression. At the Geneva Session of the Commission, provisional agreement was reached on some points and, where differences appeared, they were debated in good spirit. However, many of the differences which have come to light remain unresolved, and it is to be expected that more will emerge.

The importance of this development from the standpoint of the churches, in their own life and in their effort to promote world order, is clear. The Commission of the Churches on International Affairs, which holds consultative status with the Economic and Social Council, has set forth the views of its constituency through memoranda, informal conferences with many delegates, and formal representation to the Commission on Human Rights. Similarly, Christian leaders and committees in different countries have been instrumental in influencing the positions advanced by their governments. The texts of articles on religious freedom now contained in the draft Declaration and Covenant, as well as in provisions in related articles, strongly reflect the recommendations submitted on behalf of the churches.

Actions of the General Assembly

While the Commission on Human Rights has the initial task of study and recommendation, other organs as appropriate will apparently assume responsibility actually to promote respect for and observance of human rights.

The General Assembly has recognised the need for a further definition of the rights and freedoms which are referred to but not enumerated in the Charter. In its condemnation of genocide, the Assembly related the conception of individual rights to those of racial, biological and cultural groups and authorised the preparation of a Convention. It approved an international conference on freedom of information. It further referred the Panamanian Declaration on the Rights of Man to the Commission on Human Rights and to the member states for study and recommendation. In calling upon the Union of South Africa to treat the Indian minority within its territory in accordance with treaty obligations and with the relevant provisions of the Charter, the General Assembly took unprecedented action. Herein it revealed an intention to lift the violation of human rights from the area of domestic jurisdiction and to regard it as a matter of international concern.

The approval of eight Trusteeship Agreements marks an important step in the definition of the concept of rights and freedoms contained in the Charter. The provisions bear directly upon religious liberty and missionary freedom. The articles on human rights in the Trusteeship Agreement with Togoland under British administration will serve to illustrate these provisions:

Article 13 : The Administering Authority shall ensure in the Territory complete freedom of conscience and, so far as is consistent with the requirements of public order and morality, freedom of religious teaching and the free exercise of all forms of worship. Subject to the provisions of Article 8 (holding or transfer of lands and natural resources) of this Agreement and the local law, missionaries who are nationals of Members of the United Nations shall be free to enter the Territory and to travel and reside therein, to acquire and possess property, to erect religious buildings and to open schools and hospitals in the Territory. The provisions of this Article shall not, however, affect the rights and duty of the Administering Authority to exercise such control as he may consider necessary for the maintenance of peace, order and good government and for the educational advancement of the inhabitants of the Territory, and to take all measures required for such control.

Article 14 : Subject only to the requirements of public order, the Administering Authority shall guarantee to the inhabitants of the Territory freedom of speech, of the Press, of assembly, and of petition.

Analysis of Developments through the United Nations

The United Nations is still in its infancy. Many changes may naturally be expected as it develops to the full strength permitted under its Charter and perhaps beyond that, through processes of amendment, to a form of world government. However, certain lines are rather clearly marked out in the Charter and substantiated by the manner in which the various organs in their early sessions proceeded to put the provisions of the Charter into effect. These provisions and trends should be carefully studied in order to understand what competence the United Nations has to promote the observance of human rights.

The new factor which has been introduced into man's age-old struggle for freedom in society is the recognition of an international responsibility. This is vastly different from the diplomatic protection of citizens abroad or intervention in the name of humanity. It goes beyond previous international action in special fields such as slavery. It is potentially more inclusive than the Versailles provisions to protect minorities and the objectives sought by the Mandates Commission of the League of Nations or by the International Labour Organisation. The Charter provisions seem to indicate that a check of some kind is intended upon the constitutional and legal provisions as well as the practices of separate states. At the same time, it should be noted that the United Nations Charter contains a general article designed to protect the prerogatives of its individual member states (Article 2, section 7) :

"Nothing contained in the present Charter shall authorise the United Nations to intervene in matters which are essentially within the domestic jurisdiction of any state or shall require the Members to submit such matters to settlement under the present Charter ; but this principle shall not prejudice the application of enforcement measures under Chapter VII." (Chapter VII sets forth action which the Security Council may take with respect to threats to the peace, breaches of the peace, and acts of aggression.)

In face of the restriction here imposed, to what extent can international responsibility to promote the observance of human rights be effective? This crucial question has not yet been definitely answered. At the present stage, one can only point out what seems to be possible under the terms of the Charter as those terms are being interpreted and applied in the early transactions of the United Nations.

The Charter recognises that there are human rights and fundamental freedoms, but does not specify them. Two features of its provisions are important. First of all, the Charter makes only broad reference to rights and freedoms and thus it does not identify any single right such as religious liberty. This general approach resulted from the reluctance of the San Francisco Conference to become embroiled in a specification of particular rights. At the same time, it opened the way to a conception of necessary interrelationships among separate rights and to the possibility of their effective interplay in experience.

In the second place, the Charter stresses observance " without distinction as to race, sex, language, or religion." While non-discrimination is commendable, provision for it without an adequate enumeration of human rights is dangerous. This can readily be seen in the case of religious liberty. A government hostile to religion of any kind could, without discrimination, curtail or deny the right of religious liberty to all its citizens and still comply with the requirements of the Charter. It could say in substance that religious liberty is not a human right, or that the limited construction which it is disposed to place on religious liberty represents the extent to which the right exists. A similar situation could develop with respect to the various social, civil and economic rights. The provisions of the Charter will become full of meaning at this point only when rights and freedoms have been clearly and adequately defined. Encourage-ment may be found in the apparent intention of the United Nations to proceed with this task of definition and in the modest progress which has already been made.

The Charter states that the United Nations shall seek to achieve international co-operation in promoting and encouraging respect for human rights and fundamental freedoms, but does not specify the methods whereby this shall be done. The task of achieving international co-operation is assigned generally to the entire organisation, and more specifically to the General Assembly, the Economic and Social Council and the Trusteeship System. So far as the Economic and Social Council is concerned, it is required to set up a Commission on Human Rights. Nowhere in the Charter, however, is direct reference made to the manner in which the United Nations or any organ is authorised to proceed in order that human rights may actually be exercised. In all probability, affirmative steps can be taken to encourage member states to move toward the accomplishment of this purpose. The presence of human rights clauses in the Trusteeship Agreements and the current effort to draft an International Bill of Rights reveal ways in which such encouragement can be provided. The atmosphere which is thus created can itself offer an incentive to action by member states.

More baffling than the method of *encouragement* is the method of *action* which the United Nations can undertake. The Commission on Human Rights as presently constituted has no power to act. One indication of this appears in the somewhat evasive method now used in handling those communications which deal with reported violations.

The Charter empowers the United Nations—in most instances, the Security Council—to take action in six types of situations which are understood to fall not within domestic but within international jurisdiction. These are (1) an act of *aggression*; (2) a *breach* of the peace; (3) a *threat* to the peace; (4) a *dispute*, the continuance of which is likely to endanger the maintenance of international peace and security; (5) a *situation* which might lead to international friction or give rise to a dispute; (6) a *question* relating to the maintenance of peace and security, to armaments or disarmament, or to general principles of co-operation. Action by the United Nations under these circumstances was clearly designed in the interest of international peace and security. It may therefore be assumed that action on violations of human rights will be possible under the Charter in the first instance when international issues are involved.

Further exploration of methods of enforcement, particularly as related to domestic situations, has been authorised and begun. Preliminary discussions have referred to petition, inquiry, judicial decision, recommendation for action, observation of results, and, if recommendations are not followed, public censure, and perhaps remedial action. The fact that the Covenant on Human Rights is now being viewed as a treaty will permit the use of methods generally followed in bringing compliance with treaty provisions.

In seeking ways to promote universal observance of human rights, education must be given a place of first importance. Whatever specific legal means for enforcement may finally be devised, the weapons of publicity and public censure must be reckoned among the most effective. The nature of the world organisation as now constituted makes reliance upon such means imperative.

2. RELIGIOUS LIBERTY IN TYPICAL SITUATIONS

The emergence of an international responsibility for the protection of human rights is a distinctive and encouraging mark of political developments following the Second World War. It remains a fact, however, that human rights are normally observed or violated in more restricted political and cultural areas. Fair appraisal of religious liberty on the current scene must accordingly take into account problems which appear in national or local settings. The solution of these will first of all command the attention of the people immediately involved. As an international approach is strengthened, its impact may become progressively effective.

The world scene, in so far as it involves conditions affecting the exercise of religious freedom, is extremely complex and varied. By way of illustration, a few typical situations are here briefly described.[1]

Where national independence or autonomy emerges

For the first time in a long history, INDIA is going to have a written constitution for her government. The process of writing it has brought to the fore the question of the fundamental rights of man : Are there any rights which inhere in each and every person apart from affiliation of caste, creed, organisation or race ? While initial developments in answering this question have been encouraging, the division into two dominions carries the dangerous possibility of granting the Hindu a position of advantage in India and of establishing Pakistan along the lines of the traditional Islamic states. Whatever conflicts arise will surely centre in the problem of religious liberty. The limitations of " law, order and morality," particularly as related to conversion, are very wide and therefore open to abuse. Also, closely related social laws, as in the case of marriage and property, can serve to curtail the free expression of religious belief. The

---

[1] For the information on which these descriptions are based, the author is indebted to a group of contributors. The statements as originally submitted have been considerably abbreviated and are now intended primarily to set forth certain types of problems which must be faced. The reader must recognise that political conditions in a country may be radically changed at any time—as, for example, in Czechoslovakia. The extent to which such changes affect the observance of human rights may not be immediately discernible. The types of problems must still be taken into account even though their manifestations in national settings may vary.

solution of these issues at the domestic level can be considerably aided by an international agreement on the rights of man and on the limitations to which these rights may validly be subjected.

Where a stable government is sought following internal dissension

The people of CHINA, whether communists or nationalists, want peace, unity and democracy. However, behind the political conflict, there is the struggle for power, indeed for absolute power. When a country is torn by internal strife, the free exercise of human rights is endangered. Where communists rule, there is a tendency toward a hard and fast regimentation of community life. While the National Government is seeking a democratic pattern, it must contend not only with internal weaknesses, but also with the inertia of immense population and territory, time-honoured customs, widespread illiteracy, and the appalling destruction of the Second World War. In this situation it is of greatest importance that restrictions be kept at a minimum, and that the stage be set for the full recognition and observance of human rights when internal peace has been achieved.

Where a colonial status is apparently continuing

Varying types and degrees of encroachment on human rights, including certain aspects of religious liberty, can be seen in colonial AFRICA. In some portions of French Africa, there is a tendency to impose national points of view, and to favour religious and other bodies from outside which support this position. Where German missionaries have been at work, as in Tanganyika, the effort to identify those who supported the Nazi ideology has carried the danger of impairing religious freedom, even though the Government is committed to an objective study of each individual case. In the Belgian Congo, the manner in which Government subsidies for education have been distributed has resulted in sharp inequalities and in discriminatory practices. While the terms of the Concordata and missionary agreement between the Holy See and the Portuguese Government have not been literally applied, nevertheless the practical identification of church and state results in a curtailment of the religious rights of people in Portuguese territory overseas. Each of these problems demands separate attention. However, the solution of them all can be aided by international action to promote respect for human rights.

Where a long-standing racial minority suffers discrimination

There is no restriction by law on religious freedom in the UNITED STATES. None of the laws in those states where some form of discrimination is made legal bears directly on religion. Yet there is a curtailment of religious liberty, varying in different parts of the country and in local situations, which stems directly from racial attitudes and practices. The system of " racial caste " generally imposes the segregated church upon American Christianity and at times limits inter-church fellowship where racial lines must be crossed. In some parts of the country, there is an apparent correlation between sociological reaction and theological dogmatism. At times, there is manifest a tendency to seek implications of Christian ethics which will not undermine prevailing racial views and practices. Many Christian people are disturbed by the racial situation in the United States and are seeking to come to grips with it. Their efforts may be stimulated by the prospect of a growing international concern and the possibility of a wider international responsibility for the observance of human rights everywhere.

Where strengthened constitutional provisions are desired

Religious freedom and the rights of the churches in CZECHO-SLOVAKIA are legally recognised by two kinds of provisions, namely, the general principles of religious liberty in the constitution and the laws regarding the rights of individual church bodies or groups. A *qualified* majority of the General Assembly is required to change the constitution, while all other laws may be changed by a *formal* majority, that is, fifty-one per cent. of the Assembly. With all eventualities in mind, there would be great advantage if some of the rights now merely set forth by law and therefore subject to change by a formal majority, were made specific in the constitution of the Republic. The solution of this problem calls for united action by all bodies which are represented in the Council of Churches in Czechoslovakia.

L

Where Christian activity touches the Muslim community

The growing tendency to identify nationalism with Islam in the independent Muslim countries of the NEAR EAST intensifies the critical attitude of governments towards foreign missions, the Christian minority, and the convert from Islam. The first two are charged with introducing an alien element within the cultural unity of Islam, which is now regarded as the foundation of national greatness. The convert to Christianity is in popular eyes a traitor to the Muslim community. Islamic nationalism threatens to oust the democratic principles of equal treatment for all, irrespective of their religious affiliation, which underlies the Constitutions of these countries. This situation bears adversely upon the activities of the churches in worship and evangelism and works hardship upon Christians by restricting their social and economic opportunities. Religious liberty in the Near East is not likely to come through treaties with foreign powers. In all probability, desired improvements can be better encouraged by provisions to safeguard the rights of minorities in an International Bill of Human Rights.

Where Protestant missions involve tension with a Roman Catholic situation

In LATIN AMERICAN countries, religious liberty is theoretically guaranteed in every constitution. The problems which are there encountered arise not so much from relations between the state and the individual as from relations between the minority and the presumed majority churches. Representatives of the Roman Church, operating directly or through such states as are subservient to it, have in numerous instances brought about a denial or curtailment of freedom. The persecution of minorities is often stimulated by the contention that the essence of Latin American culture is identical with the old religion and that any new religion will necessarily destroy cultural and national values. Difficulties occasioned by this contention appear in countries where legislation favours the Roman Catholic Church, but in varying degrees are also encountered in lands where similar freedoms are to be enjoyed by all religions or where certain restrictions are uniformly imposed.

Where a Protestant minority seeks adequate safeguards of freedom

Apparent contradictions in the new constitution of ITALY give rise to some concern about the manner in which its provisions will actually be applied in the case of minority religious groups. The constitution provides that no distinction shall be made among citizens in the enjoyment of their guaranteed rights, and all religious confessions shall be equal before the law. At the same time, relations between the state and the Roman Catholic Church are to be regulated by the Lateran Pacts of 1929. Fidelity to the detailed terms of the Lateran Pacts would make impossible the full application of the general constitutional safeguards of religious freedom. Government authorities have given assurance that the general constitutional provisions will be made to prevail in practice. However, the fact that contradictions continue to stand in the fundamental law makes the basis for religious freedom measurably insecure. The danger of adverse administrative decisions at local levels adds to the concern of the Protestant minority. The position of Italy, by virtue of its commitment to terms in the peace treaty and its prospective relation to the United Nations, opens the way for a beneficial effect of any development to promote the observance of human rights through international action.

Where Christianity encounters political controls

Political conditions in the U.S.S.R., and the distinctive character of the Russian Church in its history and present life, make it virtually impossible to state the problem of religious liberty in a manner acceptable to all parties. Those who view the situation from without welcome the apparent improvement with respect to opportunities for worship and education and the apparent change in public attitude toward religion and its manifestations. At the same time, they are disturbed by what appears to be a relatively complete control over people by a totalitarian government. The failure to provide adequate legal safeguards for religious freedom and the tendency to effect changes by bureaucratic rather than popular decision serve to place more liberal current practice on an insecure foundation. The inability of people to take positions which are critical of governmental policy and their inability corporately to enter into fraternal relations with churches of other lands represent curtailments in domestic practice. Where Soviet influence becomes controlling in other countries, similar restrictions are in varying degree attempted. The disturbance of observers is accentuated by the manner in which U.S.S.R. representatives in international deliberations interpret religious freedom and related human rights, and the part which the state should play in the recognition of them. An appraisal of religious freedom in Russia, acceptable to Christians within and outside, must await the time when the situation can be discussed in unimpaired consultations. Such consultations are earnestly sought by those who are bent upon the promotion of world order, with peace and justice.

3. SUMMARY OF CURRENT SITUATION

The nations have declared their intention to achieve international co-operation in promoting respect for and observance of human rights. Effort is under way to define the rights of man and to devise means whereby the recognition of these rights may become universal. Under present world conditions, it is to be anticipated that the attainment of desired results will require a considerable period of time.

Meanwhile, problems arising from threatened or actual denial of human rights appear in many national and local situations. New constitutions and legal forms are being written which will tend to govern future practice. In many instances, the need for action, both remedial and preventive, is imperative.

Christian effort to promote the observance of human rights must reckon both with the international and national aspects of the current world scene. In normal circumstances, action in national and local situations will have to be taken by the Christians immediately involved. However, the resources of world Christianity must be available when assistance is sought. Moreover, as these co-ordinated resources move to influence the direction of international action, an atmosphere can be created which will have its beneficial effect upon local issues.

To carry on this work with prospect of greatest effectiveness, there is needed a precise statement of what Christians throughout the world believe is involved in the exercise of religious freedom. Such a statement must flow from a distinctively Christian point of view, but must be couched in terms which can win general acceptance. An instrument would thereby be provided both for appraising national problems with a view to remedial measures and for indicating requirements to be met in documents intended to safeguard human rights in the future. As background for a statement of this kind, the position of the churches as set forth in ecumenical conferences and in national church groups must be carefully analysed.

II. THE POSITION OF THE CHURCHES

With a diligence increasing in recent years, the churches have addressed themselves to the task of building a society where the exercise of religious freedom is possible. In ecumenical conferences and in national church groups, they have announced their views on the meaning of religious freedom and on procedures whereby the exercise of religious freedom may be realised. These developments ought to be brought together in brief compass. They ought also to be scrutinised in the light of recent political procedures and current need. This is necessary in order that the churches may determine what changes are called for to permit their most effective, continuing contribution.

I. STATEMENTS BY ECUMENICAL CONFERENCES

Representatives of the non-Roman churches have set forth the requirements of religious freedom, drawn particularly from the standpoint of the work which the churches seek to do. Further, they have expressed their conviction about the international significance of religious liberty and the responsibilities upon states to create conditions favourable to its exercise. These findings are here reproduced and then briefly analysed to ascertain the extent to which they are pertinent to the current international trend and to the manifestation of problems in national situations.

Requirements of Religious Liberty

Detailed statements enumerating the rights and freedoms which are necessary for the fulfilment of the churches' mission have been offered by the Oxford and Madras Conferences. The first of these is contained in the Report of the Section on Church and State at Oxford, 1937:

" We recognise as essential conditions necessary to the church's fulfilment of its primary duty that it should enjoy : (a) freedom to determine its faith and creed ; (b) freedom of public and private worship, preaching and teaching ; (c) freedom from any imposition by the state of religious ceremonies and forms of worship ; (d) freedom to determine the nature of its government and the qualifications of its ministers and members and, conversely, the freedom of the individual to join the church to which he feels called ; (e) freedom to control the education of its ministers, to give religious instruction to its youth and to provide for adequate development of their religious life ; (f) freedom of Christian service and missionary activity, both home and foreign ; (g) freedom to co-operate with other churches ; (h) freedom to use such facilities, open to all citizens or associations, as will make possible the accomplishment of these ends ; the ownership of property and the collection of funds."

The second appears in the findings of the Conference on the World Mission of the Church, convened by the International Missionary Council in Madras, 1938.

" There are minimum rights of religious freedom upon which the Church should insist, else it will be unfaithful to its calling, and its own power and effectiveness crippled. Without endeavouring to make a final or exhaustive statement on the content of these rights, we hold that they should comprise at least the right :

(a) to assemble for unhindered public worship
(b) to formulate its own creed
(c) to have an adequate ministry
(d) to determine its conditions of membership
(e) to give religious instruction to its youth
(f) to preach the Gospel publicly
(g) to receive into its membership those who desire to join it.

There are other elements of religious freedom closely connected with these, the recognition of which the Church should also claim, such as the right :

(a) to carry on Christian service and missionary activity both at home and abroad
(b) to organise local churches

    (c) to publish and circulate Christian literature

    (d) to hold property and to secure support for its work at home and abroad

    (e) to co-operate and to unite with other churches at home and abroad

    (f) to use the language of the people in worship and in religious instruction

    (g) to have equality of treatment in countries predominantly Roman Catholic, similar to that accorded by Protestant governments

    (h) to have legal recognition for Christian marriages between nationals."

International and National Aspects of Religious Liberty

The Report of the Section on the Universal Church and the World of Nations at Oxford in 1937 clearly recognised the significance of religious liberty for world order and viewed it as an international problem:

"An essential element in a better international order is freedom of religion. This is an implication of the faith of the church. Moreover, the ecumenical character of the church compels it to view the question of religious freedom as an international problem : all parts of the church are concerned that religious freedom be everywhere secured. We are, therefore, deeply concerned with the limitations that are increasingly being imposed in the modern world. We affirm the primary right to religious worship and the converse right to refuse compliance with any form of worship unacceptable on grounds of conscience. We affirm the right to public witness of religion and the right to religious teaching especially in the nurture of the young. In pleading for such rights we do not ask for any privilege to be granted to Christians that is denied to others. While the liberty with which Christ has set us free can neither be given nor destroyed by any Government, Christians, because of that inner freedom, are both jealous for its outward expression and solicitous that all men should have freedom in religious life. The rights which Christian discipleship demands are such as are good for all men, and no nation has ever suffered by reason of granting such liberties."

In an Additional Report of the Section on Church and

State, Oxford cited the general responsibility which rests on the state in relation to religious liberty:

" On the other hand, the church knows that man has been created in the image of God and has therefore an indestructible value, which the state must not impair but rather safeguard. The destiny of man and the different social activities in their proper functioning—such as marriage, the family, the nation and culture—constitute an irremovable limit of the state which it cannot with impunity transgress. A state which destroys human personality or human associations, or subordinates them to its own ends, is therefore incompatible with the Christian understanding of life. The state ought, on the contrary, to employ its resources to ensure that human freedom should find growing expression in the service of the neighbour and should not be used according to the prompting of natural inclination for self-assertion and irresponsible behaviour. In this task it cannot dispense with the co-operation of the church. It is therefore in no sense an attempt to meddle with what does not belong to it, but a simple act of obedience to God who is righteous and loving when the church, so far as circumstances allow it, becomes the champion of true human freedom in co-operation with the state and when necessary in criticism of its measures."

Analysis of Ecumenical Statements

Appraisal of these statements in the light of subsequent international developments reveals that a substantial beginning has been made. It also brings to light the need for further study by the churches in order that their position may be effectively integrated with present-day world movements to protect human rights.

The statements define the *requirements* of religious liberty largely in terms of the claims made by the churches. This is entirely legitimate. The churches must first see what is involved in religious liberty in the light of a Christian conception of man and in the light of the Church's divinely appointed task. An important first step has here been taken. With full recognition of the contribution in this first step, a further development of the Christian position now seems needed. The rights which Christians claim for man in society should be defined in terms of the rights of all men without discrimination on grounds of race, sex, language, or religion. From the rights of man will be derived the rights of the religious group.[1] Moreover, in setting forth the requirements of religious liberty, a clearer recognition of the interrelationship between religious freedom and other human rights is required. Christians may properly contend that religious freedom is primary. At the same time, they know its exercise depends upon the recognition of related rights. This harmonises with the broader approach through the United Nations. It also fits more naturally the needs of man in society where many human rights are complexly interwoven. A formulation which proceeds from the rights of man and which indicates the necessary interplay of various rights will enable the churches to communicate their claims more objectively and more effectively to governmental authorities, both international and national.

Further, the statements call attention to the *responsibility of governments* for the protection of religious freedom. The ecumenical conferences recognised the significance of religious liberty for world order. A foundation of lasting importance was here laid. From this base, national church groups moved to secure acceptance of international responsibility in safeguarding human rights through the United Nations. From this base, the churches throughout the world must now provide moral guidance as to the manner in which international responsibility can be met within the framework of the United Nations. The ecumenical conferences also clarified the responsibility of national states in relation to the work of the churches. The general principles they advanced need to be made more specific in terms of method, and correlation must be attempted between national and international responsibility. In doing this the churches will in no sense be repudiating a previous stand. By moving in the ecumenical tradition they will press for a more effective current application of Christian principles.

The position taken by the Conference on " The Churches and the International Crisis," convened by the Provisional Committee of the World Council of Churches at Geneva in 1939, stands as a connecting link—both in time and in concept—between the

[1] The broad term *religious group* is used here and in subsequent references rather than the specific term *church*. This is necessary because religious freedom must apply similarly to all religious associations. In a world society the churches can claim no rights which are not equally recognised for other religious groups.

major ecumenical conferences and the work of national church groups during the war.

" *All human beings are of equal worth in the eyes of God* and *should be so treated in the political sphere.* It follows that the ruling power should not deny essential rights to human beings on the ground of their race or class or religion or culture or any such distinguishing characteristic."

2. DEVELOPMENTS FOLLOWING THE ECUMENICAL CONFERENCES

During the war and in the period thereafter, activity of the churches in the field of religious liberty was carried on most intensively in separate countries. Effort was made to keep the churches of other lands informed about studies and action undertaken locally. A modest degree of international Christian co-operation was thus attained. In the main, the approaches taken emphasised an international responsibility and recognition of the interplay of religious freedom and related human rights. The correspondence of this approach with the procedures advocated by other than church agencies was in no small measure the result of an influence exercised by Christian action. A brief review of happenings since the Geneva Conference of 1939 reveals the manner in which the lines originally established in ecumenical thinking have been followed in the effort to come to grips with problems of religious liberty in an interrelated world.

Human Rights and the World Organisation

As the Second World War progressed to its conclusion, the nations united against the Axis powers became increasingly committed to the establishment of a world security organisation. From the outset, commissions of the churches emphasised the inadequacy of any world agency which was concerned merely with security and ignored the economic, cultural and humanitarian forces in international society. They sought more comprehensive provisions whereby the peoples of the world might live together constructively and creatively. In this effort, they gave substantial place to the demand for international co-operation to promote respect for human rights. Concurring action was taken by the Federal Council of the Churches of Christ in America and the Foreign Missions Conference of North America in the form of the following resolution :

" That the Department of State of the United States and the

Department of External Affairs of Canada be urged to seek the establishment of an agency on 'Human Rights and Fundamental Freedoms' along with the Social and Economic Council set forth in the Dumbarton Oaks Proposals."

This action was transmitted to the foreign offices of the United States and Canadian Governments. It was brought to the attention of delegates to the United Nations Conference on International Organisation at San Francisco. Similarly, the British Council of Churches and church leaders in Australia brought to the attention of their national delegations to San Francisco the need to strengthen provisions for safeguarding human rights in the Charter of the proposed world organisation. In behalf of the churches which had given expression to their views, representation was made by the consultants to the United States Delegation at San Francisco. It may be accurately stated that the findings of the ecumenical conferences, when expanded and made more explicit in the thinking of national church groups, became an instrumental factor in achieving the provisions for human rights in the United Nations Charter.

Statements on Religious Liberty

Concentrated study and action on issues of religious liberty, more broadly on all human rights, were pursued in the United States and in Great Britain, under the auspices of Joint Committees on Religious Liberty. The activities of these committees were comprehensive and far-reaching. Reference is here made only to two documents which indicated the further development of concepts which find their roots in the ecumenical conferences. Attention has previously been called to the stand for freedom by Christian people under totalitarian governments and in occupied countries, and to the significance of their contribution in advancing the cause of human rights. It is now necessary to consider activities which quite directly affect the process of drafting international agreements in the establishment and work of the United Nations.

The Statement on Religious Liberty, prepared by the United States Joint Committee on Religious Liberty, was formally adopted by the Federal Council of Churches and the Foreign Missions Conference of North America respectively in March, 1944, and April, 1944. It was used by the Committee as a basis for its various negotiations with the United States Government and was widely distributed throughout the world.

The Statement proceeds from the broad assumption that there are rights which derive from the dignity of the human person as the image of God. It claims that these rights must be set forth in agreements into which the nations may enter and must be vindicated in treaty arrangements, and in the functions and responsibilities assigned to international organisations. It specifies related freedoms which must be recognised in order that religious liberty may be inclusively observed. The Statement concludes with a brief assignment of responsibility both to the state and to the people.

In the American Statement an international approach to the protection of human rights is advocated and at the same time the obligations of individual states are recognised. The point of departure is taken in the broader concept of human rights. However, the manner in which the requirements of religious liberty are advanced does not explicitly reveal the interrelationship of religious freedom and the other rights essential thereto.

A Statement on Human Rights and Religious Freedom, prepared by the British Joint Committee on Religious Liberty, was adopted by the British Council of Churches, April 22, 1947. It was formally submitted to the United Nations Commission on Human Rights.

The Statement begins with a Christian affirmation on the meaning of human freedom and the responsibility of the state for the protection of its citizens. In the form of a Charter, religious freedom is more closely analysed in terms of its requirements and is specifically related to the civil rights which are essential to its expression. The points of the Charter are further broken down to indicate provisions which are needed to make them materially effective. The Statement concludes with a consideration of the problem of religious minorities and proposes the method of making a just treatment for religious minorities incumbent on all states alike, without any special or possibly invidious reference to individual states.

In calling attention to international responsibility and to obligations upon separate states, the British Statement sustains the idea which is rooted in ecumenical decision. With greater clarity than appears in any other statement formally adopted by the churches, nationally or internationally, it relates the exercise of religious liberty to the various civil rights which are essential thereto. Without specific definition, it allows for enforcement through internationally imposed sanctions and through the power of world public opinion.

3. RECAPITULATION OF THE DEVELOPMENT IN THE CHRISTIAN POSITION

The position of the churches with respect to religious freedom in our day has thus been explained and made more explicit. The Oxford Conference recognised the significance of religious liberty for world order and viewed it as an international problem. Oxford and Madras enumerated the requirements of religious freedom from the standpoint of the life and work of the churches. Geneva added the broader setting of all human rights.

Through the action of national church groups, the conception of international responsibility was attached to an emerging world organisation of the United Nations. The relationship between religious freedom and other human rights was pointed out with increasing definiteness. World-wide Christian conviction must now make its impact on the process whereby the United Nations seeks (1) to define, through an International Bill of Rights, the human rights and fundamental freedoms which the Charter refers to but does not enumerate ; and (2) to devise the ways by which the rights and freedoms, when they are defined, may actually be observed in a world society. A more effective Christian impact may result when the findings of ecumenical conferences and of national church groups are brought together. As a step toward this synthesis, an analysis of the requirements of religious liberty is now proposed.

III. REQUIREMENTS OF RELIGIOUS LIBERTY

The requirements of religious liberty in our day may be projected on a two-fold background. On the one hand, there is a Christian approach to the issues of religious freedom which finds its roots in the ecumenical movement and its development in the studies and actions of national church groups. This phase of the background provides in the main the *substance* or *content* which must find place in the requirements of religious liberty to-day. Accordingly, the analysis here following has drawn upon statements in ecumenical conferences, and upon the positions which became clarified under varied experiences of Christians in many countries since the outbreak of the Second World War. On the other hand, there is an emerging international political responsibility which is at least in part a response to Christian insights. This second aspect of the background gives clue to the *form* in which the requirements of religious liberty must be stated. While form is important in the analysis of requirements, it will be even more significant in fashioning an instrument which may be used for Christian representation to political authorities.

The point of view with which the churches should determine the requirements of religious liberty may be characterised by three considerations.

1. *Religious liberty must be sought for man as an individual person moving in the relationships of society.* The point of departure ought to be in the rights and freedoms of man as an individual, and in the responsibilities he must assume as a member of society. This is clearly distinguished from the starting point in the church or religious group. The claims of the religious group upon society are derived from the rights of man and should be considered only after the rights of man as an individual have been established. Whether rights and freedoms are viewed basically from the standpoint of the individual or in derived fashion from the standpoint of the religious group, they must be understood to apply to all men, no matter what their religious faith may be.

Attention is therefore centred upon *individual man in society*. In looking at him, the Christian sees what the biologist, the sociologist and the psychologist see. But he finds something more than human science alone can discern. To the Christian, every man on the contemporary scene is the concern of an eternal God. Beset by the demands of living in a complex world, man may yield to confusion or lower self-interest ; or, utilising most effectively the resources which God has placed at man's disposal, he may become "a living sacrifice, holy and acceptable to God." Whether viewed from the standpoint of science, or of an eternal dispensation, to every man is given an appointed potentiality. The realisation of his potentiality rests with man and with society. Every man ought to have the chance to become what God intended him to be. Upon society rests the responsibility to give every man that chance.

In realising the opportunity which is due to him, man cannot ignore the obligation which he owes to society. He must bring into proper balance the different and somewhat antithetical factors which operate in his growth. These factors find parallels in the paradoxes of life. The individual must be in a position to act freely, but he must also act responsibly. He must use his own resources, but he must combine them with the spiritual inheritance of the human race. He must seek his highest personal development, but he must also seek to contribute most richly to the wellbeing of his fellow men. These factors, which on the surface appear to be contradictory, must become complementary. This is man's responsibility. He will have opportunity to meet it only if he is in a position to experience religious liberty.

2. *Religious liberty which is sought for man in society is subject to biological, environmental and ethical limitations.* In some respects man can never be free. He is born into this world with the limitations of biological inheritance. Not only in physical structure, but also in mental and emotional competence, his boundaries are fixed. To say that all men should be free does not imply that all men are equal. Freedom is forced to operate within the limits of each person's biological inheritance. Man is also born into this world with the limitations of environmental inheritance—religious, cultural, political, economic, social. While these are not perforce permanently binding, they cannot be ignored. Man may rise above the environment of his birth and childhood. Nevertheless, the obvious reality of environment—as a minimum influential and as a maximum determining—makes it impossible to hold all-inclusive claims for religious liberty. Another limitation—to be sure, of a far different kind—needs to be added to those imposed by heredity and environment. It grows out of the point of view with which the Christian insists that religious liberty shall be sought for all men. Freedom is not intended to open an inviting door to the lowest levels of conviction and action. Rather, it is intended to encourage an achievement of the highest that is possible for each individual and for the world society of which he is a member. Religious liberty is properly exercised only when faith and love combine to make a free man his brother's servant. This limitation, while not inherent in the nature of man and of society, flows imperatively from the Christian presuppositions about man in his relation to his fellow men and to God.

3. *Religious liberty must be sought with full recognition of the interdependence of all rights and freedoms.* " Religious liberty is not an isolated reality. It exists or is denied in the midst of a complex of institutions, attitudes and practices. These are inseparable from measures of liberty in general and from certain specific liberties such as those of free expression and free association. Religious liberty is supported by related liberty ; the effort to secure religious liberty is, both in history and in contemporary society, a force working largely toward the associated liberties."[1]

With these considerations in mind, the requirements of religious liberty will be viewed in terms of (1) man as an individual in society ; (2) the religious group ; and (3) the responsibility of government. While separated for the purposes of analysis, the requirements as they affect man, the group, and government are interrelated in actual experiences.

I. MAN AS AN INDIVIDUAL

The achievement of religious liberty in society will require that every man, by freely but responsibly combining his own resources with the spiritual inheritance of the human race, may seek his highest personal development and, at the same time, contribute most richly to the wellbeing of his fellow men. What does man need in order that he may be in a position to exercise the religious freedom which is his right ? To answer this question, the particular functions which man must be free to perform are sketched. A brief discussion of each function is intended to bring to light the completing factors which are necessary to make the freedom personally possible and the limiting factors which are necessary to make the freedom socially beneficial.

(1) *Man in his innermost, personal life should be free to determine his own beliefs.* Here is involved that aspect of conscience which touches the individual alone—the operation of conscience as it was previously formed and the shaping of conscience in the contacts of life. Belief grows out of voluntary acceptance and therefore cannot be the result of compulsion or force. It is frequently claimed that freedom of conscience, in so far as it concerns only individual beliefs and not social actions, cannot be denied. This is untrue. For, while a person is free to believe as he sees fit within the scope of the information at his disposal,

[1]M. Searle Bates, *Religious Liberty : an Inquiry*, pp. 343, 344.

the kind and the amount of information open to him decidedly limit the decisions to which he commits himself.

A first requirement for freedom of belief, therefore, is the right of access to information. To say that a person may believe as he desires, and at the same time to prevent him from coming into contact with ideas to which he may react, is an empty gesture. Freedom of access to information should be sought for all men with a clear understanding of its reasonable limitations. Within the limits prescribed for all religious freedom, parents have the right to determine the kind of religious influence to which their children shall be exposed during childhood. A religious group has the right to determine the kind of beliefs and action it seeks to cultivate, subject to a recognition of the rights of other religious groups and to the claims of the larger community to which it belongs. A nation, with representative government, may determine its policies and practices in the light of the religious outlook which at any time is predominant in its constituency, provided its government permits criticism from its own constituency and from peoples of other countries. Neither the religious organisation nor the state has an obligation to *provide* information beyond that which it has customarily made available, except when a consistently open-minded study of " foreign " points of view reveals a worth previously unavailable to its constituency. Both have a responsibility to *permit* the mature individual to relate himself to sources of information in such a way as to allow personal decision and belief.

If the right of access to information as a first requirement for freedom of belief is to be personally and socially beneficial, the individual person, in exercising his rights, must meet related requirements. His mind must be open to entertain new points of view, or when dissatisfied with beliefs he holds, he must actually seek additional information. In the process, he must be held free to change his beliefs. He must use judgment in appraising the information to which he has access or he must rely upon the judgment of others in whom he has confidence. In reaching decisions, he must consciously take into account his higher self-interests and the implications of his beliefs for the wellbeing of his fellow men.

(2) *Man in his innermost, personal life should be free to enjoy the fruits of his belief.* Here is an area where every person can enjoy his freedom to the utmost. A Christian description of the

M

experience may be given in the words of Galatians v, 22, 23 :
" . . . The fruit of the Spirit is love, joy, peace, long-suffering,
gentleness, goodness, faith, meekness, temperance ; against such
there is no law." The only serious obstacle which arises to
interfere with this enjoyment is the impossibility of access to
information which a person considers necessary to the refinement,
strengthening, or modification of his belief. While freedom to
enjoy the inner fruits of faith can neither be granted nor denied
by human authority, it must be mentioned as an important
aspect of individual religious liberty.

(3) *Man should be free to join with those who hold similar beliefs
with a view to carrying on such activities as do not involve direct participation by others who believe differently.* Freedom to organise with
people on the basis of common beliefs should carry with it freedom
to worship according to conscience, freedom to preach,
freedom to educate members of the group and their children, freedom of fellowship and service. The rights of the individual
must then be transferred to the group. Pursuit of the group's
activities will require that it be granted, through its members,
freedom of speech and of Press ; freedom of organisation and of
public meeting ; and freedom to acquire and hold such property
as may be necessary to corporate life.

In exercising his freedom to join with others who hold similar
beliefs and in becoming party to their activities, each person
must be alert to implications for himself, for his children, and for
the broader society in which the group moves. On grounds of
personal belief or on grounds of community good, he should
always have the right of withdrawal from a religious group
without suffering loss of any privileges beyond those which
rightfully attached to his previous membership.

(4) *Man should have freedom to express his belief in a social and
political community where differing religious convictions are held.* Many
communities are not characterised by cultural or religious
homogeneity. The more the nations and peoples of the world
become closely inter-knit, the more diverse will the outlook and
practices in communities tend to become. Freedom of conscience
in its wider sense demands that man as an individual—whether
he stands alone or as a member of a religious group—has the
opportunity to express his beliefs in all social and political
relationships. Objectively conceived, this gives the proponent
of one religious view no position of advantage over the proponent

of another religious view. The strength of any religious conviction must ultimately be found in the truth upon which it rests. A social or political community may thwart the effective application of a truth. When the ideal of religious liberty is spun out in society, that risk must be run. Notwithstanding, the individual must be free to express his belief. This freedom is his right. It is also an imperative for social growth. Progress is made not so much by adjusting the conduct of an individual to the accustomed standard of the community, but by adjusting the conduct of the community to a standard higher than that which it had previously accepted.

In order that this freedom may be real, man needs freedom of speech as involved in the spoken word and in publication. Free speech, by way of criticism or commendation, is essential in order that man may make his contribution in shaping the conduct of the community. It is also essential to enable him to propagate his own beliefs ; or, looking at propagation from the side of the recipient, freedom of speech is necessary in order that others than the speaker may have access to the information and beliefs which he holds. The community in which this freedom to propagate beliefs is to operate must not be narrowly conceived in terms of municipality or nation ; it must move from the smallest social unit ultimately to include the world community of nations. In addition to freedom of speech, the individual should have the right to govern his conduct in the political and social group by conscience. The opportunity to act in accordance with belief is indispensable to full freedom.

Individual freedom of speech and action in a society of differing religious convictions becomes possible only when social and political institutions play their part. The right of man to determine what he says and what he does by conscience must first of all be a recognised premise for interrelationships in the community. Responsible people in social and political institutions must be disposed, as a matter of principle, to heed the stand which the individual has taken and to appraise fairly the conviction on which the stand is based. They must grant immunity from discrimination and from legal disability on grounds of a person's convictions, at least to the point where recognised community interests are adversely affected. Their judgment of what actually constitutes community interests may be warped and progress may be accordingly retarded ; but their judgment, in so far as it reflects the will of the people whom they represent, is the only criterion by which they can shape policy and practice.

To this situation, man must bring a measure of competence to justify his freedom. Obviously, he must recognise that other people who hold different beliefs have the same right of expression which he claims for himself. He needs the courage of his convictions. He must have respect for authority, even when his conscience forces him to take issue with the positions advocated by authority. The representation of his beliefs should be accompanied by an open-mindedness which will make him seek to appreciate other views and by a willingness to modify his position when justified. With full recognition of the complementary rights of the individual and of society, he must be ready, if need be, to suffer persecution and deprivation, in order to be true to his conscience.

The effort to place in proper functional relationship the various factors which may foster individual religious liberty in a complex society has forced an anticipation of factors which fall appropriately in the functional consideration of religious groups, and social and political institutions. This need in no sense be disturbing. In fact, it is unavoidable when religious liberty is viewed in the stream of living.

2. THE RELIGIOUS GROUP

The achievement of religious liberty in society will require that any religious group, fully recognising the rights of other religious groups and the demands of social wellbeing in a community, may freely but responsibly pursue its chosen activities among its own members and, at the same time, proclaim its way of life to others for their acceptance or rejection.

In the make-up of current society, whether viewed on a world scale or in the narrower compasses of national states, appears a multitude of different religious groups. Honesty compels us to recognise that each group either believes that it alone is right or that it is more right than any other group. Each group therefore seeks to pursue a programme of life that will not only affect its own constituency, but will also win new adherents to its faith. The intensity of the effort at self-propagation and growth varies considerably. Nevertheless, it must be assumed as valid that when a group holds convictions strongly enough, the desire to have others hold similar beliefs is inevitable. To preserve religious liberty for the individual person, the claims of competing or co-operating religious groups must be adjusted.

As far as the individual is concerned, Protestant Christianity finds a starting point in the recognition of man's right of access to information. In obeying the commission to preach the Gospel to all men everywhere, a commission which roots in the experience of the earliest Christian community, the churches place at man's disposal the information they possess. The evangelical conception of the message thus proclaimed prohibits compulsion or the use of force. Man is free to accept or to reject. Individual freedom of religion is not impaired.

In determining relations among religious groups, imperfection in man and in society must be taken into account. In the provisional dispensation which imperfection establishes, many different religious points of view will inevitably be held and proclaimed. When Protestant Christianity claims freedom for itself, it must also grant freedom to others. While it credits other religious groups with equal sincerity, it will jealously guard its heritage and seek continuously to refine that heritage with the help of God. It will use all its resources to place what it cherishes at the disposal of all men. At the same time, it must grant equal right and freedom to other religious groups. To the extent that its conduct exemplifies this point of view, it can reasonably expect that other religious groups will proceed with similar animation.

The freedoms claimed for religious groups are rooted in the freedoms claimed for the individual. Every person should have the right to organise with others. As he affiliates himself with those who have similar convictions, his individual rights become corporate rights. Freedom for the religious group should be interpreted to include freedom to worship according to conscience and to bring up children in the faith of their parents ; freedom for the individual member to change his religion and his group affiliation ; freedom to preach, educate, publish, and carry on missionary activities ; and freedom to maintain and to develop an organisation, and to acquire and hold property, for these purposes.

Each of these freedoms in varying degree impinges upon, or presupposes the recognition of certain civil and social rights. Governments and social institutions, in so far as lies within the province of each, have an obligation to see that these rights are observed. Freedom to worship, interpreted to include public worship, is dependent upon the right of public meeting and, to a certain extent, of organisation. It may involve freedom of speech and freedom of Press. Freedom to bring up children in the faith of their parents, if it is to include education beyond that which the home provides, is dependent upon freedom of speech, of the Press, of organisation and public meeting. Freedom for the individual to change his religion will call into play most of the civil and social rights as soon as he practises the religion which he has come to profess. Freedom to preach and to educate demand freedom of speech, of Press, of organisation and public meeting. Freedom to publish corresponds with freedom of the Press. Freedom to organise with others and freedom to acquire and hold property are in themselves civil and social rights. Freedom to carry on missionary activities basically bespeaks the right to testify to one's conviction in any part of the world. It may involve all or many of the other freedoms. By its very nature, however, it carries implications which the other freedoms may not contain. These implications grow out of the historical fact that missionary activity more frequently and specially involves the nationals of foreign states, their ingress, egress, and activities as aliens. It is justified in the first instance on the right of individuals everywhere to access to information. It therefore requires that social and political institutions permit freedom of access and exposure to the cultures, ideas and beliefs of other peoples and freedom of cultural exchange.

As religious groups are granted the freedoms here indicated, they will recurringly be brought into close relationship with each other and therefore will encounter the dangers of competition and friction. An ethical code would tend to minimise or remove tensions and religious organisations would contribute materially to the practice of religious freedom by developing and accepting such a code of " professional ethics."[1]

3. RESPONSIBILITY OF GOVERNMENT

The achievement of religious liberty in society will require that governments, both national and international, assure to all citizens, in their individual and group relations, freedom from direct or indirect

[1] Principles for a voluntary code to guide behaviour of religious bodies are suggested in M. Searle Bates, *Religious Liberty: an Inquiry*, pp. 562, 563.

compulsion in matters of religion, and guard them against discrimination and legal disabilities on account of religion.

The purposes and prerogatives of government may be defined in many different ways. When viewed in the light of religious liberty as a fundamental human freedom, governments bear a clear responsibility to individual man as a member of society. Negatively, it is not within their province to prohibit or to curtail the exercise of religious liberty by their citizens or to impose religious practices upon them. Positively, they have an obligation to create conditions which are favourable to the freest development and expression of conscience consistent with the best interests of the entire community under their jurisdiction. Historically, governments have in varying degree failed to meet this responsibility under two broad conditions : (1) when governments as a matter of consistent policy claimed that the people existed for the state, not the state for the people ; and (2) when governments, under adverse pressure from other states, found it necessary to protect the interests of their people and in the process of aggressive or defensive action, limited or prohibited the exercise of normally recognised rights.

In face of the present situation, the exercise of religious liberty as a human right must in the first instance be made possible through the action of separate national states. The decisions of the United Nations can be an instrumental factor in influencing member states to respect and observe human rights for all persons within their jurisdiction. It is important, therefore, to mark out the requirements which should be met by all forms of governments, international as well as national and local. Many of the requirements upon government have already been indicated in relation to the exercise of religious liberty by the individual and by the religious group. They are here brought together to reveal the part which governments should play.

1. *Governments should assure to all people within their jurisdiction— as individuals and in corporate relations as members of a religious body— freedom of religious belief and action subject only to such limitations as are prescribed by law and are necessary to protect public order and welfare, and the rights and freedoms of others.* This will require the right of access to information, freedom to worship according to conscience, freedom to bring up children in the faith of their parents ; freedom for the individual to change his religion ; freedom to preach, educate, publish ; freedom to carry on missionary

activities ; and freedom to organise with others, and to acquire and hold property for these purposes. These rights and freedoms should be equally assured to majority and minority groups. The group which claims the freedoms when it is a minority in a country has a reciprocal obligation to recognise equal freedom for all when it is a majority in another country. Where such rights and freedoms are observed without distinction, people will be free from external compulsion in matters of religion.

When political authorities reach the conclusion that the exercise of freedoms violates laws designed to protect community wellbeing, they have the right to interfere. However, such interference should not be with the purpose merely of granting one religious group a more favoured position than another body. It must be on the basis of community wellbeing. It must be with a consideration of man's place in the human family and not his place in relation to the majority religious body. As has been previously pointed out, the judgment of political authorities or the laws by which they judge an action to be harmful may be wrong. This risk cannot be avoided. It will be minimised when, through closer relations among the peoples of the world, a higher " world morality " is achieved.

2. *Governments should create conditions favourable to the exercise of the freedom in religious belief and action which is the recognised right of the individual and of the religious group.* A first contribution of government will be to safeguard its citizens against discrimination and legal disability on account of religion. This responsibility stands even though minorities and individuals, to the extent that they differ from the majority in conviction and practice, normally suffer certain disadvantages. In assuring their people freedom of religious belief and action and in creating conditions in society which are favourable thereto, national governments should seek as a minimum to comply with the highest standards in a world society. To the degree that they exceed such standards, they will be contributing to the progressive elevation of a " world morality." As the prerogatives of national sovereignty yield to the demands of world order and security through international collaboration, national states and the world organisation must co-operate to secure to every man the enjoyment of human rights and fundamental freedoms.

CONCLUSION:
PROCEDURES FOR ECUMENICAL ACTION

A survey of the present status in man's effort to make religious freedom a reality has revealed an emerging international responsibility and, at the same time, the continuation of disturbing problems in national settings. An investigation of the positions advanced by the churches indicates that the ecumenical conferences made substantial progress in their study of religious liberty and that, subsequently, national church groups have further developed these findings in relation to changing needs and practices. An analysis of the requirements of religious liberty in our time has identified the needs of the individual and of the religious group in society, and has set forth the basic responsibilities to be met by government.

There is urgent need for the churches to fashion a procedure for ecumenical action whereby the observance of all human rights and particularly of religious liberty may be promoted. Of primary importance in this procedure is the wide acceptance of a statement or declaration wherein the Christian view of religious liberty is set forth in a form which is designed to guide remedial and preventive action by the churches. Such a declaration will be helpful in appraising situations where violations are reported to have occurred and in revealing what changes in legal provision or practice are needed. It will provide direction for those who are seeking safeguards for religious liberty in national constitutions and laws, and in international treaties, declarations, or conventions ; it will be usable as an instrument to determine the adequacy of proposed or enacted juridical forms. In addition to a statement on religious liberty, the procedure should indicate the distinctive responsibilities to be assumed by the churches. The conclusions here set forth are presented as a basis for the study and discussion from which a needed plan of action may be formed :

I. A Declaration on Religious Liberty.

II. Responsibilities in the Life and Work of the Churches in Demonstrating Religious Liberty.

I. A DECLARATION ON RELIGIOUS LIBERTY

An essential element in a good international order is freedom of religion. This is an implication of the Christian faith and of the world-wide nature of Christianity. Christians therefore view the question of religious freedom as an international problem. They are concerned that religious freedom be everywhere secured. In pleading for this freedom they do not ask for any privilege to be granted to Christians that is denied to others. While the liberty with which Christ has set men free can neither be given nor destroyed by any Government, Christians, because of that inner freedom, are both jealous for its outward expression and solicitous that all men should have freedom in religious life. The nature and destiny of man by virtue of his creation, redemption and calling, and man's activities in family, state and culture establish limits beyond which the government cannot with impunity go. The rights which Christian discipleship demands are such as are good for all men, and no nation has ever suffered by reason of granting such liberties. Accordingly :

The rights of religious freedom herein declared shall be recognised and observed for all persons without distinction as to race, sex, language, or religion, and without imposition of disabilities by virtue of legal provisions or administrative acts.

1. *Every person has the right to determine his own faith and creed.*

The right to determine faith and creed involves both the process whereby a person adheres to a belief and the process whereby he changes his belief. It includes the right to receive instruction and education.

This right becomes meaningful when man has the opportunity of access to information. Religious, social and political institutions have the obligation to permit the mature individual to relate himself to sources of information in such a way as to allow personal religious decision and belief.

The right to determine one's belief is limited by the right of parents to decide sources of information to which their children shall have access. In the process of reaching decisions, everyone ought to take into account his higher self-interests and the implications of his beliefs for the wellbeing of his fellow men.

2. *Every person has the right to express his religious beliefs in worship, teaching and practice, and to proclaim the implications of his beliefs for relationships in a social or political community.*

The right of religious expression includes freedom of worship, both public and private ; freedom to place information at the disposal of others by processes of teaching, preaching and persuasion ; and freedom to pursue such activities as are dictated by conscience. It also includes freedom to express implications of belief for society and its government.

This right requires freedom from arbitrary limitation of religious expression in all means of communication, including speech, Press, radio, motion pictures and art. Social and political institutions should grant immunity from discrimination and from legal disability on grounds of expressed religious conviction, at least to the point where recognised community interests are adversely affected.

Freedom of religious expression is limited by the rights of parents to determine the religious point of view to which their children shall be exposed. It is further subject to such limitations, prescribed by law, as are necessary to protect order and welfare, morals and the rights and freedoms of others. Each person must recognise the right of others to express their beliefs and must have respect for authority at all times, even when conscience forces him to take issue with the people who are in authority or with the position they advocate.

3. *Every person has the right to associate with others and to organise with them for religious purposes.*

This right includes freedom to form religious organisations, to seek membership in religious organisations, and to sever relationship with religious organisations.

It requires that the rights of association and organisation guaranteed by a community to its members include the right of forming associations for religious purposes.

It is subject to the same limits imposed on all associations by non-discriminatory laws.

4. *Every religious organisation, formed or maintained by action in accordance with the rights of individual persons, has the right to determine its policies and practices for the accomplishment of its chosen purposes.*

The rights which are claimed for the individual in his exercise of religious liberty become the rights of the religious organisation, including the right to determine its faith and creed ; to engage in religious worship, both public and private ; to teach, educate, preach and persuade ; to express implications of belief for society and government. To these will be added certain corporate rights which derive from the rights of individual persons, such as the right : to determine the form of organisation, its government and conditions of membership ; to select and train its own officers, leaders and workers ; to publish and circulate religious literature ; to carry on service and missionary activities at home and abroad ; to hold property and to collect funds ; to co-operate and to unite with other religious bodies at home and in other lands ; to use such facilities, open to all citizens or associations, as will make possible the accomplishment of religious ends.

In order that these rights may be realised in social experience, the state must grant to religious organisations and their members the same rights which it grants to other organisations, including the right of self-government, of public meeting, of speech, of Press and publication, of holding property, of collecting funds, of travel, of ingress and egress, and generally of administering their own affairs.

The community has the right to require obedience to non-discriminatory laws passed in the interest of public order and well-being. In the exercise of its rights, a religious organisation must respect the rights of other religious organisations and must safeguard the corporate and individual rights of the entire community.

II. LIFE AND WORK OF THE CHURCHES

The ideal of ecumenicity demands that the churches in their various branches set an example to the world of toleration for all, and specifically for members of minority Christian communions. The occasion to further the cause of international understanding lies immediately to hand and is within the power of the churches to use forthwith, namely, " to do good to all men and especially toward them that are of the household of the faith."

1. *Christians should seek to promote respect for and observance of human rights by processes of education and friendly adjustment.*

them to do what they do not like doing. The great powers amongst the nations are those who can, if they wish to, subjugate the small ones to their will, either directly or indirectly. To have power does not necessarily mean to use it, although its mere existence has an effect similar to actual use, wherever it is not certain how this power will be used.

Power over others is desired by most men for two reasons : First, power over another man is as it were reduplication of one's own existence. Instead of one, I have two human organisms at my disposal. I can make the other work and live for me without worrying about his life beyond his utility for me. The second reason is of a more inward nature. Power means also enhancement of value, prestige, whether in my own estimate or in that of others. We therefore understand that men desire power and that few who have it, abstain from using it, whether in the first more objective or in the second more subjective sense.

Power is the more desirable as the goods of this world are already portioned out, because by power this distribution can be changed in favour of the one who has power. That is why a large part of human life is a struggle for power or the use of power in the struggle for goods. This power and its use can take varied shapes. Everything by which the capacity to compel others is increased, can become a means of power : bodily strength and ability ; shrewdness in using one's own superiority in the right place ; possession of things that others must have or desire to have ; these things may be of the most different kind—economic goods or the keys to Heaven—or of the doors to the high places in society or state. It is impossible to separate physical power from spiritual, even with regard to compulsion. The power of the state, for instance, by which it can compel the citizens, is not merely, nor even predominantly, its police and military force which stands behind its commandments, but it is composed of innumerable factors, the sum of which may be called the spiritual authority of the state.

Because power means the ability to compel, it stands at first in opposition to freedom. The power of the one over the other is the dependence of the second upon the first. Power and freedom are related like the convex to the concave. The surplus of freedom of the one, which is power, is the deficit of freedom of the other. Power creates dependence. But not all dependence is created by power, because there is also a dependence due to free will. Furthermore, a dependence created by power may become spontaneous. The good citizen of a good state wants the state to be powerful. He accepts its compulsive power with his free will. The freely chosen leader of a group has power which the group accepts, and is not therefore felt as compulsion. This freely willed power must not be confused with a merely psychic dependence or bondage which is a strange mixture of acceptance and refusal of the power of another.

Because power taken in itself is opposed to freedom, there is a tendency in every society to order and to canalise power in order to limit its danger for the less powerful. The most important means to order power is law, which in itself is nothing but ordered power or order of power. It is a necessity of civilised life that the ultimate use of power, power over the lives of others, should be centralised. This centralisation of ultimate power is the state, or an institution like the state. It originates from the tendency to localise ultimate power in a few hands and to canalise it by certain rules. What we call the state is the centralised monopoly of the exercise of ultimate power. Power, not merely social organisation, is the characteristic essence of the state. The social organisation of society is in itself something quite harmless. The state begins at the moment when this " harmlessness " disappears, *i.e.*, where the state stands behind this social organisation, with its ultimate power, its power over men's lives. This instrument, the state, is necessary as a safeguard of peace, because it is only by this monopolisation of ultimate power that the tendency of men is checked to use their powers to the utmost limit, for their own benefit, to the point of killing. The will-to-power and recklessness in using it is so strong in man that again and again he will not refrain from actual killing. Until this possibility is taken away by monopolisation of this ultimate power by the state, peaceful civilised life cannot develop. In this sense the state is the presupposition of cultural life.

This centralisation of ultimate power in the state, however, is only one step in taming the dangerous power-element. The second step is the ordering of centralised power by law. Ultimate power and the power of the state in general should be exercised only within definite limits, for definite purposes, and in a definite manner. The power of the state should only be used in the service of the life of the people and in defence of their rights. The state must be the guarantee of peace, order and justice. It is clear that the state is not the source of law, but rather its guarantor. The state is the servant of men and not their master. Its *raison d'être* is to protect the lives and the rights of men. That is why the monopoly of ultimate power is given to it. State law is primarily law for the state and not law of the state. State law is limitation and canalisation of the power of the state. We call it public law, in distinction from private law which the power of the state has to protect. It is by public law that society orders and disciplines the dangerous although necessary power of the state, which is monopolised ultimate power.

Private law, however, *i.e.*, law ordering the spheres of individual power, does not originate necessarily or primarily from the state. It precedes the state, but it needs the state for its protection. The rights of individuals and their lawful relation are not created by the state, but they are publicly acknowledged and protected by the coercive power of the state.

A third step, however, is necessary in order to guarantee this purpose of the state. This third step is the plurality of the bearers of power in the state ; what we call the division of power. This explains the creation of Parliament, and this also was the meaning of a much older institution : courts independent of government. The absolute king united all state functions in his person. He was ruler, law-giver and judge. The principle of " division of power " is much older than Montesquieu, but Montesquieu was the first to have clearly recognised its importance. In the people of Israel there already existed a certain division of power: the law was not given by the King, but by God, through prophets and priests, and the King had to obey and to protect this law. The Roman Republic represents a well thought out division of power, which was the result of age-long struggles. Montesquieu's principle *le pouvoir arrête le pouvoir* is the most essential element of a constitutional state as distinguished from absolutism and tyranny.

It would be unfair to claim that this conception of power is exclusively Christian, but it is deeply rooted in Christian faith. The sovereignty of God forbids any human power being made absolute. It excludes both the absolute sovereignty of the state and the absolute sovereignty of the people. All human sovereignty is limited by divine sovereignty and by divine law. Furthermore, the Christian conception of sin reveals the dangers inherent in

N

power. The Christian knows better than anyone else the temptation to the abuse of power. Power is misused whenever it is used against the law of God, and contrary to its God-given purpose.

When St. Paul deduces the power of the state from the divine order and commands Christians to obey it, he is not thinking of the absolute sovereignty of the state or monarch. The divine origin of power is at the same time a divine limitation. According to St. Paul, this limitation is given with the purpose of the state, which is peace and justice. In stressing the power of the sword, as a means of divine revenge, St. Paul gives that interpretation of the state as monopolised ultimate power, which we have just outlined. By this reference to the power of the sword, the state is not reduced to a police function, as has often been said. This reference to the sword is merely an expression of biblical realism. It shows that the monopoly of ultimate power is the very essence of the state, as the basis of peaceful civilised life. This conception of the state and of power is the correlate of the biblical conception of sin. Wherever the power of sin and the temptation to sin belonging to power is seen, it becomes impossible to understand the state as merely social organisation, as is the case on the basis of an optimistic understanding of man as good.

The concentration and canalisation of power in the state is more important the greater are the conglomerations of power within society. Society does not consist of individuals merely, but of groups, some of which wield tremendous power. In our capitalist age there are concentrations of financial and industrial power, compared with which the individual is powerless. The credit system combined with industrialisation has produced an accumulation of economic power unknown in previous times : it is that which is called " big business," mammoth corporations controlling hundreds of thousands of men and enormous capital, capable of limiting the freedom of all these hundreds of thousands, of controlling the economic life and welfare of whole nations and influencing the state machinery to a dangerously high degree. By their more or less monopolistic character, they exert coercive power almost like that of the state. But this is only one side of the picture. On the other side, we see accumulations of power created by organisation of those who individually are powerless, i.e., the tremendous power of Trade Unions, which in some countries are at least equal in power to their capitalist counterparts. Experience has proved that large numbers of men combined by organisation are equal in power to large numbers of dollars, and, in the long run, even superior. The development of these two concentrations of power breeds a new danger. These colossæ, both business corporations and Trade Unions, have become, so to speak, " states " within the state, being capable of challenging the authority of the state and thereby endangering the primary purpose of the state. The purpose of the state is to serve the interests of all. Those economic mammoth organisations, however, are so powerful that they are able to force the state to do their will. This situation explains in part why so many people want to strengthen the economic power of the state, and are calling for a general state-control and even nationalisation of economy.

The last decades, however, have confronted us with a phenomenon more dangerous than any other, for freedom and general welfare—the totalitarian state. The stronger the state, the more dangerous its power. The whole constitutional, democratic and liberal movement had sprung from the desire to combat the danger lying in state absolutism. At that time, state absolutism was represented by the absolute monarch. Parliament and constitutional government were an effective attempt to bridle it. Monarchy has either disappeared or been eliminated as the bearer of power. The democratic principle of the sovereignty of the people has conquered the western world.

It is, however, only now that we are beginning to see that this sovereignty of the people, manifesting itself in the election of government by the people, is not in itself a safe guarantee against a new kind of state absolutism. It is possible to conceive a totalitarian state on a democratic basis. To think of democracy and totalitarianism as opposites is just as wrong as to identify totalitarianism with dictatorship. Totalitarianism of the state is not a form of government. The form of a state decides how and by whom political power is to be wielded. Totalitarianism, however, means the extension of political power to life as a whole. The nationalisation of economy is the decisive step towards this totality of political control over life as a whole. If neither individuals nor groups have independent economic means they have no real political freedom. If everyone is a functionary of the state, and if nobody can make his living independent of the state machinery, if the Press, the cinema, the wireless, are state

controlled, if there are no other schools but state schools, the free
society is lost, opposition and the public expression of independent
opinion become impossible. Every deviation from the programme
of the state becomes rebellion and sabotage. Even if this state has
the democratic form, *i.e.*, government elected by the majority vote
of the people, it amounts to a complete suppression of liberty ;
it will not be long, before even the so-called " free election "
becomes illusory, because the state machinery controls all the
means of propaganda.

Compared with this modern totalitarian state, the absolute
monarchy of old times looks harmless. Private property of
individuals and groups and the absence of state-controlled
education and public opinion left a considerable area open for
free disposition. In the totalitarian state, however, this space
for free decision hardly exists and therefore a free development
of cultural life is almost totally excluded, for cultural self-
expression is dependent on material means. But all these
material means are in the hands of the state. To take one
example : if the state decides who is to get the paper available
for printing, would you believe that an opposition Press could
exist ? The state even controls the time of every individual
citizen. No one could say : I prefer to earn less in order to have
time for this or that cultural, moral or religious activity. State
economy can exist only if it has complete control of the working
time of everybody. It dictates almost entirely on what things
money may or may not be spent. It not only controls schools
and universities, but also the schools and exhibitions of art, it
controls the theatre, all the actors being state employees. In
theory it is not forbidden to do whatever you like outside of the
state ; so long as it does not cost anything and needs no material
controlled by the state. All this means that totalitarianism,
even at its best, is the grave of freedom.

Furthermore, even a democratic totalitarian state must
necessarily degenerate, because state power is unlimited. It
produces an all-powerful bureaucracy of functionaries and a semi-
militaristic hierarchy. This hierarchy necessarily leads to a
supreme Ruler. The principle of the division of powers becomes an illusion. Its place is taken by the rivalry of the
different sections of the state machinery, but all of them are
hanging from one and the same pinnacle of the bureaucratic
hierarchy. The democratic fiction will still be preserved whilst

actually there is a tyrannical dictatorship. In all this we are not describing merely one of the totalitarian systems of the present time ; all these are the necessary inevitable results of complete nationalisation of economy. We have seen during war-time how—whether we like it or not—war-time economy produces almost all of these worst features of totalitarianism, secret police, administrative jurisdiction, control of public opinion, etc., and that, even within states of solid democratic tradition and of intact democratic institutions, complete nationalisation of economy is militarisation of the state.

For all these reasons the totalitarian state, being the absolute maximum of accumulated power, is the worst and most dangerous social evil which we can conceive. It is the very devil of our time. Whatever analogies totalitarianism may have had in previous centuries, real totalitarianism became possible only in our age, where the techniques of production and transport, the aeroplane, the wireless and the machine-gun made state power omnipresent, all powerful and all pervasive.

Now we have to turn to a last no less gloomy aspect of the power problem, the power relation between the states. Mankind has somehow succeeded in eliminating the most destructive effects of power within a given territory by concentrating ultimate power in the state. It has succeeded, furthermore, in bridling the power of the state itself by law and the constitutional division of power. But now the formation of the powerful states has created a new problem : the struggle for power between the states, endangering the life and freedom of humanity. Thus far, all attempts to bring the power relations of the states under the control of justice and humanitarian interests have been almost without effect.

It may be said that at a time when the divine law and the moral order exerted considerable influence over the nations and their rulers, this purely spiritual limitation of power exerted a certain smoothing and muffling influence. The states, however ruthless in their international behaviour, did not quite do everything lying within their power. By treaties, they created a certain kind of international law which proved effective to a certain extent, although its effects were limited because the treaties could not be enforced. They created institutions of international justice and peace like the Permanent Court of International Justice at The Hague, and the League of Nations which to a certain extent eliminated the use of power by law.

But these institutions proved incapable of solving the most important and dangerous conflicts arising from the dynamic character of history because they were limited by the principle of the sovereignty of the individual states. The League of Nations certainly was an attempt to limit individual state sovereignty by a supra-national federal structure. This attempt, however, proved futile, because the great powers did not really intend to abandon their sovereignty to the will of the federation, and because some of the most powerful states were not members of the League. Horrified by the disastrous results of the second world war, the nations made a second attempt in the same direction in forming the United Nations. Although a few years only have elapsed since its formation, it must be admitted that this second attempt has also failed, so far as the present is concerned. The condition of international anarchy, therefore, still prevails, which leaves the feeble nation at the mercy of the powerful and which threatens humanity with a new conflagration that, should it become a reality, would most probably mean the end of human civilisation.

There remains the question of a world state. Why should it not be possible to overcome international anarchy in the way in which it has been overcome within a given territory by the little Swiss or by the big American federation, which combine regional autonomy with the overarching supremacy of the federation? Apart from the fact that at present such a proposal is purely academic, the question remains whether such a universal world state having the monopoly of ultimate power would not be the greatest danger for freedom and higher culture. Only a federal structure combined with a strict division of powers would prevent it from degenerating into tyranny. A centralised non-federative world state, or, if I may use the phrase, a monolithic world state, would necessarily become a power monster of totalitarian character, whilst a federative structure always includes a certain risk for the peace of the world.

A truly Christian solution of the power problem from the economic, political or international point of view, does not seem to be a realistic prospect. The ideal of a reign of peace and justice in which the lust for power would not only be tamed, but overcome from within, is not possible in a world of sinful men. Either we believe that within this temporal world sin, lust for power, can be overcome, or we do not see that real peace is irreconcilable with sin. Both these views contradict the Christian conception of man and history. Because as Christians we see the close connection between power and sin, we accept St. Paul's idea, that only by monopolised ultimate power, *i.e.*, by the state, can sinful anarchy be overcome. Whether it will be possible some time to overcome the anarchy between the powerful states themselves by subordinating them to a super-power without endangering justice and freedom, we cannot know, although we may hope for it.

In spite of all this, we cannot follow Jakob Burckhardt in his *Weltgeschichtliche Betrachtungen*, who opposes power to culture and makes culture, so to speak, the innocent martyr of power. How often did it happen that the most generous patrons of science and arts have been also most ruthless in their power politics, misusing their power ! It is not culture, it is only respect for justice, love and reverence for the divine law, which are capable of overcoming the lust for, and the misuse of power. It is only that mind which rather would suffer injustice than do it which is willing to " overcome evil with good " which is capable of resisting the temptation even of very great power. The greater the power, the greater the temptation of being godlike. Against this temptation no education or culture can prevail. The " demonism " of power is overcome by Jesus Christ alone. Therefore the most important thing that can be done at any time against the evil effects of the power motive, is the spreading and deepening of true Christian discipleship. The most dreadful thing, however, is the will to power in a Christian camouflage of which occidental history is full. If anywhere, it is here that we can see the cunning of the devilish power taking the shape of an angel of light, and in so doing, hiding the one who alone is capable of driving out the spirit of power.

(b) THE WORLD OF POWER

Kenneth G. Grubb

I

It is a cause of general apprehension that the world is the scene of the existence and possession of excessive power, and men's minds are dominated by the fear of it. There are many forms of power, and the word itself is used in many different senses.

It is not necessary here to attempt a definition, or to analyse these meanings. Most men, when the word is used in an apprehensive sense, have in mind that sort of power which contains the danger of war. It is with this meaning mainly, but not exclusively, in view, that we have to glance at some of the problems raised by power for the Christian and for all men.

Mainly, but not exclusively. For power in many of its different meanings is a necessary element in human affairs. It is the means of executing authority, and the source of technical progress. In the form of influence, the power of one mind over another, it has moved men to noble action and enduring example. Light on spiritual power, as Christians understand it, the power of the Holy Spirit and the power of God over the ultimate destinies of men, is thrown by the theology of Christianity and by the Bible. But when men speak of power in the political world, and in particular in international relations, they do not have in mind this kind of power. They think of the concentrations of power which will enable small groups of men to coerce the wills and limit the freedom of their fellows. They think also of those manipulations of economic power which deprive men of effective decision about their own lives. They think, also, of the discrepancy between the nations in resources of power, which often dictates their conduct. And, most pervasively of all, they think of all those forms of power which, whatever be their constructive possibilities, clearly imply a readiness, a willingness, or an intention, either to vindicate or to pursue a cause by force. To most men, the final, the supreme act of power, which confers on it its sinister semblance, is the readiness to use force, and to justify power by the success of force. To Christians, the supreme act of power is, in the central Christian paradox, in the weakness of the Cross, the power of God unto salvation.

If the difference between the Christian and the general conception of power is so great, is it possible to define the Christian attitude to power in any terms other than the most hostile? The Church, however, is, in common experience, involved at many points with the world. Christians cannot refuse to come to some terms with the actual existence of power for several necessary reasons. Many of the nations and civilisations that are the large-scale employers of organised power, in the modern sense, are the children of a Christian tradition. The uses of power are not necessarily malevolent, but are very often beneficial. Power is an indispensable concomitant of life : without power love cannot act. The churches are concerned in those aspects of power which construct the social and political order, the power necessary to maintain order and execute the behests of duly constituted authority. The churches have also to consider the relation of power to justice and the acute problems posed by wars which increasingly involve a visitation of destruction for all men, just or unjust.

Political Power

The power of authority, that is of governments, has extended enormously in recent decades. The liberal conception of the function of government as that of keeping order and holding the ring for progressive development and productive inter-play of social and economic forces, has proved inadequate. Accordingly, governments have set themselves the task of social leadership and education. Many of the problems thus raised seem best soluble by some measure of centralisation and uniformity. Inasmuch as authority anyhow tends to favour administrative centralisation for the maintenance of its own prestige, the stage is set for a vast increase of its influence. Behind this development has stood wholly laudable motives of social progress. As that progress has grown, men's conscience and sense of freedom are quickened, and authority has to contain, and benefit from criticism, and at the same time to govern wisely and well. Not always has it been possible to solve this question by a reasonable harmony between order and criticism, and governments have instead increased their own authority, until states which yesterday merely maintained police have to-day become police states. The pace of progress is partly responsible for this, for a due balance between order and freedom requires maturity, and maturity is the fruit of time. Time is of the essence of a rightly ripening and ordered progress, but it is not always available.

The expanding power of political authority has also found expression in empire. Of the modern empires, the British is the most conspicuous example. Yet the conception of imperial power has in general ceased to be attractive to the British mind ; indeed, as a formula, it has never in this century had the attraction of imperial influence. Precisely because the idea of centralisation was absent from its dominant scheme, the idea of power seemed an inappropriate description of its driving motive.

Economic Power

Economic power takes on complex forms : it has had attention in other papers of the World Assembly series[1] and need not receive more than a reminder here. The power of vast corporations is great ; their usual instrument for securing political decisions is not force but influence. Even that influence need not be overtly exercised ; it is usually most penetrative when least felt. The existence of a sufficient aggregation of economic power is sufficient by itself to compel crucial political decisions. This is often wholly right, for man does not live by politics and culture alone, but it may also be undesirable. The feeling that it is undesirable is one of the reasons why economic power is transferred to the state, in the belief that it will be manipulated for the benefit of all. This hope is widely held to be in process of realisation : what is still obscure is not what is gained but what is lost in the process. The state becomes the trading agent of the nation, either as the active promoter and conductor of its business, or as the regulator and guide of its citizens' activities.

Scientific Power

Technical and scientific power has reached enormous development, and volumes have been written on the power of man over nature. Constantly we are told that man's mental stature has outgrown his spiritual : no one seems happy about it, but no one is certain of the next step. It is not only a question of man's control over nature ; but that nature itself is transformed by man, and the transformation, in turn, takes on new forms. Power over nature has found new and unprecedented development through the uses of atomic energy. Power over man himself has been advanced through the control of behaviour by physical and chemical means. It is possible that we are here only on the threshold of developments whose ultimate significance it is impossible not to view with the misgivings derived from initial experience. Yet such is the fascination of power that men will possess it before they can see its uses or envisage any system for its control.

Power in Propaganda

Another use of power is found in the technique of propaganda and the censorship. By the former the mind is fed and by the

[1] See Dr. J. H. Oldham—" Technics and Civilisation," Vol. III, p. 29.

latter the eyes are closed. Those who profess their immunity from propaganda often succumb easily to it, while the suspicion of the existence of propaganda is, among others, an effective inducement to total cynicism. The power of propaganda should be taken seriously by the churches, for the Gospel itself is propagated by preaching, writing and other means. Modern propaganda may finish by defeating its own possibility of success, but not because it has left men capable of a discrimination which goes behind the advertisement, but because it has shouted them into deafness. Meanwhile, it is a powerful instrument in the hands of those who use it ruthlessly and with psychological insight.

The Use and Misuse of Power

Centralised authority, economic organisation, scientific control of nature, and the regulation of public opinion, can be used for peace. But when they are developed together, they form a powerful preparation for war. The classic forms of might, armies, navies and air forces, can also be used for peaceful purposes such as organised relief work, but their primary purpose is war.

National self-consciousness developing into overweening national ambition, sometimes supported by a crusade to impose political forms and doctrines, is an important cause of war. The deep-seated demands and foundations of nationalism cannot be ignored because of the hope of an internationalism which, in the politically effective sense, is still a dream of the future. Nationalistic aspirations may be tribal or economic or imperial or allegedly ideological ; they do not necessarily either grow or decline in proportion to the degree of popular advancement or education. The urge to nationalism in the creation of new " sovereign states " has apparently not yet reached its term. There has been much enthusiasm recently for such development, but every new nationalist state adds to the potential conflicts of national power. Where sources or means of considerable power are controlled by the state, the national cause is easily given an overwhelmingly emotional appeal of honour, and the situation becomes sinister. False, but none the less menacing, concepts of blood and destiny, or the fanaticism of intolerant political convictions, quickly resort to violence and torture for the maintenance of an authority which may be indistinguishable from tyranny, and for the suppression of freedom, criticism and the ability of the people to change the government. At this stage, the problem of power has become acute for the Christian conscience, and only those who have had to experience its effects can properly speak of it.

II

Internationally, it is customary to use such phrases as the " Great Powers," the " Middle Power," " the Balance of Power," " power politics." The idea of power, and the existence of " powers " are inseparable.

The Great Powers are presumably the U.S.A. and the U.S.S.R., and to a lesser degree, in varying gradations, Britain, France and China. Great Powers are such because of their economic resources, fighting strength, possessions, political organisation and certain other considerations. It is not necessary, therefore, that Great Powers should combine and manipulate all the menacing aspects of power described above. Britain has been great through political background and free tradition, imperial expansion and naval strength ; France, for broadly similar reasons but with the emphasis in different places ; the U.S.A. is a Great Power through her extension, economic wealth and political institutions ; the U.S.S.R. through her centralised authority, spectacular administrative and social achievements, and the success of her armies. And so on. These concepts may be remote from the Christian conception of greatness—if there is such which is applicable to the world of nations, but they are the dominant ones in the assumptions of the peoples.

If the desires and policies, legitimate or excessive, of a nation are challenged by others, a settlement may conceivably be reached through arbitration, or through the good offices of the United Nations, but if one of the parties can see their way to superior power, or the issue is hotly contested, war is possible. War is a use of power as a supreme arbitrator among the nations. It is an arbitrator not by the standards of justice, but by its own standards, which is the will and ability of the stronger. Visitors may endeavour to use their conquests justly, but what they win is the right to impose their will. There are some who hold the causes of war to be mainly economic. Others have fought violently against imperial power. Others have taken arms for freedom. The authority and ambition of a few men controlling the instruments of force may commit a nation to war in the name of national honour, to positions from which it has no escape, and the really dangerous wars are those between nations. If the different forms of power are together developed by the state and its policy is challenged, the outcome is likely to be war. But all the instruments of power can be used for good causes or bad and that is true of war. Equally power cannot of itself cause moral advance ; war, even in a good cause, usually hinders it.

In the relations of Great Powers to each other and to lesser powers, arguments of justice may have a place, or ever-dominant national self-interest may be temporarily met by a concession which satisfies honour without yielding substance, but the ultimate sanction is the possession of superior power and the readiness to use it in war. But it is an ultimate, rather than an immediate sanction, for the risks of war are many and its rewards often slight. Power is, therefore, as useful to sustain a bluff as a battle. If a Great Power is great enough, it need not necessarily be bellicose ; if its whip is long, the dogs will not bark. But since power is only decisive when it directs superior force, if one nation is powerful, another will seek to be more so.

Accordingly, it has been argued that the best solution of the problem of power, internationally, is for the world to have a master. That may be so, but it is not practicable to-day. The worst misfortune is for it to have two or three powerful masters, for when they fight the lesser nations will be crushed between them. The best chance of such nations is that one be much better armed than the others, preferably that one whose general outlook agrees with their own fundamental political and moral assumptions, and whose policy most suits their own self-interest. Here again, there is little that is Christian about a world of this kind.

The situation is bad because the Great Powers have become relatively greater ; and the small ones relatively smaller. The massive organisation and supplies needed for modern war can only be compassed by nations of prodigious resources. In such a world, so time-honoured a policy as that of the balance of power, becomes impossible. The enormous technological and scientific equipment required for modern war needs vast wealth and man-power. This is true of the development of atomic energy, and may also be true of other unknown and even more powerful weapons, said to be in preparation. Although scientists have themselves raised their protest, it is unlikely that men will cease from these discoveries, or that they can be limited to peaceful uses. As the world is to-day, the status of a Great Power requires the sanction of superior war potential for the final arbitrament. It is quite obvious that there is no reason to assume that by the use of this sanction anything other than power, for example, justice, is vindicated or advanced. Indeed, power, used as force, is most likely to breed a greater concentration of power.

The discovery of nuclear energy has deepened the problem. At present it seems that only Great Powers, or powers possessed of considerable economic and technical resources, will be able to develop atomic energy on any scale in the near future, especially for the purpose of war. The distance between Great Powers and others is, therefore, increased. That the United Nations should have come into existence at the time when the first atomic bombs were dropped ought to have been regarded as a last chance offered to mankind. In fact, no progress has been made towards effective control. Whatever be the responsibility for the dropping of the bombs, it may be questioned whether a government could, under the circumstances, be expected to go any further than the United States has at the United Nations. The Federal Council of Churches in the U.S.A. stated, some two years ago, that " our nation, having first used the atomic bomb, has a primary duty to reverse the trend which it began." But at present it seems likely that a discovery which ought to enrich the nations will be so handled as to reduce the peoples to poverty and fear.

The Christian attitude to war has not been rendered any easier by recent developments of destructiveness, and Christians are still divided about the issues. There are those who would agree with Machiavelli that " that war is just which is necessary ; and those arms are merciful when no hope exists save in them." Many will feel that an even more earnest concentration by Christians on the causes of war and their removal is possible and urgent. " War consisteth not in battle only, or the act of fighting ; but in a tract of time, wherein the will to contend by battle is sufficiently known. . . . So the nature of war consisteth not in actual fighting ; but in the known disposition thereto, during all the time there is no assurance to the contrary. All other time is Peace " (Hobbes). If the defence of justice is justification for war, it is not a crucial point whether the war be between states, or civil war. There are many who hold that revolution for the overthrow of tyranny is justifiable to the Christian conscience. Those who attach a universal significance to the methods of non-violence practised by Gandhi would say that it is not. But it is also legitimate to doubt whether modern tyrannies of power can be overthrown by such means.

It is instructive to note what the Oxford Conference has said on this matter : " The necessity for the use of force, however difficult and morally questionable it may be, must be admitted in principle, since without it the State would not be able to maintain the system of law and order which it protects. But there is much well-grounded difference of opinion on the question whether certain kinds of force are, under all circumstances, forbidden to the Christian, and at what point, in concrete instances, the line should be drawn ; these differences come out particularly clearly in the attitude to war. But, in spite of these differences, there is a settled Christian conviction that the use of force, however unavoidable it may be for the fulfilment of the distinctive tasks of the State, is in itself absolutely opposed to the commandment of love. It can only be used as the lesser of two evils in reliance on divine forgiveness. It is, therefore, part of the political responsibility of the community to watch the ends for which the State uses its power, and also to see that the use of force is reduced to a minimum. Further, it should be insisted that the exercise of force, apart from exceptional instances of extreme emergency, should take place within the framework of generally accepted law, and should remain the exclusive monopoly of the organs of the State, in order that it should not become the instrument either of caprice or of the private and collective lust of power."[1]

So long as the fear of overwhelming reprisal is the best deterrent to war, there is a strong argument for restricting the use of the atomic bomb to those who now have it. But there is no good reason to suppose that such restriction will remain possible. The majority of Christians will perhaps recognise the legitimacy even of atomic war for a just cause, but the assumption that civilisation can be thus defended must be abandoned. It will be destroyed. Nevertheless, those who believe in the

[1] *The Churches Survey Their Task :* The Report of the Conference at Oxford, July 1937, on Church, Community and State, pp. 262, 263.

defence of justice at all costs will be slow to weaken the hands of
governments by non-participation in war. Others will take the
opposite view. " We do not believe," stated the Commission of
the British Council of Churches on the Era of Atomic Power,
" that the Church is able with its present insight to pronounce
between the two alternatives. It must throw the shield of its
protection and sympathy over those who make either choice.
Each is the expression of loyalty to one side of Christian obligation. The one is a response to the claims of what presents itself
as a moral absolute, and to an instinctive conviction that the
future of the Church as the Body of Christ cannot be staked in a
conflict in which there is no place left for mercy and the individual person counts for nothing at all. For those who make this
choice the end of citizenship has come, since society has taken a
course in which no Christian meaning can be found. The other
decision is an attempt to discharge in the most desperate of
situations the obligation which by God's appointment men owe
to temporal order ; for those who make it the greatness of the
crisis is a crowning reason why citizenship should be affirmed."

The competence of the United Nations in the control of
atomic energy has yet to be tested. Even if agreement were
reached on one Atomic Development Authority, there remain
formidable obstacles. The Authority would only be effective
if national sovereignty were surrendered to an extent which no
nation has hitherto accepted, and surrendered to an international authority in the effectiveness of which no nation can at
this stage be confident. Ideally, the stage is set for action. The
United Nations is a more fully representative international body
than any that has previously existed. It has been created
precisely at the time when the uses and dangers of atomic energy
have made a vivid impression on the conscience of mankind. It
is right, therefore, that Christian influence should be directed
to the support of its authority and prestige. In the long run,
it should be possible to build up a moral influence through the
United Nations which will be expressed in official decisions and
pronouncements, but will depend for its effectiveness on the
general attitude of the majority of its members.

Throughout history there have been attempts at peaceful
international co-operation. The League of Nations was the best
organised, most far-reaching, least successful and least durable.
Its efforts were supplemented by a host of international instru-

ments, regional arrangements and treaties. Most were mainly ineffective. It is certainly arguable, on this record, that one of the failures has not been the concoction of pacts but the readiness to enter into them too lightly. It is also true that certain uses of power in war, such as gas, have not been revived, and that the horror of an instrument of mass massacre may cause a universal revulsion from it. The relative relationships of the powers of attack and defence must, however, be weighed before gathering any comfort from this argument, and as a long struggle deepens, men will embrace what they profess to abhor.

If the failures of the past be taken with the misgivings of the present, it seems to be the wrong moment for elaborate schemes of international control of atomic power. Such schemes involve sacrifices by the nations of precedent and constitutional authority that they are not prepared to face. They ask for a confidence in the control itself that they are unwilling to give. They demand an understanding and trust in one another that only folly can suppose to exist. For the present, even if it is a situation which is bound to break down, it is better and safer that the matter should be left in the hands of the United States.

It remains to ask whether the relations between the powers, great or small, can be conceived in terms more satisfactory than those of " power politics." This depends on whether the nations can be persuaded that they have common interests and obligations which are essential to their survival. If they have common interests which they believe to be not incompatible with their self-interest, the chances of a conflict of force are greatly reduced. But it is not possible to hold and realise such common interests without some acceptance of common obligations.

The tradition of Natural Law at one time supplied first a common interest in Europe, and subsequently a source for the conception of international law. It failed to maintain its hold when the idea of progress took vigorous possession of men's minds and has never been effectively restored. Perhaps the most pervasive common interest to-day is in the desire for security. It is a most important interest to meet, because until nations enjoy security they rarely indulge in morality. In national life, morality results from having margins to spare. It is a luxury which is not afforded by nations which are struggling for exist-ence, and which imagine themselves to be thwarted and baffled in what they hold to be their legitimate ambitions. Nations

o

which are strong and prosperous have frequently some morality to spare. But if a desire for security is a common interest, it may not of itself be of decisive importance. It does not follow that if a nation were truly and finally assured of security it would be content with its present position and influence.

To some, war seems the worst of all evils. To others, violence in a just cause is better than a state of deception and perfidy, torture and persecution. But modern war itself by its scale and the methods it employs, by its own destructiveness and deception, does not necessarily cure these evils—or rather it may cure a disease to create an epidemic. Nevertheless, the view of fighting which tends to regard it as a supreme wickedness is strange to many Christian minds, and to the history of the Church. It is bad, but there are worse evils. What seems certain is that it cannot be isolated from other evils and eradicated alone. The object of peace is not to make a world safe for covetousness, coercion or unrestricted indulgence. They err who hope to equate the evasion of war with the attainment of pleasure.

Meanwhile, the Churches would be well advised to consider their own strategy and relationship in regard to the situations likely to be created by war. These things should, as far as possible, be planned in advance. This is not a counsel of despair, but one aspect of a reasonable common sense. At the same time, it is not right to forget that power is also being used to-day for beneficent ends ; that, although frustration dulls the edge of high endeavour, yet purpose, pursued by right means for right ends, in and through the strength of God, does not always fail of fulfilment. The ministries of love, even in the presence of war, are not done in vain. Self-deception must be avoided, but despair has no final justification for the Church. Above all, men have yet to learn to tread the hard path of humiliation and confession of need for forgiveness and to throw themselves on the mercy of God.

MEMBERSHIP OF ASSEMBLY COMMISSION IV ON "THE CHURCH AND THE INTERNATIONAL DISORDER"

(The Commission consists in part of members of the permanent Commission of the Churches on International Affairs. The list includes only those members of Assembly Commission IV who were appointed before the volume went to press.)

MR. KENNETH G. GRUBB, London *(Executive Chairman)*
PROFESSOR O. FREDERICK NOLDE, New York *(Director)*
PROFESSOR H. S. ALIVISATOS, Athens
PROFESSOR BARON F. M. VAN ASBECK, Leyden
THE REV. C. BAETA, Gold Coast
SR. A. BAROCIO, Mexico City
PROFESSOR F. BEDNAR, Prague
PROFESSOR N. BERDYAEV, Paris (Deceased)
THE RT. REV. EIVIND BERGGRAV, Norway
PROFESSOR G. W. BROWN, Toronto
THE RT. REV. THE LORD BISHOP OF CHICHESTER, England
THE RT. REV. JOHN CULLBERG, Wästerås, Sweden
MR. JOHN FOSTER DULLES, New York
PROFESSOR J. L. HROMADKA, Prague
DR. C. L. HSIA, China
PROFESSOR WERNER KAEGI, Zürich
MR. JOHANNES LEIMENA, Java
DR. RAJAH B. MANIKAM, Nagpur
REV. W. MENN, Frankfurt
S. A. MORRISON, Esq., Cairo
THE RT. REV. G. A. OLDHAM, Albany, N.Y.
DR. G. PAIK, Korea
MRS. A. A. PEREZ, Philippines
MR. W. F. RENNIE, New York
PROFESSOR R. SMEND, Göttingen
THE RT. REV. J. SZERUDA, Warsaw
MRS. L. E. SWAIN, Craigwill-on-Cape Cod, Mass.

INDEX

(a) Subjects

FIRST ASSEMBLY OF THE
WORLD COUNCIL OF CHURCHES

MESSAGE

THE World Council of Churches, meeting at Amsterdam, sends this message of greeting to all who are in Christ, and to all who are willing to hear.

We bless God our Father, and our Lord Jesus Christ Who gathers together in one the children of God that are scattered abroad. He has brought us here together at Amsterdam. We are one in acknowledging Him as our God and Saviour. We are divided from one another not only in matters of faith, order and tradition, but also by pride of nation, class and race. But Christ has made us His own, and He is not divided. In seeking Him we find one another. Here at Amsterdam we have committed ourselves afresh to Him, and have covenanted with one another in constituting this World Council of Churches. We intend to stay together. We call upon Christian congregations everywhere to endorse and fulfil this covenant in their relations one with another. In thankfulness to God we commit the future to Him.

When we look to Christ, we see the world as it is—His world, to which He came and for which He died. It is filled both with great hopes and also with disillusionment and despair. Some nations are rejoicing in new freedom and power, some are bitter because freedom is denied them, some are paralysed by division, and everywhere there is an undertone of fear. There are millions who are hungry, millions who have no home, no country, and no hope. Over all mankind hangs the peril of total war. We have to accept God's judgment upon us for our share in the world's guilt. Often we have tried to serve God and mammon, put other loyalties before loyalty to Christ, confused the Gospel with our own economic or national or racial interests, and feared war more than we have hated it. As we have talked with each other here, we have begun to understand how our separation has prevented us from receiving correction from one another in Christ. And because we lacked this correction, the world has often heard from us not the Word of God but the words of men.

But there is a word of God for our world. It is that the world is in the hands of the living God, Whose will for it is wholly good; that in Christ Jesus, His incarnate Word, Who lived and died and rose from the dead, God has broken the power of evil once for all, and opened for everyone the gate into freedom and joy in the Holy Spirit; that the final judgment on all human history and on every human deed is the judgment of the merciful Christ; and that the end of history will be the triumph of His Kingdom, where alone we shall understand how much God has loved the world. This is God's unchanging Word to the world. Millions of our fellow-men have never heard it. As we are met here from many lands, we pray God to stir up His whole Church to make this Gospel known to the whole world, and to call on all men to believe in Christ, to live in His love and to hope for His coming.

Our coming together to form a World Council will be vain unless Christians and Christian congregations everywhere commit themselves to the Lord of the Church in a new effort to seek together, where they live, to be His witnesses and servants among their neighbours. We have to remind ourselves and all men that God has put down the mighty from their seats and exalted the humble and meek. We have to learn afresh together to speak boldly in Christ's name both to those in power and to the people, to oppose terror, cruelty and race discrimination, to stand by the outcast, the prisoner and the refugee. We have to make of the Church in every place a voice for those who have no voice, and a home where every man will be at home. We have to learn afresh together what is the duty of the Christian man or woman in industry, in agriculture, in politics, in the professions and in the home. We have to ask God to teach us together to say No and to say Yes in truth. No, to all that flouts the love of Christ, to every system, every programme and every person that treats any man as though he were an irresponsible thing or a means of profit, to the defenders of injustice in the name of order, to those who sow the seeds of war or urge war as inevitable ; Yes, to all that conforms to the love of Christ, to all who seek for justice, to the peacemakers, to all who hope, fight and suffer for the cause of man, to all who—even without knowing it—look for new heavens and a new earth wherein dwelleth righteousness.

It is not in man's power to banish sin and death from the earth, to create the unity of the Holy Catholic Church, to conquer the hosts of Satan. But it is within the power of God. He has given us at Easter the certainty that His purpose will be accomplished. But, by our acts of obedience and faith, we can on earth set up signs which point to the coming victory. Till the day of that victory our lives are hid with Christ in God, and no earthly disillusion or distress or power of hell can separate us from Him. As those who wait in confidence and joy for their deliverance, let us give ourselves to those tasks which lie to our hands, and so set up signs that men may see.

Now unto Him that is able to do exceeding abundantly above all that we ask or think, according to the power that worketh in us, unto Him be glory in the Church by Christ Jesus, throughout all ages, world without end.

REPORT OF SECTION IV

THE CHURCH AND THE INTERNATIONAL DISORDER

Received unanimously by the Assembly and commended to the churches for their serious consideration and appropriate action

THE World Council of Churches is met in its first assembly at a time of critical international strain. The hopes of the recent war years and the apparent dawn of peace have been dashed. No adequate system for effecting peaceful change has been established, despite the earnest desire of millions. In numerous countries, human rights are being trampled under foot and liberty denied by political or economic systems. Exhaustion and disillusionment have combined with spiritual apathy to produce a moral vacuum which will be filled, either by Christian faith or by despair or even hatred. Men are asking in fear and dismay what the future holds.

The churches bear witness to all mankind that the world is in God's hands. His purpose may be thwarted and delayed, but it cannot be finally frustrated. This is the meaning of history which forbids despair or surrender to the fascinating belief in power as a solvent of human trouble.

War, being a consequence of the disregard of God, is not inevitable if man will turn to Him in repentance and obey His law. There is, then, no irresistible tide that is carrying man to destruction. Nothing is impossible with God.

While we know that wars sometimes arise from immediate causes which Christians seem unable to influence, we need not work blindly or alone. We are labourers together with God, Who in Christ has given us the way of overcoming demonic forces in history. Through the churches, working together under His power, a fellowship is being developed which rises above those barriers of race, colour, class and nation that now set men against each other in conflict.

Every person has a place in the Divine purpose. Created by God in His image, the object of His redeeming love in Christ, he must be free to respond to God's calling. God is not indifferent to misery or deaf to human prayer and aspiration. By accepting His

Gospel, men will find forgiveness for all their sins and receive power to transform their relations with their fellow men.

Herein lies our hope and the ground of all our striving. It is required of us that we be faithful and obedient. The event is with God. Thus every man may serve the cause of peace, confident that—no matter what happens—he is neither lost nor futile, for the Lord God Omnipotent reigneth.

In this confidence we are one in proclaiming to all mankind:

I. WAR IS CONTRARY TO THE WILL OF GOD

War as a method of settling disputes is incompatible with the teaching and example of our Lord Jesus Christ. The part which war plays in our present international life is a sin against God and a degradation of man. We recognise that the problem of war raises especially acute issues for Christians today. Warfare has greatly changed. War is now total, and every man and woman is called for mobilisation in war service. Moreover, the immense use of air forces and the discovery of atomic and other new weapons render widespread and indiscriminate destruction inherent in the whole conduct of modern war in a sense never experienced in past conflicts. In these circumstances the tradition of a just war, requiring a just cause and the use of just means, is now challenged. Law may require the sanction of force, but when war breaks out, force is used on a scale which tends to destroy the basis on which law exists.

Therefore the inescapable question arises—can war now be an act of justice ? We cannot answer this question unanimously, but three broad positions are maintained:

(1) There are those who hold that, even though entering a war may be a Christian's duty in particular circumstances, modern warfare, with its mass destruction, can never be an act of justice.

(2) In the absence of impartial supra-national institutions, there are those who hold that military action is the ultimate sanction of the rule of law, and that citizens must be distinctly taught that it is their duty to defend the law by force if necessary.

(3) Others, again, refuse military service of all kinds, convinced that an absolute witness against war and for peace is for them the will of God, and they desire that the Church should speak to the same effect.

We must frankly acknowledge our deep sense of perplexity in face of these conflicting opinions, and urge upon all Christians the duty of wrestling continuously with the difficulties they raise and a praying humbly for God's guidance. We believe that there is a special call to theologians to consider the theological problems involved. In the meantime, the churches must continue to hold within their full fellowship all who sincerely profess such viewpoints as those set out above, and are prepared to submit themselves to the will of God in the light of such guidance as may be vouchsafed to them.

On certain points of principle all are agreed. In the absence of any impartial agency for upholding justice, nations have gone to war in the belief that they were doing so. We hold that in international as in national life justice must be upheld. Nations must suppress their desire to save " face." This derives from pride, as unworthy as it is dangerous. The churches, for their part, have the duty of declaring those moral principles which obedience to God requires in war as in peace. They must not allow their spiritual and moral resources to be used by the State in war or in peace as a means of propagating an ideology or supporting a cause in which they cannot whole-heartedly concur. They must teach the duty of love and prayer for the enemy in time of war and of reconciliation between victor and vanquished after the war.

The churches must also attack the causes of war by promoting peaceful change and the pursuit of justice. They must stand for the maintenance of good faith and the honouring of the pledged word; resist the pretensions of imperialist power; promote the multilateral reduction of armaments; and combat indifference and despair in the face of the futility of war; they must point Christians to that spiritual resistance which grows from settled convictions widely held, themselves a powerful deterrent to war. A moral vacuum inevitably invites an aggressor.

We call upon the governments of those countries which were victors in the second world war to hasten the making of just peace treaties with defeated nations, allowing them to rebuild their political and economic systems for peaceable purposes; promptly to return prisoners of war to their homes; and to bring purges and trials for war crimes to a rapid end.

2. PEACE REQUIRES AN ATTACK ON THE CAUSES OF CONFLICT BETWEEN THE POWERS

The greatest threat to peace today comes from the division of the world into mutually suspicious and antagonistic blocs. This threat is all the greater because national tensions are confused by the clash of economic and political systems. Christianity cannot be equated with any of these. There are elements in all systems which we must condemn when they contravene the first Commandment, infringe basic human rights, and contain a potential threat to peace. We denounce all forms of tyranny, economic, political or religious, which deny liberty to men. We utterly oppose totalitarianism, wherever found, in which a State arrogates to itself the right of determining men's thoughts and actions instead of recognising the right of each individual to do God's will according to his conscience. In the same way we oppose any church which seeks to use the power of the State to enforce religious conformity. We resist all endeavours to spread a system of thought or of economics by unscrupulous intolerance, suppression or persecution.

Similarly, we oppose aggressive imperialism—political, economic or cultural—whereby a nation seeks to use other nations or peoples for its own ends. We therefore protest against the exploitation of non-self-governing peoples for selfish purposes; the retarding of their progress towards self-government; and discrimination or segregation on the ground of race or colour.

A positive attempt must be made to ensure that competing economic systems such as communism, socialism, or free enterprise may co-exist without leading to war. No nation has the moral right to determine its own economic policy without consideration for the economic needs of other nations and without recourse to international consultation. The churches have a responsibility to educate men to rise above the limitations of their national outlook and to view economic and political differences in the light of the Christian objective of ensuring to every man freedom from all economic or political bondage. Such systems exist to serve men, not men to serve them.

Christians must examine critically all actions of governments which increase tension or arouse misunderstanding, even unintentionally. Above all, they should withstand everything in the press, radio or school which inflames hatred or hostility between nations.

3. THE NATIONS OF THE WORLD MUST ACKNOWLEDGE THE RULE OF LAW

Our Lord Jesus Christ taught that God, the Father of all, is Sovereign. We affirm, therefore, that no State may claim absolute sovereignty, or make laws without regard to the commandments of God and the welfare of mankind. It must accept its responsibility under the governance of God, and its subordination to law, within the society of nations.

As within the nations, so in their relations with one another, the authority of law must be recognised and established. International law clearly requires international institutions for its effectiveness. These institutions, if they are to command respect and obedience of nations, must come to grips with international problems on their own merits and not primarily in the light of national interests.

Such institutions are urgently needed today. History never stands still. New forces constantly emerge. Sporadic conflicts East and West, the attainment of independence by large masses of people, the apparent decline of European predominance, the clash of competing systems in Asia, all point to the inevitability of change. The United Nations was designed to assist in the settlement of difficulties and to promote friendly relations among the nations. Its purposes in these respects deserve the support of Christians. But unless the nations surrender a greater measure of national sovereignty in the interest of the common good, they will be tempted to have recourse to war in order to enforce their claims.

The churches have an important part in laying that common foundation of moral conviction without which any system of law will break down. While pressing for more comprehensive and authoritative world organisation, they should at present support immediate practical steps for fostering mutual understanding and goodwill among the nations, for promoting respect for international law and the establishment of the international institutions which are now possible. They should also support every effort to deal on a universal basis with the many specific questions of international concern which face mankind today, such as the use of atomic power, the multilateral reduction of armaments, and the provision of health services and food for all men. They should endeavour to secure that the United Nations be further developed to serve such purposes. They should insist that the domestic laws of each country conform to the principles of progressive international law, and they gratefully recognise that recent demands to formulate principles of human rights reflect a new sense of international responsibility for the rights and freedoms of all men.

P

4. THE OBSERVANCE OF HUMAN RIGHTS AND FUNDAMENTAL FREEDOMS SHOULD BE ENCOURAGED BY DOMESTIC AND INTERNATIONAL ACTION

The Church has always demanded freedom to obey God rather than men. We affirm that all men are equal in the sight of God and that the rights of men derive directly from their status as the children of God. It is presumptuous for the State to assume that it can grant or deny fundamental rights. It is for the State to embody these rights in its own legal system and to ensure their observance in practice. We believe, however, that there are no rights without duties. Man's freedom has its counterpart in man's responsibility, and each person has a responsibility towards his fellows in community.

We are profoundly concerned by evidence from many parts of the world of flagrant violations of human rights. Both individuals and groups are subjected to persecution and discrimination on grounds of race, colour, religion, culture or political conviction. Against such actions, whether of governments, officials, or the general public, the churches must take a firm and vigorous stand, through local action, in co-operation with churches in other lands, and through international institutions of legal order. They must work for an ever wider and deeper understanding of what are the essential human rights if men are to be free to do the will of God.

At the present time, churches should support every endeavour to secure within an international bill of rights adequate safeguards for freedom of religion and conscience, including rights of all men to hold and change their faith, to express it in worship and practice, to teach and persuade others, and to decide on the religious education of their children. They should press for freedom of speech and expression, of association and assembly, the rights of the family, of freedom from arbitrary arrest, as well as all those other rights which the true freedom of man requires. In the domestic and in the international sphere, they should support a fuller realisation of human freedom through social legislation. They should protest against the expulsion of minorities. With all the resources at their disposal they should oppose enforced segregation on grounds of race or colour, working for the progressive recognition and application of this principle in every country. Above all it is essential that the churches observe these fundamental rights in their own membership and life, thus giving to others an example of what freedom means in practice.

5. THE CHURCHES AND ALL CHRISTIAN PEOPLE HAVE OBLIGATIONS IN THE FACE OF INTERNATIONAL DISORDER

The churches are guilty both of indifference and of failure. While they desire more open honesty and less self-righteousness among governments and all concerned with international relations, they cannot cast a first stone or excuse themselves for complacency.

Therefore, it is the duty of the Christian to pray for all men, especially for those in authority; to combat both hatred, and resignation in regard to war; to support negotiation rather than primary reliance upon arms as an instrument of policy; and to sustain such national policies as in his judgment best reflect Christian principles. He should respond to the demand of the Christian vocation upon his life as a citizen, make sacrifices for the hungry and homeless, and, above all, win men for Christ, and thus enlarge the bounds of the supra-national fellowship.

Within this fellowship, each church must eliminate discrimination among its members on unworthy grounds. It must educate them to view international policies in the light of their faith. Its witness to the moral law must be a warning to the State against unnecessary concession to expediency, and it must support leaders and those in authority in their endeavour to build the sure foundations of just world order.

The establishment of the World Council of Churches can be made of great moment for the life of the nations. It is a living expression of this fellowship, transcending race and nation, class and culture, knit together in faith, service and understanding. Its aim will be to hasten international reconciliation through its own members and through the co-operation of all Christian churches and of all men of goodwill. It will strive to see international differences in the light of God's design, remembering that normally there are Christians on both sides of every frontier. It should not weary in the effort to state the Christian understanding of the will of God and to promote its application to national and international policy.

For these purposes special agencies are needed. To this end the World Council of Churches and the International Missionary

Council have formed the Commission of the Churches on International Affairs. The Assembly commends it to the interest and prayers of all Christian people.

Great are the tasks and fateful the responsibilities laid on Christians today. In our own strength we can do nothing; but our hope is in Christ and in the coming of His Kingdom. With Him is the victory and in Him we trust. We pray that we may be strengthened by the power of His might and used by Him for accomplishing His design among the nations. For He is the Prince of Peace and the Risen and Living Head of the Church.

RESOLUTION

WHEREAS the uprooted peoples of Europe and Asia are far more numerous than at the close of the war, and whereas this problem constitutes a challenge to the Christian conscience
IT IS RESOLVED :

(i) That the World Council of Churches give high priority to work for the material and spiritual welfare of refugees; and appeal to its member churches in countries capable of receiving any settlers, both to influence public opinion towards a liberal immigration policy and to welcome and care for those who arrive in their countries.

This priority in work for the material and spiritual welfare of refugees includes not only those within the care of the International Refugee Organisation and refugees of German ethnic origin, but all refugees and expellés of whatever nationality.

Especial attention should be given to the needs of children, particularly in countries where children have been severed from family care.

(ii) That the International Refugee Organisation, in pursuance of its task of resettling refugees, be requested to continue to urge governments which recruit able-bodied persons from among these displaced persons, to receive and settle their dependent relatives also, and thus respect the unity and integrity of family life.

(iii) That the Council authorise the World Council of Churches Refugee Commission to take such steps as may be appropriate to bring persons of German ethnic origin within the protection of the United Nations International Refugee Organisation. Further, the Assembly directs the World Council of Churches Refugee Commission to work for the inclusion of all refugees and expellés within the mandate of the International Refugee Organisation.

(iv) That the World Council of Churches, having already requested its member churches to support the efforts of the United Nations Secretariat on behalf of Arab and other refugees from the conflict areas of Palestine, appeal to the Jewish authorities throughout the world to co-operate in this work of relief, and to facilitate the return of the refugees to their homes at as early a date as practicable.

(v) WHEREAS the World Council of Churches notes with satisfaction that the United Nations has accepted as one of its major purposes the promotion of respect for and observance of human rights and fundamental freedoms for all without distinction as to race, sex, language or religion,

AND WHEREAS the Assembly, conscious of the magnitude and complexity of the task of placing the protection of human rights under the ægis of an international authority, regards a Declaration of Human Rights, which is neither binding nor enforceable, although valuable as setting a common standard of achievement for all peoples and all nations, as in itself inadequate
BE IT RESOLVED

That the Assembly calls upon its constituent members to press for the adoption of an International Bill of Human Rights making provision for the recognition, and national and international enforcement of all the essential freedoms of man, whether personal, political, or social.

That the Assembly call upon its constituent members to support the adoption of other conventions on human rights, such as those on Genocide and Freedom of Information and the Press, as a step toward the promotion of respect for and observance of human rights and fundamental freedoms throughout the world.

(vi) WHEREAS the churches are seeking to promote the observance of religious liberty throughout the world
BE IT RESOLVED

That the World Council of Churches adopt the following *Declaration on Religious Liberty* and urge the application of its provisions through domestic and international action.

A DECLARATION ON RELIGIOUS LIBERTY

An essential element in a good international order is freedom of religion. This is an implication of the Christian faith and of the world-wide nature of Christianity. Christians, therefore, view the question of religious freedom as an international problem. They are concerned that religious freedom be everywhere secured. In pleading for this freedom, they do not ask for any privilege to be granted to Christians that is denied to others. While the liberty with which Christ has set men free can neither be given nor destroyed by any Government, Christians, because of that inner freedom, are both jealous for its outward expression and solicitous that all men should have freedom in religious life. The nature and destiny of man by virtue of his creation, redemption and calling, and man's activities in family, State and culture establish limits beyond which the government cannot with impunity go. The rights which Christian discipleship demands are such as are good for all men, and no nation has ever suffered by reason of granting such liberties. Accordingly:

The rights of religious freedom herein declared shall be recognised and observed for all persons without distinction as to race, colour, sex, language, or religion, and without imposition of disabilities by virtue of legal provisions or administrative acts.

1. *Every person has the right to determine his own faith and creed.*

The right to determine faith and creed involves both the process whereby a person adheres to a belief and the process whereby he changes his belief. It includes the right to receive instruction and education.

This right becomes meaningful when man has the opportunity to access to information. Religious, social and political institutions have the obligation to permit the mature individual to relate himself to sources of information in such a way as to allow personal religious decision and belief.

The right to determine one's belief is limited by the right of parents to decide sources of information to which their children shall have access. In the process of reaching decisions, everyone ought to take into account his higher self-interests and the implications of his beliefs for the wellbeing of his fellow men.

2. *Every person has the right to express his religious beliefs in worship, teaching and practice, and to proclaim the implications of his beliefs for relationships in a social or political community.*

The right of religious expression includes freedom of worship both public and private; freedom to place information at the disposal of others by processes of teaching, preaching and persuasion; and freedom to pursue such activities as are dictated by conscience.

It also includes freedom to express implications of belief for society and its government.

This right requires freedom from arbitrary limitation of religious expression in all means of communication, including speech, press, radio, motion pictures and art. Social and political institutions should grant immunity from discrimination and from legal disability on grounds of expressed religious conviction, at least to the point where recognised community interests are adversely affected.

Freedom of religious expression is limited by the rights of parents to determine the religious point of view to which their children shall be exposed. It is further subject to such limitations, prescribed by law, as are necessary to protect order and welfare, morals and the rights and freedoms of others. Each person must recognise the right of others to express their beliefs and must have respect for authority at all times, even when conscience forces him to take issue with the people who are in authority or with the position they advocate.

3. Every person has the right to associate with others and to organise with them for religious purposes.

This right includes freedom to form religious organisations, to seek membership in religious organisations, and to sever relationship with religious organisations.

It requires that the rights of association and organisation guaranteed by a community to its members include the right of forming associations for religious purposes.

It is subject to the same limits imposed on all associations by non-discriminatory laws.

4. Every religious organisation, formed or maintained by action in accordance with the rights of individual persons, has the right to determine its policies and practices for the accomplishment of its chosen purposes.

The rights which are claimed for the individual in his exercise of religious liberty become the rights of the religious organisation, including the right to determine its faith and creed; to engage in religious worship, both public and private; to teach, educate, preach and persuade; to express implications of belief for society and government. To these will be added certain corporate rights which derive from the rights of individual persons, such as the right: to determine the form of organisation, its government and conditions of membership; to select and train its own officers, leaders and workers; to publish and circulate religious literature;

to carry on service and missionary activities at home and abroad; to hold property and to collect funds; to co-operate and to unite with other religious bodies at home and in other lands, including freedom to invite or to send personnel beyond national frontiers and to give or to receive financial assistance; to use such facilities, open to all citizens or associations, as will make possible the accomplishment of religious ends.

In order that these rights may be realised in social experience, the State must grant to religious organisations and their members the same rights which it grants to other organisations, including the right of self-government, of public meeting, of speech, of press and publication, of holding property, of collecting funds, of travel, of ingress and egress, and generally of administering their own affairs.

The community has the right to require obedience to non-discriminatory laws passed in the interest of public order and well-being. In the exercise of its rights, a religious organisation must respect the rights of other religious organisations and must safeguard the corporate and individual rights of the entire community.